Real Knockouts

Real Knockouts

The Physical Feminism
of Women's Self-Defense

Martha McCaughey

NEW YORK UNIVERSITY PRESS

New York and London

NEW YORK UNIVERSITY PRESS
New York and London

Library of Congress Cataloging-in-Publication Data
McCaughey, Martha, 1966–
Real knockouts : the physical feminism of women's self-defense /
Martha McCaughey.
p.   cm.
Includes bibliographical references (p.) and index.
ISBN 0-8147-5512-7 (cloth : acid-free paper)
ISBN 0-8147-5577-1 (pbk. : acid-free paper)
1. Self-defense for women—Social aspects. 2. Feminist theory.
3. Women—Crimes against—Prevention. I. Title.
GV1111.5.M38 1997
613.6'6'082—dc21   97-4774
                      CIP

New York University Press books are printed on acid-free paper,
and their binding materials are chosen for strength and durability.

Manufactured in the United States of America

10 9 8 7 6 5 4 3 2 1

Contents

Acknowledgments

This project owes much to all the women with whom I shared the exhilarating experience of learning self-defense, and to those who took time to speak with me about their understandings of self-defense. I am equally indebted to the instructors who shared their time and perspectives in interviews with me. Many of them shared materials with me, helped me make contacts with other people involved with women's self-defense training, and even read a draft of this book. I am also grateful to the many people, from a variety of self-defense-related organizations, who sent me photographs, articles, and other valuable information.

My gratitude goes to Robin Lloyd for suggesting that I take a self-defense class. Some years before that, Walter Allen encouraged intellectual aggressivity in me and his other students, and Luis Sfeir-Younis taught the importance of nonviolence and love. Without these people this book would not have been written. My thanks go to the friends, family members, and colleagues, too numerous to name, who clipped articles from newspapers, told me about a television show or book related to women's self-defense, or shared some information with me. Thanks to Kelly Nugent and Trina Seitz for obtaining data and other materials for me. Christine and John Watkins generously housed me while I conducted research on the East Coast, and the University of California at Santa Barbara funded some aspects of my research.

The following people made helpful intellectual contributions at various stages of my research and writing: Lisa Brush, Laura Grindstaff, Elisabeth Jordan, Ann Kilkelly, John Mohr, Frances Montell, Niko Pfund, and Beth Schneider. Niko Pfund and his staff at New York University Press have been encouraging, diligent, and witty through each phase of the publishing process. I am most grateful to Avery Gordon, Neal King, and Richard Widick, who made extraordinary contributions from the formative to the final stages of the book.

Thanks also go to the many female students I had at UCSB who made unsolicited revelations, in confidence, of their experiences of sexual violence. Their stories remind me of the frequency and pain of sexual violence and of the need for change. I've been encouraged by the many students to whom I lectured who got excited about "mean women" and made a point of telling me so.

Finally, this work owes a debt to all the feminist activists before me who challenged the notions that women shouldn't speak in public, pursue higher education, play sports, and wear blue jeans—some of my favorite unladylike activities. It also owes much to those contemporary feminists who have challenged rape laws, self-defense laws, and standards of heterosexual normativity, making possible this modest attempt to push those ideas further.

Preface

This book offers a way to understand and experience women's self-defense. As a participant-observer studying and describing women's self-defense training, I have connected an array of happenings, courses, sentiments, and statements into a coherent "movement." *Real Knockouts*, then, like all ethnography, is as much a means of experience as it is a record of it. Armed with the insights of feminist scholarship, this analysis of self-defense highlights its potential for undermining violence against women and sex inequality more broadly.

Of course self-defense cannot be the only way of resisting male domination, or even male violence specifically. Nevertheless, self-defense has important implications beyond the trained woman who thwarts an assault and the person who tries to attack her. Women's increasing involvement in self-defense disrupts the gender ideology that makes men's violence against women seem inevitable. Beyond this, it prompts us to question some of the assumptions that have been driving feminist theory and politics.

Rather than attempting a sweeping survey of self-defense organizations and their participants, *Real Knockouts* offers a deep description of women's self-defense. It analyzes how self-defense training transforms the female body and then assesses the impact that self-defense could have on our culture, including the educational efforts, political organizing, and theorizing of feminists who first called our attention to sexual violence as a social problem. My hope is that clarifying the political and philosophical stakes of women's self-defense might expand the possibilities for women's legitimate use of aggression against men's, as well as for our negotiation of categories with which we understand and organize ourselves politically.

This book does not attempt to answer the question, "What do I do if someone tries to rape me?" (an issue addressed in Pauline B. Bart and Patricia H. O'Brien's *Stopping Rape: Successful Survival Strategies*, 1985, and in countless self-defense manuals). Nor does it hope to provide an institutional history of women's self-defense or a survey of the many women's self-defense organizations and programs.[1] The self-defense programs that I describe here are far from obscure, but neither are they exhaustive of the many programs available. This book does not provide statistical information on the who, what, where, why, and when of violence against women. It does not suggest how a woman should choose a form of self-defense training, discuss all of the ethical matters one must consider when training to defend oneself from attack, or provide a history of women fighters (see Helen Grieco's *Demystifying Violence: What Women and Girls Need to Know to Be Safe*, 1997).[2] Finally, my book does not recount women's self-defense victories (see Caignon and Groves's *Her Wits about Her: Self-Defense Success Stories*, 1987).

Anytime one attempts to write a grounded, serious book about a widespread political and cultural phenomenon in an engaged scholarly fashion, one faces the inevitable dilemma of deciding for whom one is writing. In this particular case, I am writing for two groups of people who know surprisingly little about each other, making this dilemma all the more exaggerated. On the one hand, self-defense activists, participants, instructors, and students tend not to be immersed in feminist theory, in which this book is, after all, rooted. On the other hand, feminist scholars and other academics are, in my experience, unlikely to have more than a fleeting, impressionistic knowledge of those engaged in self-defense. Phrased differently, how many women at the Modern Language Association or the annual sociology convention know how to shoot a gun or how to kick someone in the jaw? And how many women in self-defense courses have read up on their Judith Butler, their Catharine MacKinnon, or their Michel Foucault? I hope I will not be perceived as disparaging when I say that the number of folks who travel in both circles is statistically rather marginal. So, what to do? In this book, I endeavor to speak to both groups and, in doing so, must ask for your understanding if at times you weary of hard theory and yearn for an anecdote or a personal narrative, or, if you would like to see specific theoretical points explained more intricately or succinctly. This book, then, is written for both ordinary educated readers interested in women's empowerment and resistance to violence, and scholars interested in debates about subjectivity, agency, and embodiment. If successful, it will show how the latter matters bear upon the former.

Feminist philosophers and theorists have challenged central threads of modern thought. Unfortunately, however, their books have appeared remote from the concerns (and vernacular) of everyday women. Self-defense provides an excellent vehicle through which to render those sometimes abstruse ideas comprehensible and relevant to the lived realities of women and men. And, by providing some history of the construction of gender and sexual violence, and the social intolerance of women's aggression, I hope to enable a greater historical consciousness in the self-defense community.

Some women may wrongly take rape for granted as natural male predation from which they must learn to protect themselves. Other women may never learn about Western culture's historical intolerance of female aggression and may assume that our legal system would have no objections to their self-defensive violence. Still others may not understand their entitlement to safety and freedom as part of a historically feminist movement. Just as young women in the United States today take for granted their rights to vote, to make reproductive choices, and to work outside the home, they might also assume an entitlement to self-protection training without the historical memory of oppression and without the determination to advance the position of women in society. Unless women's self-defense training is situated in a larger framework of sex inequality, it could end up an individualized and less effective force for social change.

Self-defensers—a neologism I employ throughout the book to refer to the women who take or teach self-defense—are inventing new ways to conduct their lives and define themselves as women. The "fighting spirit" women achieve in self-defense courses complements, and sometimes pushes the envelope of, other efforts central to feminism. Women's studies has been trying to correct the male bias in scholarship. Take Back the Night marches have been an important step in claiming women's right to take up space and to have freedom to move around in the world. Feminist artists and performers have offered new ways to represent women. Self-defense is another arena that helps women question the culture they live in—and the culture that lives in them. Women can change society. We can transform our relationship to tradition. The mobility women achieve through self-defense complements the mobility and freedom sought by feminist artists, performers, activists, and philosophers.

The emotional, corporeal, cultural, and political transformations that self-defense makes possible can best be understood through the insights of contemporary feminist theory. As a practice that rescripts the female body, self-defense not only highlights women's ability to redefine the body, but the significance of corporeal change for consciousness. Elizabeth Grosz (1994) has argued that feminism must overcome a traditional duality of mind and body that has implicitly positioned the body as ahistorical and acultural. Grosz named an important agenda for feminism: "Corporeal feminism" moves away from earlier feminist approaches that either construed the body as naturally sexed or ignored the body altogether. Corporeal feminism understands the body as part of agency, consciousness, and reflection—notions typically construed as solely interior (Grosz 1994, viii)—in a way that does not reduce to essentialism or biologism. While much of feminist thought has focused on how men and women come to incorporate sexist ideologies into their psyches, corporeal feminism insists on examining the ways such ideologies become inscribed and contested at the level of the body. The "physical feminism" of women's self-defense illuminates precisely this process. Women's self-defense demonstrates that power is not simply about ideology (traditionally conceived as a matter of ideas, values, or attitudes) nor physical violence enacted on bodies. Rather, power is disseminated and resisted through the lived body.

I would not argue, though, as many would, that radical feminists such as Andrea Dworkin and Catharine MacKinnon commit the theoretical sin of construing the body as presocial and naturally sexed. The accusation that they claim men are inherently prone to rape and women are inherently violable (e.g., Gatens 1996, 78, 87-88) is, in my view, unfair and simplistic. While radical feminists have emphasized women's vulnerability to violence (and have done so for good reason), they have analyzed, not employed, biologism as a political myth that supports sex inequality.[3]

At the same time, however, many feminists have neglected to consider seriously women's self-defense training as a means of subverting the embodied ethos of rape culture. To be sure, it is the ultimate goal of rape crisis centers to end sexual violence altogether. Take Back the Night rallies and conferences on violence against women might offer a self-defense workshop. But self-defense lacks a political theory, and theorists don't discuss self-defense.

This void may have contributed to the misreading of feminists such as Dworkin and MacKinnon as naive essentialists. It might also account for Katie Roiphe's (1993) suggestion that Take Back the Night marches and other aspects of the anti-sexual assault movement only solidify women's identities as helpless victims. Unlike Roiphe, I do not suggest that women can embrace agency and thereby will themselves out of victimization—as though self-defense offered women the choice of agency *over* victimization. Women's victimization and agency must be understood together, since they operate simultaneously in women's lives. Offering a theory and politics of women's self-defense, then, need not imply that women can kick and scream their way out of systematic oppression. That said, women's resistance in its context of domination is an overlooked, undertheorized topic.

The failure to emphasize and theorize women's concrete resistance to male domination might explain not only why some feminists are denounced for positioning women as naturally powerless victims, but also why some feminist philosophers get accused, paradoxically, of having the very opposite problem MacKinnon is accused of having. The work of Judith Butler (1990) and other feminist philosophers who emphasize the discursive construction of sex has been, far from regarded as essentialist, admonished for being immaterial and ignoring the pain of violence on real bodies. They are repeatedly asked, in accusing tones, "If everything is text, what about violence and bodily injury?" (Butler 1993, 28). Butler and others have provided rich understandings of how the gendered social order is implanted at the level of the body. Although identifying, for instance, how and why women "throw like girls," as Iris Marion Young (1990) has, does not mean that such bodily dispositions are natural, ethically desirable, or unchangeable, these theorists have not discussed how we might embody alternative ideologies.

I insist that the ideas of both theorists such as Dworkin and MacKinnon and theorists such as Butler, Grosz, and Young are relevant for theorizing women's self-defense. Thus it should not surprise readers to see such works integrated in the service of elucidating women's contestation of sexed embodiment. Self-defense culture challenges feminism to elaborate the ways women can resist their subordination in a culture that demands specific kinds of bodies. It demands that feminism take seriously the corporeality and pleasure of that resistance. It demands that feminism get physical.

This is why feminism has as much to learn from self-defense as self-defense has to gain from feminist analysis. At the same time that I make an interpretive intervention in self-defense culture, then, I take a position from within the community of self-defensers about feminism, suggesting how feminism might rethink some of its assumptions that ground an uneasiness over women's efficacious and pleasurable relation to aggression. For it was as an occupant of both categories—academic feminist and self-defenser—that I came to this conclusion. The pleasure of mock combat made it easy to become a fan of the women who take and teach self-defense, which in turn made it difficult to dismiss them as dupes of male domination.[4]

My participant-observation research put me through an intense bodily experience where two of the most important theoretical lessons hit me. Before this research began, I had analyzed, in the typical disembodied academic manner, sex discrimination and sexual violence. Because I had identified a "masculine" ethic as part of the problem of our rape culture, I was opposed to any form of violence and firmly against guns. The power and pleasure of hitting, kicking, screaming, and shooting drastically altered my vision of feminist resistance. Second, although I knew we needed to undo hegemonic modes of thinking, as a self-defenser I started living—not just understanding—it differently. This made me realize the relevance of physicality to consciousness.

En route to these theoretical considerations, *Real Knockouts* tells a story about something that has generated considerable controversy and abounding excitement. I want to live in a culture where it seems perfectly reasonable for a woman to stop an assault aggressively. The corollary, of course, is that it would seem unreasonable, indeed unthinkable, for a man to assault a woman in the first place, and we would finally live in a world in which the latter, not the former, was deemed the improper, aggressive act.

The danger exists that my study of the pleasure of mock combat takes away from the terror of assault, whether or not one fights back. No one—no matter how well armed, physically trained, or emotionally prepared—wants to be confronted by someone who attempts to do her harm. While writing a portion of this book, I lived in a large house for the summer. Spending much time alone in an unfamiliar area led me to imagine what I would do if someone walked in and tried to hurt me. Even though I knew that I would fight back, the thought of having to have that fight left me feeling wretched. And I am still afraid I might lose the battle. I do not want, nor do I want readers, to lose sight of the terror, pain, and injustice of sexual assault as I discuss the power and benefits of women's self-defense. (In chapter 4 I discuss two opposing feminist worries about self-defense, first that self-defense will reduce the political significance of rape, and second that self-defense will uncritically elevate the "natural" significance of rape and sexuality.)

Similarly, in writing on the pleasures of sparring and shooting, my inclination is not to dash hopes, readers' or my own, for a utopian future in which conflicts are resolved peacefully. Promoting self-defense as an important component of the women's movement must not be understood as a position of relinquished social ideals or as a compromised ethical stance toward assailants and the social institutions that support them. No matter how enthusiastic about self-defense, we must not blame the victims (whether or not they fight back) but rather place the ethical and legal responsibility with whom it belongs—the perpetrators.

Finally, many feminists will undoubtedly be suspicious of, or downright unhappy with, my willingness to embrace even the armed wings of women's self-defense efforts. While I address some of these concerns in chapters 4 and 5, I do not wish to bring closure to debates about sexual violence and resistance. This book aims to spark some fruitful discussions among conscientious groups concerned with women's freedom. I hope less to persuade readers to adopt a specific program or argument than to move the debate to a new level.

Looking Ahead

In the introduction that follows, I explain the potential of women's self-defense to disrupt our culture of normalized violence against women and even feminist politics and theory. As I show, a surprising degree of ambivalence about women's aggression keeps many feminists strongly opposed to, or at best, indifferent toward women's self-defense. Chapter 1 covers the theoretical ground necessary to illuminate how self-defense not only changes the individual woman but also constitutes an intervention in the discourses of sex difference which fuel male violence against women. I explain the political context of sexed embodiment in which male aggression and female vulnerability are cultural corporeal paradigms. The naturalized embodied ethos of rape culture makes women easy, and easily rationalized, targets for men's violence. I discuss the popular fiction of male physical power and female vulnerability in visual representations, and the presence of these representations in traditional rape and self-defense laws, and in many crime prevention and self-defense manuals for women. Establishing the historical and cultural processes that constrain the imagined possibilities for a female body is important for understanding how self-defense instruction can be a critical juncture for the facilitation of new, previously unimagined realities.

The next two chapters, based on my ethnographic research, provide a picture of self-defense training and its impact on the women engaged with it. In chapter 2, I describe what women learn in a variety of self-defense courses, as I experienced them as a participant-observer. Readers anxious to know what goes on in women's self-defense classes might want to read this chapter first. Chapter 3 provides a more abstract and detached analysis of self-defense as a discourse that challenges traditional views and creates a new female body. Presenting interviews with self-defense instructors and students, I develop a theoretically informed interpretation of contemporary self-defense culture, hoping to prompt both the community and feminist theorists to see their projects in new ways.

The last two chapters show how self-defense bears on central tensions in feminist theory, involving how we conceptualize sameness and difference, violence, discursivity, agency, subjectivity, corporeality, and resistance. Chapter 4 anticipates feminist apathy and skepticism toward women's combative bodily practices, locating those sentiments in two overarching philosophical assumptions about violence and the body. Chapter 5 proposes that feminism place the body at the center of its political and analytic agenda—that is the *physical* of physical feminism—and explains how self-defense can be understood within a feminist analytic framework—the *feminism* of physical feminism. It also suggests how and why the women's self-defense movement might find new allies in sexual assault prevention education, in popular culture, and in feminist politics.

Real Knockouts

Introduction: The Challenge of the Self-Defense Movement

I was once a frightened feminist. I knew much about male violence and little about stopping it. When my odyssey into self-defense culture began, I was neither fan nor critic, but simply a feminist with strong opinions and a lack of confidence in speaking out. When I lectured on sexual violence at the university where I worked, I found myself intimidated by the hostile men who would inevitably approach me afterward. Furthermore, I had recently begun living alone in a first-floor apartment, and had been reading and lecturing on interviews with convicted rapists (see Scully 1990). The stories these men told—accounts of hiding in women's bedroom closets until they went to sleep at night—crippled me psychologically. I couldn't come home in the evening and relax without checking my closets and all the other hiding places that the men talked about. Attending Take Back the Night rallies, hearing one testimony of victimization after another, left me feeling hopeless.

That's when I took a self-defense class and discovered that North American women in unprecedented numbers are learning to knock out, maim, and shoot men who assault them. Mace tear gas spray sales have skyrocketed. Model Mugging, a nationwide aggressive self-defense course, has trained over twenty thousand women in the United States. Over fourteen million American women own handguns. Hundreds of corporations have sponsored self-defense training for female employees. Increasing numbers of women have found self-defense training available at health clubs under names like "Cardio Combat" and "Aerobox."

My initial interest in self-defense was not academic; my approach to it was devoid of theories or hypotheses. But what at first moved me viscerally eventually moved me intellectually. I realized that I was holding, in the ball of my fist, key tensions in contemporary feminist theories—theories that are often dismissed as too abstract and impenetrable to make sense of real lives. At the same time that enacting an aggressive posture felt empowering, it felt taboo—in my case doubly taboo as a woman and a feminist. For even as current feminist philosophy suggests that power operates at the level of the body, much of feminism—which always stood for a heightened consciousness of patriarchal modes of acting and thinking—rejects the possibility that anything good could come from violence. Women's embrace of their aggressive potential prompts a reexamination of our understandings of violence and resistance to it, of ideologies of gender, and of feminist theory itself. This is why I wanted to investigate women's self-defense and to offer an interpretation of it.

As I chose to continue self-defense courses as an ethnographer, I took field notes (although never during the classes) and asked students and instructors for interviews. Throughout my fieldwork, I gathered articles of the movement: buttons, bumper stickers, books, videos, newspaper articles, key chains, T-shirts, whistles, personal alarms, pepper sprays, mini batons, and advertisements for self-defense courses and products. I became a member of several self-defense organizations and subscribed to their newsletters and to magazines like *Fighting Woman News* and *Women and Guns*. I wanted to get a sense of self-defense culture: what people discuss and what they do not; how the importance of self-defense is construed; and how self-defense is or is not connected to other issues facing women. I did not take only one self-defense course, or simply a beginner-intermediate-advanced series of one form of self-defense training (although I did that, too). I surveyed, experientially, a wide variety of self-defense instruction: self-defense with firearms; aggressive unarmed self-defense against padded attackers; women's self-defense in the martial arts; and a number of other courses sold as self-defense in martial arts dojos (Krav Maga), aerobics studios ("Cardio Combat"), and fitness centers ("Boxing for Fitness").

Participating in self-defense lessons established an experiential and appreciative relationship with the various practices and people I discuss here. I talked informally with fellow self-defensers. I read the magazines. I wore the T-shirts. I carried the mini baton—and heard the ensuing "well-I-won't-mess-with-you-then" gibe from countless men. Most significantly, I went through the self-defense metamorphosis. I learned to jab, punch, poke, pull, kick, yell, stomp, shoot, and even kill with my bare hands. But the fighting spirit is more than that: self-defense transforms the way it feels to inhabit a female body. It changes what it means to be a woman.

Aggression is a primary marker of sexual difference. By this I do not mean that one major way in which men and women naturally differ is in their capacity and propensity for aggression. I mean that aggression is one way that we culturally tell men and women apart. The construction and regulation of a naturalized heterosexual femininity hinges on the taboo of aggression, and often what challenges femininity is labeled "aggressive."

Our culture is wedded to distinguishing bodies as male and female. Sex is materialized through regulatory norms surrounding the use of aggression. Cultural ideals of manhood and womanhood include a cultural, political, aesthetic, and legal acceptance of men's aggression and a deep skepticism, fear, and prohibition of women's. This set of assumptions fuels the frequency and ease with which men assault women, and the cultural understanding that men's violence is an inevitable, if unfortunate, biological fact. Ironically, a significant amount of feminist activism and scholarship has fallen into this trap, failing to critique men's presumably natural power to rape and batter, and neglecting to stress the possibility of women's physical resistance. Self-defense instruction shows women how to thwart assault aggressively, and in so doing throws open for critique the gender ideologies to which we have all become more or less habituated.

The Self-Defense Movement

The forms of self-defense that I examine are connected by their explicit goal to teach women (and sometimes men also) to defend themselves against sexual violence. Though women face a variety of criminals, self-defense courses teach women to hand over their cars, money, and other possessions and to fight back only when an attacker attempts or threatens to strike, rape, and/or take them from point A to point B. I do not include in this analysis certain methods women employ to diminish the likelihood of sexual assault, such as home alarm systems, baggy clothes, cellular phones, dogs, husbands, safe-walk programs, and nighttime ride services. Although risk-reducing strategies are widespread and important, models of "rape prevention" that keep women indoors after dark or otherwise put a restrictive onus on women do not challenge men's freedom relative to women's, nor men's reputed appetite and ability for physical coercion. Nor do they repel the particular men most likely to cause women harm; consequently, they have never been controversial. Women's uses of weapons and their own bodies for self-defense are publicly scrutinized in a way that husbands and home alarm systems are not—probably because they injure men, and because they provide women with greater autonomy while restricting men's behavior, rather than the opposite. This project also concerns women who defend themselves without being exposed to any formal self-defense training, such as women who kill battering husbands.

While many women have fought back against attackers without any self-defense lessons, significant trends in popular culture and features of contemporary social life have made self-defense training an increasingly appealing project. For it is not only a perception of vulnerability or a context of feminist antirape politics that leads women to self-defense courses. Women's self-defense is also made popular and meaningful by a social context of new images that make women's verbal and physical assertiveness appealing; a social milieu that gives the body a certain meaning; and a culture of fitness that makes women's body work more common.

During the 1980s, a "postfeminist" decade in which women were thought to have finally made it into the ranks of privileged men, the media began to cover more cases of sexual violence. Perhaps this was, as some have suggested (e.g., Faludi 1991), part of a "backlash" to remind women that they can be victimized. The 1989 sexual assault of the white female yuppie jogging in New York's Central Park perhaps best exemplifies the way in which women were reminded that even the most modern and powerful among us are vulnerable (Coward 1992).[1] But whatever its cause, the anti–sexual assault movement and the battered women's movement have begun to receive the attention they deserve in popular media and in high school and college classrooms. Additionally, a growing cultural concern with violent crime (including rape, murder, car-jacking, and nonsexual assault) has led to debates over violence, firearms, and the Second Amendment. If all of this popular attention to violent crime and the dangers of male sexuality has made more women feel vulnerable to assault, it has also made more women interested in learning how to stop it. Some of New York's aerobics self-defense classes are a direct response to heightened fears caused by the attack on the Central Park jogger and the intense media coverage it received.

On the heels of these trends has emerged a popular discussion of—and concern over—what feminism has made women into. Interestingly, this debate involves the double accusation that feminists have made women too aggressive and unfeminine—witness Rush Limbaugh's invention of the term *femi-nazis*—*and* too helpless and victimized—Katie Roiphe's (1993) belief that women have become whining victims. Further, debates about what kind of women we are in the 1990s collide with debates over women's responses to sexual assault. In May 1994, *Ms.* magazine featured a handgun on its cover with the question "Is this power feminism?" The rise of a popular discussion of women's rights and the dangers of male sexuality, then, has also contributed to a growing interest in challenges to gender ideology and debates about which of those challenges are most appropriate.

The recent cultural fascination with images of women who know how to shoot and fight reflects these concerns. Between 1990 and 1993, female characters in popular television shows such as *Murphy Brown, Roseanne,* and *Beverly Hills 90210* took self-defense classes and, in those same years, several major Hollywood films featured women who shot guns (*Aliens, Blue Steel, Eve of Destruction, Thelma and Louise,* and *Point of No Return,* the remake of *La Femme Nikita*) and entered into hand-to-hand combat with men (*Aces: Iron Eagle III, Double Impact*). When it comes to sex and violence, the dominant representations in North American film and television display and eroticize women's inability to defend themselves or characterize them as enjoying forced sex. A set of alternative images is emerging, however. Scenes from the 1990s include the following: In *Terminator 2,* Linda Hamilton clobbers men, warning the one who moans that she's just broken his arm, "There are 215 bones in the human body. That's one." Susan Sarandon, in *Thelma and Louise,* points a gun to the head of a man in a parking lot, whom she catches in the act of rape, and orders, "You let her go, you fuckin' asshole, or I'm gonna splatter your ugly face all over this nice car," after which she becomes angered at his defiant attitude and shoots him straight through the heart.

These media images offer new fantasies of what women can be which rest on women's abilities to set boundaries, defend themselves, and enter into combat, especially with aggressive men. This cultural shift to a new, aggressive woman in popular films, television shows (e.g., *American Gladiators*), comic books (e.g., *Hothead Paisan, Silver Sable*), and advertisements (e.g., Diet Coke, Revlon) is not only visual. The sassy rap, rock, and punk "riot grrrl" bands sound this fresh female brassiness. From singing the praises of independent womanhood (Salt 'n Pepa) and proclaiming to men that "you're not knockin' this hiney" (Roxanne Shante), to shouting out the lyrics, "Dead men don't rape" (Seven Year Bitch) and enacting on stage a fantasy of retaliation against gang rape, cutting off a fake penis with a knife while singing "Frat Pig" (Tribe 8), new women's bands exemplify a fantasy of female entitlement and an offbeat anger at men's violence against women.

In this context of media-enhanced fear of violent crime, media-produced "mean women" moguls, and new courses and products for "personal protection" and "urban security," self-defense erupts as an increasingly popular body project. Body projects are a defining feature of life in modern Western society. The body is increasingly the site of conscious control, of identity reflexively negotiated and lived out, and thus the foundation for a sense of self (Giddens 1991). The body offers the possibility of constructing a reliable sense of self in a posttraditional age of uncertainty, where God is dead and political authorities and political ideals seem farcical. The many global risks and dangers we face make us yearn for something for which we can be responsible and over which we can have some control. In these times, we also have a new and remarkable level of control over our bodies, multiplying the choices we must make about them. As we decide, amid an array of possibilities, what kinds of diet, exercise, medical intervention, and adornment are appropriate for our bodies, we incarnate a collection of cultural signs and social codes. We wear our feelings—our faith in particular institutions, our politics, and our identities—on our arms.

Contemporary Westerners have come to see bodies as "malleable entities which can be shaped and honed by the vigilance and hard work of their owners" (Shilling 1993, 5). Hence the degree to which to the health and fitness movements have captured women's attention. This investment in our bodies with moral meaning makes the body all the more difficult to part with. Modern fears of death can be so great precisely because, paradoxical as it is, we are invested in the finite body as a primary source of meaning. The body's role as a reflexive project, *and* as something fated to die on us, increases women's investment in controlling their physical destinies. The AIDS epidemic intensifies that investment by making any rape potentially life-threatening. And as the body is increasingly endowed with meanings like "free person" or "equal citizen," the integrity of the body and others' respect for its physical-ethical boundaries grow all the more consequential.

Most have now heard one or more statistics suggesting that a staggering number of U.S. women will, some time in their lives, encounter a man who tries, successfully or not, to rape them. Most have also heard that women with male partners stand a horrifyingly good chance of being beaten, and of having rape accompany the battery.[2] In case it needs to be stated, some men do not rape or batter and, of course, the ones who do don't manage to victimize everybody. Ultimately it matters less exactly how many men do it, or how many women are victimized, and more that enough men are violent to make all women afraid of being attacked (Gordon and Riger 1989).

While sexual violence is not the only fear women confront or the only form of oppression they endure, women nevertheless want to know what to do if they face sexual assault. Almost all women have experienced one or more threats along the continuum of sexual violence: threatening phone calls, sexual harassment, flashing, and/or stalking, acts all the more controlling of women precisely because we fear what lies on the far end of that continuum—rape, battery, and murder. Some women know the pain of sexual violence from childhood. Other women face immediate threat from men in their lives. Still others are simply scared or tired of being scared.

Women are not the only victims of violence in our society. Men, though not nearly as often victimized sexually or by romantic partners, can also be scared of, and do face, victimization by car thieves, ATM robbers, drive-by shooters, gangs, burglars, muggers, and murderers. Men's violence against men, however, even when sexual, is usually socially recognized as violence whereas women are often blamed for precipitating, inviting, or deserving men's violence against them. When women train to fight back, they defy gender norms. It's manly, but not womanly, to protect and fight.[3] Men are supposed to protect and defend women, a notion notorious for its unreliability (no woman has a protector at all times, some don't want a protector at all, and in any case women are most often victimized by men who supposedly protect them) yet convenient for keeping women in a victimized position.

In self-defense, women master actions of which they are often deemed incapable. The presumed inability to fight in part defines heterosexual femininity. The reification of gender as natural, particularly men's invulnerability and women's helplessness—in popular media, in traditional rape and self-defense laws, and even in crime prevention advice for women and college rape prevention programs—is a central tenet of rape culture. Our society is a rape culture because sexual violence (including all gender-motivated assaults such as incest, rape, battery, and murder) and the fear of violence are subtly accepted as the norm.[4] Rape culture's models of sexuality and gender perpetuate men's violence and women's fear. Rape culture accepts men's sexual aggression against women as normal, sexy, and/or inevitable, and often regards women's refusal of it is as pathological, unnatural, and "aggressive."[5]

Women who take self-defense instruction, with whatever motivations and ideological perspectives, are offered an implicit or explicit critique of the ways in which gender is constructed in a culture of male privilege which rests on the abuse of women. What is usually taken for granted as a fact of nature—that a woman simply cannot physically challenge a man—is revealed as a social script which privileges men at the expense of women. The influence of gender ideologies on our bodily dispositions surfaces in self-defense instruction, where women gain the capacity for verbal and physical aggression. Gender ideology is thus not simply a matter of the mind; it includes embodied social values. Self-defense offers the possibility of a critical consciousness of gender's influence on what we see as male and female bodies.

As such, it is a "final frontier" of feminist consciousness-raising—an effort that has traditionally focused on the mind, not the body, as the recipient of ideology.

As increasing numbers of North American women take pride and pleasure in the deployment of their bodies in ways previously thought impossible, we learn not only the stories by which rape culture is rationalized, but also how the social order imposes itself at the level of the body. Gender ideology is not a matter of psychology *as opposed to* biology. Gender ideology affects the way we interpret and experience our physical bodies. If contemporary feminism has enabled the transformation of women's consciousness, and has spawned a critique of the way the female body has been treated, represented, and thought of, self-defense training reveals how the traditional sexist ideas actually find their way into the functioning of the body itself. Thus self-defense transforms the realm of bodily possibilities for women, and presents a new form of "consciousness" complementary, and crucial, to the feminist movement. Feminists have long considered the ways in which gender seems like biology but really isn't; self-defense illuminates the ways that gender is an ideology inseparable from, and alterable through, the lived body.

This is not to suggest that self-defensers shed the ideology which naturalizes sexism and trade it in for the "real truth." A powerful, consequential understanding about womanhood is possible, a "real truth" is not. Self-defensers come up with new versions of womanhood, new values and ideas which defy rather than accommodate rape culture. Self-defense enables us both to question the ways that we are defined, categorized, and embodied, and to define ourselves anew. This is what makes women's self-defense a social movement for social change.

The Challenge of the Self-Defense Movement

The self-defense movement not only changes the way women think about themselves and about violence. It chips away at the collective assurance men have had that women cannot and will not fight back and transforms the gender ideologies that support the incidence of rape. Self-defense exposes gender as a cultural meaning system whose status as a natural fact of human difference and the cause of women's vulnerability is a key myth of rape culture.

Self-defense culture produces a new understanding, not shared by many people, about what a woman can be. Many women who take and teach self-defense classes are not self-defined feminists, although it has clearly been feminist activists who have raised public awareness about sexual violence. The self-defenser can be any of the following: a lesbian for whom having a male protector is neither a desire nor an option; a mother who conceives of herself as a virtuous "mama bear" protecting her young; a member of the trauma recovery movement for whom learning to defend herself is secondary to the "inner" benefits of self-defense training; a Wall Street yuppie for whom aggression is part of professionalization; or a self-conscious dieter whose regular aerobics course became "Cardio Combat." Though self-defense brings together many women who do not necessarily define themselves as feminists, it offers some important lessons that could easily be considered feminist.

As I shall elaborate in chapter 1, femininity involves deferring to men, for instance men who want sex. One woman taking self-defense, after practicing to yell "No!" remarked, "That's the first time I've ever said 'no.'" Self-defense helps women undo the enslaving feminine identity of deference, kindness, and weakness that men so often take advantage of, by getting them to imagine and practice aggressively refusing men's advances. It also enables women to take themselves more seriously and to approach men's demands and whims with a different kind of thoughtfulness and consideration.

In their book based on interviews with survivors of attempted and completed rape, Bart and O'Brien (1985, 14) say that "the best overall advice we could offer women to increase the probability of avoiding rape is 'Don't be a nice girl.'" Self-defense instruction tells women how to avoid the habits of nice girls and become *mean women* instead. Women can find it difficult to use physical force against someone they know (Bart and O'Brien 1985), and since over 80 percent of assailants attack women they know (Koss and Harvey 1991), rewriting the script of feminine deference is crucial. This is precisely why women in self-defense courses unlearn the habits of polite, compliant feminine conversation.

Women learn their own value in self-defense classes, and begin to see themselves as worth fighting for. The experience of sexual violence contributes to women's weak sense of self in the first place. Abuse and violence can progressively induce in women a state of boundarilessness or "ownability" (Gidycz et al. 1993; Wyatt, Guthrie, and Notgrass 1992). Self-defense can interrupt this vicious circle of vulnerability. One study has shown that survivors of rape had a lower sense of confidence in their abilities and power to impact the world around them (what researchers call a sense of "self-efficacy") than women who had not been raped. After taking a self-defense class, though, the survivors' sense of self-efficacy had increased to the same level as that of women who had not been raped, whose sense had strengthened as well (Ozer and Bandura 1990).

Self-defense is a primary vehicle for women's achievement of a sense of authority and self-worth.

Violence—defined as physical force exerted with the intent of damaging, controlling, or stopping someone—is usually used as a form of control, to redress something the aggressor sees as a moral wrong (Campbell 1993, 13; Katz 1988). Men have typically been the ones to use violence in this way. Rape can be seen as such a form of redress: Men who feel entitled to the sex they want to have with an unwilling woman may construe her sexual unavailability or refusal as a moral wrong which warrants redress (see Beneke 1982; Scully 1990). Put differently, men who rape, like many of those who attack and murder (see Katz 1988), often get violent with a sense of righteousness—as though the woman had teased, dared, or defied them, as though they were simply defending their own rights to the identity and self-worth that a woman exercising self-determination took away. The same could be said of battering, as men who beat their intimate partners use violence and intimidation to control what they perceive to be a threatening, offensive female self-determination. By this logic, female self-determination is a moral wrong which seems to warrant violent redress. Self-defense culture turns this around: Assault, because it snubs a woman's sense of worth, is the moral wrong that warrants the redress of self-defense.

Violence between women and men has not been a form of "subject-subject" violence in which equals in status engage in combat. Rather, the point of most violence against women is to reaffirm that women are incapable of responding: "Rape engenders a sexualized female body defined as a wound, a body excluded from subject-subject violence, from the ability to engage in a fair fight. Rapists do not beat women at the game of violence, but aim to exclude us from playing it altogether" (Marcus 1992, 397). A batterer enforces his authority by causing pain. "What he is engaging in is not fighting at all; it is terrorism" (Gillespie 1989, 69).

Self-defense treats such violent assaults as scripted interactions that women are capable of interrupting. This begins to dismantle the assumption that women have victim-bodies, that is, weak, small, boundariless, and ineffective bodies. In practicing brutal resistance to men's attacks, self-defense training counters the popular attributions of the "unstoppable attacker" role to men and "disempowered victim" role to women. Self-defense courses treat sexual assault as "a scripted interaction in which one person auditions for the role of rapist and strives to maneuver another person into the role of victim" (Marcus 1992, 391). Self-defensers learn that matching an assailant verbally, without ever getting physical, will usually successfully spoil his efforts. They also learn how to physically hurt men in case verbal defense techniques do not succeed. In practicing that verbal and physical aggression, they rehearse an intolerance for men's attempts to coerce and control women.

Because violence against women depends upon the myth of male strength and female weakness, rape culture depends upon the impossibility and inappropriateness of women's aggression. Rape is not simply an unfortunate side-effect of nature. A man's ability to accomplish rape depends more on language and interpretation than unbeatable physical force (Marcus 1992). Bart and O'Brien's (1985) research showed that four of five rape attempts fail, and are particularly likely to fail if the woman puts up a fight. Another study revealed that women who fought back forcefully were more likely to avoid rape than women who did not fight back, whether or not the attacker had a weapon (Ullman and Knight 1993). Finally, no statistical evidence supports the popular contention that a woman's armed self-defense against sexual assault usually fails or results in her disarmament.[6]

Rape is both a product and a cause of gender inequality (Brownmiller 1975; MacKinnon 1989, 245). For rape is not merely sex without consent. Rape is the violent imposition of a particular sexuality. The aggressive refusal to be raped therefore resists the imposition of a sex-class status. Women's cultivation of aggressivity challenges the naturalized gender polarity that has legitimated only men's violence. Learning how to fight back exposes rape culture as an embodied ideology precisely because it gets disembodied in self-defense training. Self-defense emphasizes at once the historical production of gendered identities at the level of social interaction and at the level of the body. The self-defense movement further undermines the victim-body assumption because women need not get raped or beaten to say they are oppressed, or say rape is wrong because the body is sacred or because (consensual) sex with men is natural and good. And as self-defense changes the meanings of gender, aggression, and oppression, it also alters the meaning of rape.

Self-defense actually turns rape into an act that is understood not as the result of natural sex differences but as an act that produces the embodied idea of them. Rape is an act of social sexing (Plaza 1981, 33). Self-defense frames the rape attempt as a fight, and thus deconstructs the traditional terms of the event, which enable men's assaults and thwart women's resistance. Self-defense potentially denaturalizes rape without naturalizing sex.

Self-defense also encourages in women a sense that their bodies are not just things that house their intellects, or things to be gazed at or sexually taken. But neither are they simply the real property of women, appendages to be defended by the woman with the will, armed with assault techniques, or furious with feminist consciousness. Self-defense training transforms the female body, and in so doing, the female consciousness—in a way that destroys the distinction between body and mind. The fighting bodies struggling for dignity, survival, or just to "get this sweaty pig off of me" are not body-things but body-selves struggling to be lived and represented in different terms, "terms which grant women the capacity for independence and autonomy, which thus far have been attributed only to men" (Grosz 1994, xiii).

Traditionally, in rape interactions, women become subjects of fear; through self-defense, a rape interaction makes women into potential agents of aggression (Marcus 1992). Discarding the feminine manners that rape culture demands proves consequential for women's daily lives.[7] Furthermore, since a woman's chance of a successful self-defense claim in court decreases if it can be established that she was angry (Bochnak 1981a; Gillespie 1989; Walker 1989), women's growing entitlement to aggression and anger, through self-defense training, has important legal implications. My aim is not to get women to discover that they "really are" angry or aggressive, or to encourage women to determine who they are through self-defense skills. My aim is to examine and understand gender, aggression, and sexual assault in ways that create an opportunity for transforming our body-selves from objects of patriarchal reflection into agents against patriarchal oppression.

Often feminists are berated for analyzing oppression without offering strategies for resisting that oppression. Self-defense arrives, in our faces, as feminist resistance. We are not so oppressed that we can't make an intervention; women are challenging the inevitability of men's violence—and not just through theoretical pronouncements. Significant aspects of feminism's institutional and ideological history, however, have left much of feminism distant from, and even skeptical of, women's aggression.

Feminist Ambivalence about Women's Aggression

Feminism has been instrumental in challenging both the political construction of heterosexual femininity and the social sanctions on women who do not conform to it. Additionally, claiming the rage that women have been denied is a popular women's therapeutic practice. At the same time, though, feminist theories have emphasized women's greater sensitivity, care, empathy, and proclivity for connection (Burack 1994, 112-13). And we have been so busy analyzing women's victimization by men's aggression that we have almost reified men's power to coerce women physically, failing to highlight women's potential for fighting back.

For instance, in the recent 450-page anthology with the promising title *Transforming a Rape Culture* (Buchwald, Fletcher, and Roth 1993), there is but one article on the subject of women's counterviolence. Located in a section called "Visions and Possibilities," it presents "a tangle of difficult questions" (Clarke 1993, 403). One might suspect that the book offers ways to transform rape culture that are simply more collective and material than women's self-defense seems to be, for instance John Stoltenberg's (1993, 213–21) proposal to make rape an election issue. However, *Transforming a Rape Culture* mainly includes articles that, based on a classic feminist insistence that "the personal is political," suggest how to redefine masculinity (e.g., Miedzian 1993), how to raise girls for the twenty-first century (e.g., E. Buchwald 1993), how sex education in the public schools should teach kids about consent and bodily integrity, and how people should speak out against pornography (e.g., Stoltenberg 1993, 221–22). Those articles that do focus on activist organizations and included in the section called "Activism," for instance "Training for Safehouse" (a battered women's shelter) (C. Buchwald 1993), don't by their nature exclude self-defense. After all, self-defense is no less activist and collective—it involves education, advocacy, fundraising, instructor training and certification, conferences, and legal reform.

Put another way, training women for self-defense is no more individualistic than helping women leave battering relationships or changing men's attitudes. The book practically ignores self-defense because the authors fail to entertain the possibility that, for instance, redefining masculinity or the sex-education curriculum might include changing the sense of physical superiority boys have over girls, or that training for physical combat could help girls in the twenty-first century as much as raising their self-esteem. Tackling masculinity as well as the institutional support for violence against women is an extremely important feminist effort. But too often the effort stops there, without suggesting that women might be able to do something about the violence. Even most feminists seem reluctant to stress that until more rapists and batterers go to prison and until masculinity, sex education, and the media have been reformed, a man who does make a violent move could be stopped.

In an article called "Whose Body Is It, Anyway? Transforming Ourselves to Change a Rape Culture," Pamela R. Fletcher (1993, 440) recollects several occasions of sexual assault, lamenting disempowered responses, imagining new ones:

What if we girls in junior high and high school believed we deserve respect rather than verbal and sexual abuse from our male classmates?

What if we girls in my high school had confronted the gang of boys who raped Rachel that night in the football field twenty years ago, rather than perpetuated that cycle of abuse and shame she suffered? What if Larry and I had confronted Danny for raping Brenda that summer night in her apartment? What if Brenda had felt safe enough to tell Larry, me, and the police? What if the women in Wyoming had confronted that man while he terrorized me rather than defended him? What if they had protected, comforted, and supported me? What if we females believed ourselves and each other to be as important and deserving of our selfhood as we believe males to be? Just imagine.

What if Rachel had broken some knees on that football field? What if Brenda had ruptured Danny's testicles? Violent resistance just doesn't seem to be an option in this long list of "what ifs." But just imagine.

Feminist cultural critics have often encouraged women to resist male domination by rallying around the ways in which women have learned to be different from men. These critics locate women's strength as a cultural and political force in their failure or refusal to be violent like men (e.g., Morgan 1989). In her book *Men, Women, and Aggression*, Anne Campbell (1993, 1) argues that men and women have "separate styles" of aggression: "Women see aggression as a temporary loss of control caused by overwhelming pressure and resulting in guilt. Men see aggression as a means of exerting control over other people when they feel the need to reclaim power and self-esteem" (ibid., viii). When women see or use aggression in men's mode, Campbell (ibid., ix) suggests, they have traded in their own view for men's. In this logic, women's aggressive refusal to be assaulted can be conflated with masculinism or a political failure to resist male domination. It's just not revolutionary enough.

Feminists have opposed all sorts of violence, protesting not only rape and battery but war, the draft, and even what have come to be regarded as violent "phallotechnologies" (e.g., Caputi 1993). Standing behind phrases like "violence begets violence" and "the ends don't justify the means," many feminists have suspected that women's cultivation of aggressive personalities and bodies, especially when pleasurable, amounts to getting duped by male domination. Feminists have tried not to "play into the patriarchy" by playing men's games and sharing "male" values. From this vantage point, women's embrace of violence smacks of getting in the pigsty with the pigs.

This explains why so many feminists object to the aforementioned musical performance by Tribe 8, the all-female band that severs a fake penis on stage. Their performance at the 1994 Michigan Womyn's Music Festival was protested by a number of feminists who were offended by Tribe 8's embrace of (fantasized) violence against men (Hummel and Mantilla 1994). Protesters objected to the violence they thought the performance implied, as well as its supposed connection with sadomasochism (to which they also object because of the patriarchal violence they think it implies). Tribe 8 does not advocate the castration of rapists, but they do believe that fantasized violence can be a cathartic ritual useful for displaying women's anger at past and potential sexual aggressors (Hummel and Mantilla 1994, 16). Such a celebratory expression of women's violence appears quite misguided to feminists who oppose violence across the board.

That opposition accounts for the articles in *Ms.* magazine's 1994 issue on women and guns, which declare that "power feminism" is not a gun. Ann Jones (1994, 44) asks *Ms.* readers, "How do we arm women with awareness and the courage to live free of violence?" For Jones, it's cowardly and naive to pack a pistol. Stopping violent men is "not a job to be done piecemeal by lone women, armed with pearl-handled pistols, picking off batterers and rapists one by one." Jones argues that women are being duped, and buying into "age-old patriarchal notions of an eye for an eye" (ibid., 37). In a different forum, Jacklyn Cock (1994, 165) suggests that women's engagement with violence might be a "right-wing feminism," one in which women join the existing masculine hierarchy and cultivate a masculine sense of self. For Cock this is a feminism "stripped of its revolutionary potential" and "does nothing to challenge the status quo" (ibid.).

Even skepticism directed specifically toward women's defensive use of firearms misses the similarities in fundamental aspects of self-defense instruction and the connections among various forms of self-defense for many women involved. For instance, a woman might take a firearms course and a martial arts course as training for different types of threats. Moreover, feminists' cynicism over female aggression comes at the price of excluding women from a citizenship status that presupposes the potential to act aggressively in self-defense. Keeping women away from violence also preserves the exclusive association of violence and masculinity.

While feminists emphasize women's right to say no to sex with men, to report rape to the police, or to get respect from men, we still position women as responding to men's initiatives. Put differently, even in feminist discussions, women wind up positioned as acted upon sexually, rather than as active agents. Of course, feminists have emphasized women's victimization for two important reasons. One, women are often coerced and acted upon. Second, though in our popular culture women are represented as having sexual agency, it is a masculinist representation of female agency where that agency amounts to the active seeking of the very sexual encounters men force on women in real life (MacKinnon 1989).

But by directing laws, money, and legal criticism toward probing masculinity and making women's postrape lives more tolerable (providing therapy for survivors of rape and woman abuse, getting rapists and batterers convicted), instead of toward making male violence impossible (highlighting women's abilities to resist assault), men's power to coerce women physically becomes naturalized in the popular imagination. Attempts to stop men's violence against women solely through legal deterrence and pleas to men also subtly presume that men simply have the power to trounce, rather than assume that women might be able to sabotage men's ability to do so (Marcus 1992, 388).

When women are the focus of assault prevention efforts, attempts to reduce their vulnerability to assault commonly involve controlling or restricting their behavior, as if there were no other way women could prevent victimization. For instance, certain private colleges still maintain early curfews for female students. Some campus Rape Prevention Education Programs explicitly attempt to increase women's sense of vulnerability so that they willingly restrict their own behavior (see, e.g., Gray et al. 1990; Hanson and Gidycz 1993; Mynatt and Allgeier 1990). Other such programs implicitly confirm women's helplessness by focusing almost exclusively on men's heterosexual predation, women's vulnerability to it, and the cultural celebration of both, without offering the possibility of resistance or self-defense training.

Although these programs, like self-defense programs, attempt to challenge the cultural normativity of men's sexual violence, they do not actually challenge men's understandings of their bodies or of sexuality as much as they get men to restrain themselves around the "weaker sex"—an approach doomed to fail precisely because it fails to get men to question their sense of physical superiority and to respect women as equal citizens (McCaughey and King 1995, 376). Rape attempts are not treated as ventures that can fail, but as virtually inevitable once men have the biology, attitudes, socialization, or vocabulary of motive.

Further, by presuming that once a man goes to rape, the action is practically inescapable, we position women as intrinsically vulnerable. Perhaps some women need to be told that they are not invincible, that they could indeed be assaulted. But telling women that they are vulnerable is certainly not as preventative as rape prevention could get. By fixating on the harm of men's violence and women's vulnerability to it rather than on how women can stop it, feminists have inadvertently constructed women as victims and caregivers of victims.

Federal agencies, state and local governments, private foundations, churches, and traditional women's service organizations have been less willing to support financially those practices associated with feminism they perceive to be "radical." Consequently, the more moderate feminist social services such as hot lines and counseling for victims of violence receive more funding (Searles and Berger 1987, 78). As the antirape movement gained legitimacy, and increasingly relied on government funding, it construed rape as a crime of violence and not sex (Matthews 1994, 153) and became centered on satisfying the needs of victims. Similarly, as the battered women's movement became increasingly formalized, battering was established, often for strategic reasons, as a unique phenomenon of physical abuse rather than as an issue of power and control (Schneider 1992b). This inadvertently "psychiatrized" battered women, removing them from their place as casualties of a gender war and creating them as persons with deep, complicated psychologies (Fraser 1989, 176–77). And so this set of cultural mechanisms established contemporary feminism as a victim services squad.

Many rape crisis centers do offer self-defense classes, and some battered women's shelters have referrals to self-defense courses or have a self-defense instructor come to the shelter to teach women there. However, these offerings are limited. Women's shelters, for instance, tend not to refer women to firearms training, let alone provide it for them. Thus self-defense has as often as not developed outside the context of anti–sexual assault organizations. Again, this is in part because gender ideology makes feminist victim prevention services seem too radical. But it has also become part of the thinking and practice of much feminist activism.

Feminist politics, like other forms of resistance, have habitually held up the broken body as the way to argue that a set of social arrangements is objectively wrong. This has led feminists to construe sexuality in quite naturalized, apolitical terms. The moral inappropriateness of rape is often secured with references to the female body as a sacred place, and by implicitly contrasting consensual sex as apolitical with forced sex as a political, nonsexual matter of violence. Additionally, much feminist activism and teaching to educate men and women about sexual violence presuppose the very fictions of sexed embodiment that fuel rape culture. Finally, much feminist discourse has maintained a central assumption of bourgeois liberal individualism, namely that the body is an appendage of the self subjected to property rights (Diprose 1994). This assumption turns the body into an object rather than an agent, thus rendering women's self-defense training irrelevant, inconsequential, or even antithetical to feminist politics.

The anti–sexual assault movement and feminist theory could better challenge rape culture at its core. While knowing "in theory" that violence against women is not natural or inevitable, we have overlooked the potential of training women to fight back and have given all the power to stop violence to men. We have inadvertently preserved a fundamental association between masculinity and violence. We have not adequately challenged the rape myth that men rape because of size and strength. Nor have we adequately contested the distinction between sexuality and politics, a distinction that, while defining rape as an unnatural act rooted in relations of social inequality, preserves sexuality as a "natural" essence free from power relations. Finally, we have not thoroughly interrogated the traditional distinction between the body and consciousness.

Self-defense at its core challenges what it means to have a female body, what it means to be a man or a woman. Self-defense thus offers a critique of the way gender is written into our bodies. It transforms the bodies we inhabit and hence who we are; the meaning of sexuality; and the culture of sexual violence against women. The self-defense movement can be an impetus for feminists to reimagine the categories and practices that define feminism. Feminism must take seriously the pleasure women gain from combative bodily practices, and reconsider the primacy of corporeality to consciousness. In short, feminism must get physical.

To understand why self-defense is so transformative for women, and so disruptive of the embodied ethos of rape culture, we must first understand how proper femininity has excluded aggression. Over the course of North American history, women have been restricted through codes of feminine manners that are in large part bodily. Women no longer have to ride sidesaddle, work in long skirts, or cavort in corsets. How is it that so many of us still don't know how to hit?

1

Balls versus Ovaries

Women's "Virtue" in Historical Perspective

"Sugar and spice and everything nice, that's what girls are made of. Frogs and snails and puppy dog tails, that's what boys are made of." Institutionalized versions of this nursery rhyme abound. And while such ideas declare males and females to be innately different, a rigid enforcement of these supposedly natural differences takes place at all levels of society. In his hugely popular *Baby and Child Care*, Dr. Spock, along with many other post-World War II parenting specialists, explicitly instructed parents to encourage boys to be aggressive, cautioning against turning them into "sissies" (Spock 1945). The same expert told parents to discourage girls from hitting and other aggressive activities. But it is not only socialization into proper gender "roles" that encourages men's aggression and proscribes women's.

Aggression is fastened to the realm of the masculine in the popular imagination and in everyday language. For example, bravery and courage are male qualities. The word *mettle* is synonymous, in Webster's thesaurus, not only with *courage* and *bravery* but also with *man* and *manly*. Two entries describe female mettle, Joan of Arc and Amazon—specific historical figures who, incidentally, are hardly symbols of femininity. Our casual talk displays this same implicit understanding that courage is gendered: "You've got balls." That to "fuck" someone implies an aggressive violation is evidenced by the meaning of insults like "Fuck you!" and complaints such as "I got fucked by the IRS" (Beneke 1982). Losing sports teams get "reamed" by their opponents and someone unwilling to submit to an authority figure refuses to "bend over."

The cultural connection between aggression and manhood, then, is sexualized. We don't, after all, commend someone's manly heroism with aphorisms like, "You've really got beard" or "Man, you've got an Adam's apple." And no one can congratulate a woman for an act of heroism with "You've got ovaries." In fact, women's reproductive organs have been invoked historically to justify their exclusion from aggressive sports and a number of other prized and financially rewarding social spheres.

Of course it's now easy to see through the gender ideology that grounds women's exclusion from civil life in their reproductive organs. But many people still hold unexamined beliefs about the difference between male and female bodies which must be examined in order to appreciate the radical impact of women's self-defense training. Gender is the "knowledge that establishes meaning for bodily difference" (Scott 1988, 2). Gender does not spring innocently from our biology or become added on top of it; gender is the system that organizes the meaning of our biological bodies.

Gender is a discursive construction that produces our knowledge of ourselves as sexed individuals. Discourse is a system of signs, practices, statements, and texts across different social sites that constructs experience (see Canning 1994; Foucault 1980; Terdiman 1985; Weedon 1987). As a preassembled way to think, a discourse makes some possibilities easy to imagine and others impossible. While individual agents shape discourse, various cultural representations and discourses help produce the female and the male body as such. This chapter examines how those discourses discourage women's aggression, and encourage men's, at the level of fantasized possibility and at the level of the body.

Being a Normal, Feminine Lady

In the 1890s, U.S. social reformers sought to exclude the married woman from factory labor on the grounds that distress and disorder would result. Children would be left unsupervised and men would be driven to pubs due to the dirty living quarters resulting from their wives' absence. Not only would men and children suffer, in this logic, but women's bodies would be unable to sustain work with machines (Canning 1994). In much the same way, women's entrance into higher education was resisted on the grounds that their uteruses would be damaged, as though the brain and the uterus demanded energy from the same source, rendering one ineffective by the use of the other (Ehrenreich and English 1978, 126).[1] This mythology suggests that if we don't act on the sex differences that God or nature gave us, we will jeopardize either our own physical health or the larger social order.

Many male commentators of the Victorian era claimed that women really did have power, the power to "moralize their families and their country" (Gay 1993, 297). Indeed, womanliness was defined by the ability to teach purity and virtue. If men had the privilege of exercising authority in public, women were to think that they had an even greater and worthier authority in the home. The lack of aggression defines a "lady"—she is known for her ability to handle a difficult situation, even a man's aggression, without ever getting aggressive, or "rude," herself (Clarke 1993, 397).

Being recognized as morally superior for one's pacifism and kindness, however, grants no real social power. Mary Daly (1978) points out that the feminine virtues of altruism and self-sacrifice are virtues of subservience. Sarah Hoagland (1988, 83) suggests that vulnerability is yet another such feminine virtue, which includes nonreciprocal openness, loyalty, and dependency. Jeffner Allen (1986, 39) notes that nonviolence is also linked to the ideology of heterosexual virtue:

> The ideology of heterosexual virtue forms the cornerstone of the designation of women as nonviolent. The ideology of heterosexual virtue charges women to be "moral," virtuously nonviolent in the face of the "political," violent male-defined world. The ideology of heterosexual virtue entitles men to terrorize—to possess, humiliate, violate, and objectify—women and forecloses the possibility of women's active response to men's sexual terrorization.

The pacifism and passivity of femininity, then, are part and parcel of a system of compulsory heterosexuality.

Women's fighting and aggression have met the same kind of opposition that women's intellectual and public pursuits have, for the same reasons. This is not to say that women have not aggressively fought and survived. There have always been women who have worked hard and fought in wars. But they were rarely supposed to do so officially, and these actions certainly called their femininity into question. Whereas men fight as men, and can achieve manhood in doing so, Joan of Arc had to fight in drag—and was ultimately executed as a witch, not hailed as a hero. Women's fighting challenges a fundamental association between women and goodness. Consider the following congressional testimony from retired Marine Corps Commandant, General Robert H. Barrow (June 1991, quoted in Blacksmith 1992, 26):

> Exposure to danger is not combat. Being shot at, even being killed, is not combat. Combat is finding . . . closing with . . . and killing or capturing the enemy. It's killing. And it's done in an environment that is often as difficult as you can possibly imagine. Extremes of climate. Brutality. Death. Dying. It's . . . uncivilized! And women can't do it! Nor should they even be thought of as doing it. The requirements for strength and endurance render them unable to do it. . . . Women give life. Sustain life. Nurture life. They don't take it.

Because men's aggression is taken for granted as natural, women's seems threatening to society in a different way. The fear that women's rebellion will cause social life to crumble still exists. Look at men's reactions to *Thelma and Louise*: They declared the film "fascist" and "degrading to men" (Schickel 1991, 52). Women are discursively positioned as the moral conscience of their families, communities, and nations.

Of course, women as a group are far more diverse, and as individuals far more complex, than the culturally dominant model for female identity suggests or allows. But because we have construed the meaning of *female* as passivity, women's activities that fall outside the dominant image get construed as aggressive. A historical perspective reveals that women who have deviated from the prescriptive feminine norm have hardly been considered women at all.

Women's Deviance in Historical Perspective: Lesbian and Black Women As Aggressive

Historically, girls and women have been considered deviants or criminals for behaving in a variety of ways legally permitted for males, for example running away from home. William I. Thomas's *The Unadjusted Girl* (1923) uncritically examines such girls without questioning why the overwhelming "deviant" behaviors reported in the case notes are premarital sex,[2] prostitution, and pregnancy. Thomas (1923, 109) admits that delinquency in girls begins with the desire for "amusement, adventure, pretty clothes, favorable notice, distinction, freedom in the larger world," hinting that deviance in girls was often simply what was socially accepted as healthy in boys.

Cesare Lombroso (1911), a criminologist notorious for his assertion that men with specific, presumably less evolved, physical features were more likely to be criminals, accounted for women's less frequent criminal activity with reference to women's "piety, maternity, want of passion, sexual coldness, weakness, and an undeveloped intelligence" (Lombroso and Ferrero 1895, 151). Lombroso and Ferrero suggest that "female criminals approximate more to males . . . than to normal women, especially in the superciliary arches in the seam of the sutures, in the lower jaw-bones, and in peculiarities of the occipital region" (ibid., 28).

So difficult is it to conceive that women are not innately passive that female deviants are construed as biologically defective. These explanations of women's criminality or lack thereof presume that natural sex differences exist and explain behavior. These theories do not explain that, for instance, "running away" and "sexual misconduct" were crimes only girls could commit. Deviance is a matter of social definition. Social definitions are more interesting than the deviant individual. For the deviant status of women's aggression points to the social structures that organize gender and aggression.

It was not only criminology of the turn of the century that positioned natural womanhood in opposition to aggression, which it associated with natural manhood. Sexology and psychoanalysis did as well (see Hart 1994, 3-28 for a review).[3] Freud's theories construed women as passive and saw the girl in the clitoral phase of sexual development as a "little man" (Freud 1931, in Strachey 1981, 151). Sexologists studied the female "gender invert" who was as active as a heterosexual man in desiring a woman. Most sexologists were so wedded to womanhood as heterosexual and passive that they construed the lesbian as a deviant, too aggressive to be a "real" woman.

The understanding of women as virtuous, nonaggressive keepers of the moral order explains why lesbians have historically been seen as threatening to civilized social organization (Chauncey 1982-83, 133). "Civilization" is configured in the interests of dominant men whose privilege would be unsettled if women rejected the ideology of heterosexual virtue. What has been so upsetting to people about the existence of lesbians is not that women are the object of the lesbian's desire per se, but the masculine, aggressive form that such desire connotes (Chauncey 1982-83, 119; Hart 1994, 9). In other words, the aggressiveness implied in her object choice was what made the lesbian seem so deviant and dangerous.

This is the historical connection that makes it so easy to deride an aggressive woman as a lesbian. The aggressive woman is threatening to, although necessary for, heterosexist patriarchy; relegating this figure to a special category, lesbian, makes her containable and therefore useful (Hart 1994). The displacement of criminality onto lesbianism helps retain aggression as a male preserve, as if aggression really were not possible for women, at least "real" women. If the lesbian is still thought of as a "man" or some sort of gender invert (whether created by a "perversion" of nature or culture), then the "real woman" is still heterosexual and passive.

In the late nineteenth century, black women, lesbians, and prostitutes were lumped into one deviant category (ibid., 119-20). "Ladylike" behaviors such as physical delicacy were outside the bounds of possibility for black women—due to life circumstances in a racist society which made it virtually impossible for them to attain those signs of successful womanhood. The ideal of the helpless, corseted woman so weak and so wealthy that she retired to the fainting couch for a spell was not a real option for black women who did heavy manual labor and other work outside their homes. Black women were not supposed to devote time to their families; whites blamed crop failures on just such inappropriate black female behaviors. But at another level, all women were held accountable to the dominant standard of femininity. Hence black women, like lesbians, have been construed as failed women.

That black women's social position made the attainment of the feminine ideal practically impossible did not free them from their own form of sequestration. During Reconstruction, the threat of rape by white men made public appearances dangerous for black women, hence black men became their link to economic and political spheres (Davis 1983). These conditions, different from those cloistering white women, solidified black women's distance from public life and the mobility it implied.

If a black woman was sexually assaulted, no one with political authority cared or sided with her if she defended herself against the assailant. Black women were positioned as property to white men—not the kind of property white women were, which was valuable and virtuous, but as workers and as sexually exploitable property. Their sexuality being seen as less civilized and refined than white women's, black women were judged as either sexless "mammies" or sexually disrespectable "Jezebels." The stereotype of the mammy represents the ideal of unconditional love and nurturance, an image that rationalized black women's oppression by representing them as happily concerned with the needs of white people (hooks 1981, 41-45). This image of selfless nurturer was different from the icon of white female nurturance, but it was nurturance and maternalism just the same, thereby excluding aggression.

The stereotype of the Jezebel made black women appear sexually inviting and always available to satisfy men, which reinforced white men's real sexual access to black women. Rather than being seen as sexually virtuous, black women were seen as sexually voracious. This did not offer some sort of social freedom; to the contrary, it rationalized sexual assaults against black women. Moreover, black women have been evaluated according to the ideals of feminine virtue and passivity, and women of color more generally have served as the contrasting "others" against which white women could measure themselves.

The legacy of slavery is still with us, as evidenced by the greater degree of media coverage that assaults on white women receive. And still today, whereas white women are presumed virtuous until proven otherwise, black women are presumed to be bad and must prove otherwise. Thus while the standing as a lady has been a naturalized dominant ideal against which all women have been judged, it was attainable only for middle- and upper-middle-class white heterosexual women. Moreover, regardless of the actual appearance or behavior of lesbians and black women, stereotypes about them make it virtually impossible for them to meet the ideal in homophobic and racist imaginations.

Though it may seem obvious what a woman is, what a man is, and what aggression is, our "knowledge" about these categories is socially constructed. Aggression is an ideological category central to rape culture, with no distinct definition. Women who step out of line are perceived as aggressive. The putative naturalness of the ideal connecting passivity with women and aggression with men justifies holding the ideal as a standard against which to measure women and men. But even the categories "woman" and "man" are ideological, constructed through a cultural meaning system. Sex difference really isn't a simple matter of balls versus ovaries.

The Social Production of Sex Differences

Cultural authorities—scientific, medical, and religious—have for ages said that humans come in two sexes with complementary natures: Men are strong and aggressive, and women are weak and passive. We learn to assess all of our actions in terms of ideals of sex and by doing so maintain "real manhood" and "real womanhood" (Bem 1993). Moreover, the commitment to heterosexuality as a privileged institution and identity makes man and woman seem like a natural and inevitable pair (Dworkin 1974; Butler 1990). The myth of the interior origins of gender forecloses or explains as deviant various forms of gender dissonance, such as female aggression, or for that matter, male pacifism (Butler 1990, 1993).

To the extent that men fail, consciously or not, to develop strength in their bodies, to disrespect women, and to pursue sexual intercourse with them, they fail at heterosexual masculinity. Others can derogate such men as "sissies," "pussy whipped," and "faggots," respectively. To the extent that women choose, or are forced by economic necessity, to be strong, assertive, or emotionally or sexually unavailable to men, they fail at heterosexual femininity and may be labeled "dykes," "castrating bitches," or simply "crazy." Nobody actually lives up to the purest ideals of womanhood and manhood; but those are the ideals against which we judge ourselves and others. The point, then, is not that heterosexism, racism, and rape culture determine sexed embodiment perfectly, completely, or permanently. It is that these are idealized norms against which individuals are judged. These norms make the female body seem complementary to the male body, and make heterosexuality compulsory.

Feminists have argued that sex inequality, and rape specifically, occurs not because women are different from men, but because sex itself has been made into a social difference of profound importance and thus the basis upon which inequalities rest (MacKinnon 1989; Gatens 1996). Rape is not a result of any "natural" sexuality. Women's sexual availability to men is in part what defines womanhood. If sex itself is not a natural difference but a socially constituted one, then gender and gender inequality are not results or expressions of biological sex assignment, a matter of balls vs. ovaries. Rather, gender is a political fiction of difference which itself produces the idea of anatomically differentiated bodies.

There is no original, presocial difference, "sex," which then gets translated into social differences. In a chicken and egg reversal of profound importance, our popular ideals of gender actually produce the ideal of natural sex. Gender is a cultural fiction that produces sex as its (imaginary) natural origin (Butler 1993, 93). This is not to say that cultural assumptions supply half the population with balls, but it is to say that cultural assumptions make having balls mean what it does. Were it not for our cultural assumptions, having balls would not imply membership in a category of persons; nor would it imply anything about what kind of personality one has, what kind of sex one likes or "needs" to have, what kind of work one is capable of performing, and so on.

The criteria for what makes a body male or female have changed through time. Although we may take for granted today that the presence or absence of a properly sized and functioning penis is a natural marker of sex, it once was the presence or absence of ovaries that indicated sex classification (Kessler 1990). The knowledge we have about sexed bodies is a value-laden knowledge informed by and solidifying the power inequalities between men and women. There is no ahistorical body prior to a power/knowledge system that institutes the body as an object (Diprose 1994). Power influences the knowledge we have about bodies and, since we live out knowledge, constitutes the kinds of bodies or subjects we become.

The patriarchal power system affecting our knowledge of male and female bodies positions women as inferior to men. As Elizabeth Grosz (1994, 14) notes:

> Instead of granting women an autonomous and active form of corporeal specificity, at best women's bodies are judged in terms of a "natural inequality," as if there were a standard or measure for the value of bodies independent of sex. In other words, women's corporeal specificity is used to explain and justify the different (read: unequal) social positions and cognitive abilities of the two sexes. By implication, women's bodies

are presumed to be incapable of men's achievements, being weaker, more prone to (hormonal) irregularities, intrusions, and unpredictabilities.

The universalistic stance of scientific discourse conflates the masculine with the human, thereby confining the feminine to a secondary position that is devalued compared to the primary position. This dualistic mode of thinking creates binary differences and rationalizes a hierarchical scale of power relations (Braidotti 1994, 154). The scientific discourse of biology does not give us the "truth" of sex. Scientists don't merely notice sex differences and report their findings. Scientists choose to study sex differences, funding agencies choose to fund such studies, and the studies often reflect preconceived notions about sex.[4] Contrary to the popular notion that "seeing is believing," quite often the belief in sex actually makes us see it (Lorber 1993).

Scientists didn't simply come along and discover the passivity of females. The ideology of male activity and aggression and female passivity and vulnerability is the product of scientists who, like everyone else, were responsible for judging their behavior and ideas in terms of the gender ideals of their day. Scientists work with the ideologies available to them, such as the teachings of Aristotle, who suggested that "female" is passive and absent while "male" is active and present. The masculine represents what is valued while the feminine represents the "other" and what is devalued. Thus, for example, scientists call some *E. coli* bacteria male and others female simply because one strain of *E. coli* cells contains F plasmid and can transfer genes into the cells which lack F plasmid. Predictably, the ones which lack F plasmid and receive it are called female (Spanier 1995, 56-58). Similarly, scientists have been unable to imagine and describe the process of fertilization as anything other than an aggressive, competitive sperm fighting its way to a passive egg-in-waiting—at least until feminist critics like Emily Martin (1992) suggested that sperm are actually terrible swimmers and must be sucked in by a decidedly nonpassive egg. Scientists have instead imagined and described a heterosexual romance story with the sperm and egg (Martin 1991).

Heterosexual norms, then, are officially prescribed through scientific, medical, legal, and psychological discourses. While construing their concern with gender as an innocent matter of scientific truth—the proper translation of biology into identity, sex into gender—these discourses actually produce the idea of sex, that is, of natural difference underlying gender. Such ideational configurations have been instrumental in drawing official boundaries of proper male and female behavior, as they distinguish the sane versus the insane, the healthy versus the sick, the natural versus the perverted. They have framed men's heterosexual predation as healthy, except in cases of extreme violence or black male predation on white women (real or imagined). These discourses have framed as deranged women's behaviors that seem to challenge heterosexual norms and the naturalized gender polarity.

Popular conceptions of natural masculinity and femininity support rape culture. These fictions are not simply beliefs, attitudes, or roles we decide to play. They actually produce bodily dispositions that make heterosexual intercourse compelling and physical coercion fairly easy for men to accomplish. Male and female bodies are not given. Social/moral codes do not just govern, say, how men treat women (and vice versa). They constitute the embodied ethos of men and women; they govern what it means, in any given historical era, to be a man and to be a woman.

The point is not that all of our ideas about bodies are socially constructed and therefore immaterial or inconsequential. Rather, the traditional association between the male body and aggressivity, on the one hand, and between the female body and violability, on the other, are matters of history and culture—with significant historical effects. So long as gender is a fiction that informs our understanding of and living of our bodies, gender informs action. Male dominance demands certain specific bodily investments. Rape culture becomes an embodied ethos.

Masculinity and Rape Culture

It is a common misperception that rape is a large part of women's experience but not men's. Men do have an experience of rape—far too often as rapists—but they rarely think of it as rape, or as violence. Rape is sex without consent. But men who rape often see it as sex, and as natural at that (MacKinnon 1989; Scully 1990). To be sure, there are men who act violently, sexually and non-sexually, toward other men. But those acts of violence are often clear to all participants *as violent,* while rape can often be construed as a man's "natural instincts" responding to a woman whose appearance, behavior, or reputation "invited" it.

Many hang on to the view that men are naturally predatory. Believe it or not, feminists have always given men more credit than this. Feminists suggest that rape is a learned behavior that is mythologized as a drive rooted in natural sex differences. In popular North American cultural logic, the practice of rape, even if regrettable, is caused or enabled by some sort of primal male advantage and female disadvantage.

But rape does not depend upon superior size or strength; it depends on a fantasy of them. This fantasy is what allows men to believe in their abilities and to see women as appropriate targets for abuse. This fantasy also encourages women to believe that their efforts to fight an attacker would be futile:

> A rapist's ability to accost a woman verbally, to demand her attention, and even to attack her physically depends more on how he positions himself relative to her socially than it does on his allegedly superior physical strength. His *belief* that he has more strength than a woman and that he can use it to rape her merits more analysis than the putative fact of that strength, because that belief often produces as an effect the male power that appears to be rape's cause. (Marcus 1992, 390)

Although our cultural imagination construes rapists as physically overpowering women, men need not be particularly aggressive, strong, or physically violent to accomplish rape. Men may need to believe that they have the physical power with which to carry on around women in ways that barely consider women's desires. Indeed, the respect with which men approach other men surely has something to do with the sense that there are consequences for treating a man disrespectfully.

Popular beliefs in the physical superiority of men and the passivity of women, then, underlie the general practice of rape. This is what makes male power "the myth that makes itself true" (MacKinnon 1989, 104). Male supremacy needs biologism to sustain itself. Hence feminists have criticized the celebration of mythic male physical strength and female weakness as a central tenet of male supremacy:

> The right to physical strength as power, in a male-supremacist system, is vouchsafed to men. [One] tenet of male supremacy is that men are physically stronger than women and, for that reason, have dominion over them. Physical strength in women that is not directly harnessed to "women's work" becomes an abomination, and its use against men, that is, as power, is anathema, forbidden, horribly punished. The reality of male physical strength in an absolute sense is less important than the ideology that sacralizes and celebrates it. In part, the physical strength of men over women is realized because men keep women physically weak. (Dworkin 1979, 14-15)

Popular beliefs about the meaning of human body parts also fuel rape culture. Women's bodies are positioned culturally as spaces to be invaded while men's are positioned culturally as impenetrable invaders. (When referring to penis-vagina intercourse, we say "penetration," not "envelopment.") Hence, another myth of male supremacy is the idea "that sexual power authentically originates in the penis. Masculinity in action, narrowly in the act of sex as men define it or more widely in any act of taking, is sexual power fulfilling itself, being true to its own nature" (Dworkin 1979, 24).[5] If men's sense of social superiority feels real, physical, and visceral, through their sexual organs, and their potential for physical aggression is celebrated as natural, then clearly we have a recipe for the sustenance of a rape culture that produces its own legitimation.

The commonsense understanding of the location of a man's sense of self (a man's penis is referred to as his "manhood"), and its implicit misrecognition as a natural fact, is reinforced in childhood socialization, mainstream media, and mainstream pornography—although never absolutely. Thus the perpetual need to enact rituals of manhood, such as heterosexual intercourse (whether forced or consensual), thereby providing corporeal reassurance that manhood is natural after all. A man's need to *have a sex* (that is, an identity as a man) so perfectly coincides with a need to *have sex* that it appears to be grounded in some sort of natural biological "drive" (Stoltenberg 1989). But "proving one's manhood" is really more about establishing it. However much some men would like to think that they belong to a preexisting, precultural sex category that has certain properties, namely an essential need for heterosexual contact with certain women and an aggressive impulse to get that contact, those feelings (however authentic) are the embodied ethos of rape culture. That manhood feels real, and that men feel driven, only exemplifies the corporeal manifestation of the cultural ethos.

Heterosexual intercourse is thus crucial for solidifying a sense of oneself as belonging to a naturally existing category of manhood. Thus, sex, whether forced or consensual, often solidifies for men a sense of natural sex differences. If such a fantasy of difference is necessary for a confirmation of privileged identity, then sexual activity, specifically intercourse, might become so compelling that women's interest in it is either irrelevant or taken for granted as part of their natural makeup. In this light, sexual assaults are not *conscious* attempts to keep women down but, quite literally, boys trying to be boys.

Our understanding of masculinity goes hand in hand with an understanding of the male body as impenetrable and invulnerable. When men desire to be penetrated, they are seen as "perverted." When men are raped, almost always by other men (in prison, for instance), the act is understood as a violation. That such an act is seen as "making a woman" out of them also shows how the heterosexist norms of our culture intertwine markers of sex and aggression. We could conceivably—but do not—live in a culture in which women fondle and penetrate drunk men in bars and at parties, or in which armed women assault men on the streets and in their homes. It is a matter of culture, not nature, that we live in a world of primarily male heterosexual predation. It is a matter of culture that we even have a category of persons known as "men," with bodies understood as impenetrable.

The statement, "rape is about violence, not sex" has often misled people into thinking that when men rape women, they do so knowing the difference between consensual sex and felony rape, knowing that women experience it as oppressive, and knowing that they are violating or dominating women. But that statement was never meant to capture the assailant's experience of the event. It was meant to capture the victim's experience of rape, and to counter the misconception that men rape out of some unstoppable sex "drive," exemplified by Camille Paglia's declaration that "hunt, pursuit and capture are biologically programmed into male sexuality" (1992, 51).

A man may very well experience raping as a sexual act; but even if he does, sexual aggression is not natural, nor is it erotic for his victim. In a situation of rape, the man and the woman do not have the same experience of the event— *that* is the problem. Little compels men to see such encounters in the same way that women do (Scully 1990). Men who rape do not necessarily intend to rape; they intend to have sex. That a woman does not want sexual intercourse, sadly, seems either irrelevant to a man who rapes or relevant to him but arrogantly misconstrued as desire (ibid.).

Men may know that a woman in a short skirt isn't an invitation to rape; but some think it's an invitation to have sex—the problem being that too many men construe sex as not-rape because a woman did this or that (indicators other than saying "I want to do this with you"). Men tend not to claim that men who wear shorts with no shirts, stand naked in locker room showers, or dress in tight jeans are leading anyone on or "asking for it." We do not tend to regard men as violable beings in the same way; nor do we see men as vulnerable to or deserving of sex for which they have no interest.

Many imprisoned rapists admit to having had sex but insist that it was consensual or otherwise OK and not rape (ibid.). This, grievously, includes men who broke into the homes of women and raped them at knife point. It is not difficult to imagine that if even rapists who committed such extreme and obvious felonies do not see their action from their victim's perspective, the men who rape their dates and acquaintances under more everyday circumstances do not necessarily understand themselves to have harmed someone either. Some of these men can be so ignorant that they call their victims to ask for another date, or, when confronted by their victims, justify their behavior by insisting that the victim did not have a good enough reason to refuse the sex.

Rapists aren't the only ones who don't get it. Many people blame the victim or otherwise excuse the rapist's behavior. Rapists get their excuses and justifications from the culture in which they live. There is a societywide predisposition to minimize the culpability of men who rape. Hence men who rape are less social deviants than they are conformists (Franks 1985). The discrepancy of opinion over when a woman is allowed to determine whether or not she will have sex, and therefore whether or not what she experiences is rape, is precisely why feminists fought to make marital rape illegal. Prior to that, any sex a man had with his wife was treated as inherently consensual in the law. Feminists sought to redefine as rape acts of forced sex that many insisted were—simply because of the relationship between the people involved—consensual. How women are defined vis-à-vis men makes a significant impact on the likelihood that a given act will be seen as legitimate. When women were still considered to be their husbands' property, it was nearly impossible for most people to understand that women could be raped by their husbands.

Over two decades ago, the anti-sexual assault movement emphasized the violation at the heart of women's experience of rape; they did so specifically to denaturalize rape. The movement also emphasized rape as a violent crime so that their need for state funding of rape crisis centers and hot lines would be seen as legitimate (Matthews 1994, 151-61). Framing rape as violent rather than sexual also helped challenge some sexist aspects in and surrounding rape law. For instance, it helped overcome the problem of marital exception to rape law, relieve the stigma of being a rape victim and increase women's likelihood to report rape, and reduce the media's interest in the victim's sexual history and attire (Dumaresq 1981, 49-50). But this emphasis has tended to separate sexuality from violence falsely, thereby naturalizing consensual heterosexuality as it denaturalized rape. Some now take the statement "rape is about violence, not sex" to mean that rape is an act of violence perpetrated by a psychotic individual with violent intentions, opposing it to a freely chosen natural sexual act in which no power inequality or feeling of dominance is present.

The claim that men rape in order to dominate turns rape into an act that men presumably conduct consciously (as if all rapists knew their victims do not want it) as some sort of oppressive tactic to ensure male political privilege. Moreover, the claim that forced intercourse gives the man a feeling of dominance tends to ignore the ways in which consensual heterosexual intercourse can also give men a feeling of dominance (MacKinnon 1989; Plummer 1984; Rich 1980; Stoltenberg 1989). A widespread popular misperception of radical feminist arguments about sexuality and power is that they claim all sex is rape. This misperception may stem from the inability to conceive of the more subtle point feminists have made: that for some men the psychic rewards (e.g., a sense of masculinity, virility, pleasure, and domination) of consensual sex may be no different from those of forced sex. Feminism does not castigate all heterosexual sex as nefarious or unlawful, then, but questions the ability to separate sexuality from the power relations with which it is bound up.

Heterosexual male aesthetics involve all the things that perpetuate strength and invulnerability. Masculinity is socially conceived in ways that support men's participation in sports, development of their physical capabilities, and training with firearms (Messner 1990, 1994; Gibson 1994). Such activities render men more, not less, masculine. It's not "manly" to be servile, soft, small, or vulnerable. It's not "manly" to be too concerned about one's appearance or attractiveness, as it's not manly to have one's body looked at, penetrated, or taken. These things, in the popular imagination, represent femininity. It is to the cultural cultivation and appreciation of feminine passivity in women that I now turn.

Femininity and Rape Culture

The old saying, "It takes work to be a woman" reveals the efforts women must exert to stylize their bodies in ways that are considered appropriately feminine. Indeed women may be keenly aware that the body is invested with daily time- and money-consuming practices involving diet, exercise, clothing, makeup, hair and body cosmetics, accessories of adornment, posture, gait, attitude, and even surgery. Femininity does not come "naturally." Women are rewarded psychologically and materially for cultivating physical difference from men, and not just any difference.

Feminine manners and attractiveness require a concern for the needs of others, a degree of pleasantness to which we do not hold men accountable (Cline and Spender 1987), and a cultivated inability to defend moral and physical boundaries (MacKinnon 1989). Being looked at (rather than looking at others) and withholding one's strength help make up femininity (MacKinnon 1987; Young 1990). Women learn to be nice and deferential to men, occupying a number of personal and professional roles that demand such an ability (Hochschild 1983). Secretarial work, domestic work, waitressing, flight attending, nursing, child care, homemaking, and hooking implicitly and explicitly require feminine deference and cheerfulness in serving others. Feminine manners are anything but aggressive; in fact, feminine manners are precisely the opposite.

Women display deference to men out of economic necessity, for fear of consequences, and sometimes simply out of habit in a number of situations that men exploit. Women are taught that, in order to be liked by a man, they must reflect him in larger-than-life ways. Women's magazines are an ever-present source of such directives. One girl recalls what she learned from them: "I remember reading that girls should let boys do all the talking. Smile and say nice things to a boy, cliché things . . . like, 'Michael, what big muscles you have!' . . . I was supposed to sit and listen and smile at everything HE said, and never be bored or look bored" (Székely 1988, 92).

Femininity requires appearance as well as demeanor. Women stylize their bodies in a predictable manner: in terms of vulnerability (high heels create it); smallness (dieting and, failing that, girdles help produce it); and feminine attractiveness, which is sexual availability to men (dressing in whatever styles are current "turn ons" indicates it). This body work, whether women take it for granted, enjoy it, feel rewarded for it, resent it, reject it, or feel obligated to do it, serves as a reminder to women that gender is a physical appearance that does not simply flow from the hormones and ooze out the pores.

Femininity is a practice and social form of consciousness that not only differentiates women but signals their subordinate position in a human hierarchy. As an aestheticized appearance, hegemonic femininity renders gender inequality sensual, erotic, and attractive. Women are expected to engage in a whole host of activities for others that men would not as readily do: look nice, smell nice, feel nice, smile nice, smile more, listen well, talk softly, talk sweetly, be polite, and please others. Simultaneously, women are expected to avoid those things that will make them messy, sweaty, bruised, dirty, or large (Wolf 1991).

Of course some would have us think that many men's intense appreciation of women's femininity indicates that women actually have power over men. After all, such women are "drop-dead gorgeous," "stunning," "blond bombshells," and of course "real knockouts." The "power" that feminine beauty and manners offer, however, doesn't get women very far. Feminine manners are not strong or respectable, fierce or heroic. They're not intelligent and forthright, determined or assertive. And while a feminine woman should take a man's breath away, she should not *really* be able to knock him out. If a woman has any real institutional, physical, or political power, she is often considered aggressive and unattractive.

That femininity is defined in terms that rationalize women's subordination to men explains the stereotype of the ugly feminist. Aesthetic evaluations of what is sexy revolve around male dominance and female subordination. Hence a feminist must be ugly, angry, militant, ball-busting, and man-hating, while wife beaters (female-bashers, quite literally) and rapists (militant in their desire for sex) are seldom called woman-haters.

Our aesthetics are not innocent personal preferences outside of power relations. In art, women have been sexually provocative objects for the male voyeur. Femininity includes a distinctively textual dimension, whereby femininity as a social consciousness is produced through writing, painting, television, and film (Smith 1988, 38). Such discourses of gender provide fantasies of what women and men can be. These fantasies in turn affect our self-perceptions and bodily comportments. Film serves as a primary means of glamorizing women's helplessness and men's heroism. Usually, these two fantasies are interdependent: Who does the hero save but a helpless woman? Whose death or rape does he avenge? Who loves him in the end as her best protector?

Men in films are the active, heroic protagonists who make things happen, often because of the love or fear that the beautiful woman, the appealing object, inspires in him (Mulvey 1989, 19-20). The ideals of womanhood involve beauty, not acts of heroism as ideals of manhood do. As Naomi Wolf (1991, 59) points out, "A beautiful heroine is a contradiction in terms, since heroism is about individuality, interesting and ever changing, while 'beauty' is generic, boring, and inert." We are inundated by portrayals of beautiful young white women saved (and then later ravished) by heroic male crime-stoppers, while the reverse is practically unheard of. Feminists have pointed out that representations of women in popular culture reflect male fantasies and anxieties more than women's realities or fantasies (Mulvey 1989, xiii).

Women's sexual compliance is a common fantasized image in popular media. MTV's rock videos display the all too common formula in which a male rock star is surrounded by scantily clad, sex-starved female models (Jhally 1990). Women in these fantasies joyfully fulfill a status as sexual toys. Laura Mulvey (1989, 19) explains the pervasiveness of woman as a visual image for male spectatorship:

> In a world ordered by sexual imbalance, pleasure in looking has been split between active/male and passive/female. The determining male gaze projects its fantasy onto the female figure, which is styled accordingly. In their traditional exhibitionist role women are simultaneously looked at and displayed, with their appearance coded for strong visual and erotic impact so that they can be said to connote *to-be-looked-at-ness*. Woman

displayed as sexual object is the *leitmotif* of erotic spectacle: from pin-ups to strip-tease, from Ziegfeld to Busby Berkeley, she holds the look, and plays to and signifies male desire.

MTV rock videos represent a specifically male fantasy, not a fantasy that women and men share.[6]

Much male-constructed visual culture represents women in ways that do not mirror what women actually seek in their sex lives. If women were to make videos involving their sexual fantasies, it is doubtful that they would involve women who look as if they had not eaten in a week, grouped together, all fawning over a scruffy musician. Though women are being turned all the time into objects of display, to be looked at and stared at by men, the images projected may have little relationship to women's real lives, fantasies, fears, and desires (Mulvey 1989, 13).

Imagistic discourses do not produce desires definitively. By analogy, images of "happy darkies"[7] did not fool *everyone* into thinking that blacks enjoyed subordination, and certainly did not make black people start enjoying their subservience. Nevertheless those images had the general effect of a legitimating ideology. In the same way, images of glamorized female passivity legitimate women's circumscribed position but do not necessarily produce such desires in all women or all men.

The constant representation of women as the fantasy figures of the male spectator turns the women of visual culture into objects. Imagistic discourse suggests that men have bodies that will prevail, that are strong and impenetrable. Female bodies are not represented as active agents in this way, but instead as breakable, takeable bodies. Just as such images portray women as prey to men's violence, they allow men to imagine themselves as invulnerable, especially compared to women. The textual representations of sexed bodies are lived out as material realities—as evidenced by women's greater likelihood to put themselves on display sexually for the gaze of another. Further, the imagistic discourses of femininity and masculinity perpetuate the myths that women actually enjoy being chased and captured (i.e., that *no* means *yes*); that women invite rape and battery; that only psychotic strangers rape; that men cannot control their passions or their privates; and that men rape and batter because they are so big and strong.

Such popular images and other discourses construct women as a class of people unable to exercise the physical agency characteristic of men. Women have been "de-skilled" in heterosexist society, because the system reinforces their economic dependence on men (Hoagland 1988, 33). In addition, women have been de-skilled in terms of their potential as fighters. They are trained to be weak and thus to need a man, or the police, for protection against male violence. Thus, the ideal of passivity is particular to a system in which heterosexuality is a privileged institution and identity. The physical de-skilling of women and the stigmatization of lesbians reinforce each other: the fear of being labeled a lesbian keeps many women in line just as the heterosexist society's economic and physical de-skilling of women cultivates among them a psychically compelling, and often materially real, need for a man. Our understanding of the female body as penetrable supports not only compulsory heterosexuality but women's "rapeability."

Women's socialization has insured the continuation of rape culture, making them easy and easily rationalized targets for men's abuse. A woman's successful tutelage in the fragility of the "male ego" can turn into a habituated disavowal of her own strengths (Lerner 1988). Women are not simply stupid or duped, though there are intense social pressures on them to exhibit the qualities of femininity. MacKinnon (1987, 54) writes that "femininity as we know it is how we come to want male dominance, which most emphatically is not in our interest." Still, women might find their "part" in oppression in a way which renders them neither pure victims nor pure agents of their own distress (Rose 1986).

Women's pleasing personalities are enforced by many men's expectations; for women who refuse to "reflect men at twice their natural size," as Cline and Spender (1987) put it, have faced harsh consequences. Women are not allowed to defy "feminine" obligations and claim "masculine" entitlements with impunity. Traditionally, as I will explain later, a woman was not legally permitted to defend herself against a sexual assault, even though the assault itself, when not perpetrated by her husband, constituted a felony. Women who have defended themselves from murderous husbands have been punished as "crazy" and sent to mental hospitals. When they were lucky enough to claim self-defense in court, many were sent to jail anyway (Gillespie 1989).

When wives were acquitted on charges of first-degree murder—women like Francine Hughes, who set her battering husband's bed to burn before driving away with her children (Jones 1980, 299-300, 306-7)—newspapers printed headlines such as "Self-Defense Decision Causing Double Standard: Women Get More Than Equal Rights after Killing Spouse." Quips like this one from an attorney were also common: "Hey, it's open season on husbands" (Gillespie 1989, 10). Never mind that it has long been open season on wives and girlfriends: Women are six times more likely than men to experience violence by an intimate (U.S. Department of Justice 1995, 3); in 1994, almost two and a half times as many women in the United States were murdered by male mates than vice versa (Uniform Crime Reports for the United States 1994, 19).[8] Yet, even when defensive, women's violence is considered inappropriate and unfeminine.

Rape culture depends upon the construction of women as a category of persons desirable to men, unable to resist men's attacks, and therefore available as objects with which men can satisfy a variety of desires, including the desire to prove their manhood. Women's second-class citizenship is not simply a contributing factor, but is part of the motivation for male violence.

Women are subjected to, and sometimes willingly cultivate, a style of violability that bleeds right into rape culture and their own oppression. Male supremacist sexuality, lived out by women and men, is not just a psychological, attitudinal, or ideological matter. It's a material reality. Gender is no less bodily or material because it is discursive or textual. Social institutions seep into our bones. The standards of gender operate through meaning systems which themselves operate through the lived body.

Embodiment and Power

Many people might find believable dominant discourses that differentiate men and women along the lines of aggression not only because they see those differences in the social world but also because they feel those differences in themselves. As one female university student put it, "Gender hasn't affected the kind of person I've become. I'm not a very aggressive person *anyway*." Her statement is interesting not only for targeting aggression as that which distinguishes men from women but for admitting that she genuinely feels less aggressive than she imagines men feel. But the fact that we feel gender as a physical reality isn't so surprising and certainly doesn't controvert its discursive, ideological status. Anatomical bodies are constructed by systems of power *and* are entirely sensual, real, and consequential.

Bodies are not only marked, constituted as appropriate for their cultural requirements, through clothing, makeup, and jewelry, but also through physical habits such as patterns of movements and gestures. In other words, it is not simply that we adorn or enhance a body that is basically given through biology; discourses of gender help constitute our very biological organization (Grosz 1994, 142). Discourses of sex difference become a part of our bodily schema.

Anyone who travels outside his or her own culture notices how people embody culture: people walk and gesticulate, talk and eat in ways unique to their culture. Variations in embodiment are not always simple examples of cultural relativism, though. Pierre Bourdieu (1990) has suggested that power inequality in any given culture influences one's embodiment, specifically arguing that we learn a set of bodily dispositions that are appropriate for our class position. Political mythology is embodied, or "turned into a permanent disposition, a durable way of standing, speaking, walking, and thereby of feeling and thinking" (ibid., 69-70). Bourdieu explains:

> One could endlessly enumerate the values given body, *made* body, by the hidden persuasion of an implicit pedagogy which can instill a whole cosmology, through injunctions as insignificant as "sit up straight" or "don't hold your knife in your left hand," and inscribe the most fundamental principles of the arbitrary content of a culture in seemingly innocuous details of bearing or physical and verbal manners, so putting them beyond the reach of consciousness and explicit statement. (Ibid., 69)

The embodiment of culture is also gendered: Women not only hear "sit up straight," but also "put your knees together," as Susan Brownmiller (1984, 187) recalls from her childhood, or "keep your dress down and your drawers up," as Barbara Smith (1983, xlv) recalls from hers. Although Bourdieu does not discuss a culture of sexual violence, he does mention the gendered uses of the body: "The specifically feminine virtue . . . modesty, restraint, reserve, orients the whole female body downwards, towards the ground, the inside, the house, whereas male excellence . . . is asserted in movement upwards, outwards, towards other men" (Bourdieu 1990, 70). Bourdieu's theory can make sense of the embodied ethos of rape culture.

Bourdieu explains that practical belief is not about adhering to a set of instituted dogmas or doctrines but is, rather, a state of the body. This enacted belief, in the world of everyday life, is the commonsense knowledge or reality that is taken for granted. All of these practical beliefs are displayed and experienced as states of the body. "Habitus" refers to the embodied tastes and preferences we inherit and live out (ibid.). Habitus is where the program dwells; it is the social inside the body, the source of our strategies, that which informs action.

Women, therefore, do not so much consider feminine socialization, think it's a good idea, and then do it. Like it or not, feminist or not, it becomes a state of the body. Brownmiller (1984, 171-72) articulates her successful feminine movement and recalls some of its iconic sources:

Inspired by classical sculpture, Chinese ivories and Florentine art, I'm an adept practitioner of the oblique gesture, the softened motion, the twisting torso, the widening eyes. I rarely stand straight, preferring to lean sideways from the waist with one knee slightly flexed, one hip extended. I lower my shoulder when I lift my arm, adjusting the balance of elbow, wrist and fingers, breaking the line at each critical joint. Without conscious effort I smoke a cigarette, eat a sandwich, regard my hand, climb into a taxi with full assurance of the feminine effect.

Here, Brownmiller tries to be conscious of the feminine habitus, which is that set of unconscious gestures and postures that we take for granted. The social order is imposed through these trained habits or skills. The set of movements, experiences, and habits peculiar to one's social history is a "motor memory" (Merleau-Ponty 1962). This motor memory is gendered because we live in a world structured by sex inequality.

A society of sex inequality effects and requires gender-specific somata (Henley 1977). That is to say, bodily postures, talking, walking, and occupying space are learned habits "appropriate" for one's sex class status. For instance, men tend to address women in more familiar terms rather than polite ones, and stand closer to women than they would to male nonintimates, equals, or people they see as superior. Men tend to expect women to smile at them, but do not generally expect to reciprocate (ibid.).

Iris Marion Young (1990) explains that a person's performance of physical tasks requiring strength or muscular coordination display gender. Girls and women tend not to make full use of the body's spatial and lateral potentialities (Young 1990, 145). Men's strides and gaits are typically longer, relative to their size, than women's. Men are more likely to swing their arms, sit with their legs open, stand with their feet apart, and in general display less constricted postures and gestures. Hence, a woman learns to "throw like a girl," that is, to withhold strength, to approach physical tasks in a timid manner. The quip "you throw like a girl" is not simply based on an innocent observation that the carrying angle of the elbow is likely to be different for a person with relatively wide hips than for a person with relatively narrow hips. Such derision designates a person as an incompetent thrower. This physical incompetence is not some simple matter of body size or shape. It's a matter of how the social gets lodged inside the body.

Women's motions tend to be concentrated in one body part, rather than fluid and directed. Women tend not to reach, extend, and follow through because they are not as likely as men to have developed a relationship with their bodies as agents, as instruments of action:

Women often do not perceive themselves as capable of lifting and carrying heavy things, pushing and shoving with significant force, pulling, squeezing, grasping, or twisting with force. When we attempt to do such tasks, we frequently fail to summon the full possibilities of our muscular coordination, position, poise, and bearing. Women tend not to put their whole bodies into engagement in a physical task with the same ease and naturalness as men. (Ibid.)

Thus if a woman throws "like a girl," runs like a girl, swings like a girl, climbs like a girl, and hits like a girl, it is not because she has some natural disadvantage relative to men, but because she does not use her whole body and full strength; because she has less self-conscious direction and placement to her body motion; and because she approaches physical tasks with timidity, uncertainty, and hesitancy (ibid., 146).

Women have been trained out of physical competence and facility with mechanical devices, including firearms. In contrast, aggressive physical activity and shooting guns help establish and confirm a man's gender identity. For example, David Barringer, writing in the men's magazine *Details*, explains that his childhood relationship with guns was a romantic one, watching media heroes triumph over bullies. Even if moral issues proved to be more complicated in adulthood, his approach to guns was a matter of manhood:

The years of cinematic brainwashing may have primed me for a gun, but what finally made me jump the tracks was neither fear nor loathing, but an appeal to prove my manhood. . . . I approached it as if I were cultivating a skill every worldly man should master, one neglected by, but not inconsistent with, my liberal arts education. Inspired by the Greeks, who emphasized the development of mind, body, and spirit, who rapped with Socrates and then bashed each other with swords, I decided to buy a gun. (Barringer 1993, 112)

Girls and women lack such inspiration to shoot and fight. In fact, girls don't achieve womanhood by cultivating those skills, they compromise it. To this day, boy scouts can learn to shoot rifles and shotguns starting in the sixth grade. Girl scouts sell cookies and contribute to charities, but never learn to shoot.

The social investment in women's heterosexual passivity is revealed in the historical discouragement of women from entering sports. Historically, people thought athletics, especially competitive sports, made one assertive, and thus deemed it appropriate for boys but not for girls. Women's economic and sexual servitude to men justified the connection between sports and men. Sports have been seen as a socializing agency that prepares men for adult roles in the workplace and political life (Boutilier and SanGiovanni 1983). Various "experts" of the early twentieth century were as vehement about women's abstinence from physical education as they were about men's participation in it.

Hence North American sport has been an arena in which men could feel their manhood as powerful and natural (Messner 1994), particularly because personal identity has increasingly become rooted in particular stylizations of the body. The physical character of sports helps solidify or mythologize men's sense of sexual differentiation as a preexisting natural fact. Discouraging women from athleticism helps produce a gendered difference in bodily comportment. By the time we are adults, particularly when it comes to physical tasks, men's bodily comportment bellows, "I can," while women's bodily comportment chirps, "I can't."

Those sports in which women have been encouraged to participate are often noncombative practices (even though they require strength, skill, and stamina, and include the pleasures of body mastery), like tennis, aerobics, swimming, golf, and gymnastics. Fewer women engage in sports that emphasize force and body contact, such as those popular among boys and men (as participants and spectators), namely football, soccer, rugby, basketball, hockey, and wrestling. Here, participants learn to accomplish their goals in the face of opposition, by force. That this catechism and its mythical status as natural manly aggression fit well into rape culture is evidenced by one advertisement for men's athletic shoes, in which the male basketball hero is asked about his "biggest score"—to which he responds, "Betty, tenth grade."

A greater number of U.S. females than ever before are competent athletes, thanks in large part to the passage of Title IX of the Education Equity Act of 1972, which prohibits educational programs receiving federal funds to exclude, deny, or discriminate against someone on the basis of sex. Girls were a mere 7 percent of high school athletes in 1971. By 1991 girls were 36 percent (Phillips 1995, 116). But girls are still discouraged from participating in sports, particularly those that involve rough play or competitiveness. The cultivation of shooting and fighting skills still counts as unfeminine. Women are assessed more for their looks than for their physical abilities or personal powers. Thus while legal reforms are crucial, we must address the ideological associations that pit femininity against physical strength.

No one knows better than the girls and women who engage in aggressive contact sports what a disruption of gender their participation is to so many people. The young female athlete soon learns of a discrepancy between the bodily comportment that goes with her athletic accomplishments and that tied to her attractiveness. This conflict between beauty and athleticism is exemplified by school girls' ambivalence about wearing their school's required gym clothes (Scraton 1987). It is hardly startling, in light of these conflicts, that female athletes have always been suspected of being gender outlaws.[9] No wonder teams of female rugby players get stereotyped as "dykes." Those women are not really suspected of being in love with each other. Their actions violate heterosexual femininity because they are aggressive, combative, and powerful. Imagine the members of an all-male football team being labeled "fags"; this is so incomprehensible precisely because aggressive sports establish men as properly heterosexual and masculine.

Sports as a male preserve helps turn the political fictions of gender into practical sense. The embodied ethos of rape culture is also perpetuated through the practice of sexual violence. That violence, the experience as well as the fear of it, produces in women specific feminine dispositions. The fear of violence restricts women's mobility and encourages them to be with male "protectors." It prompts women to engage in a variety of cautious and modest behaviors to avoid crossing the line between virtuous woman and whore (for whom little sympathy is given when victimized). Women display deference to men that they would not otherwise because of rape culture. Women might, for instance, wish to attack a street harasser verbally but hesitate to do so for fear of violent consequences. Sexual violence weakens women. The acts of rape and battery teach women that they have no boundaries with men, that their bodies are objects for someone else's use, that they dare not impose themselves or their desires onto the world. We learn that this is the privilege of men, not women.

When a woman is actually the target of male violence, her bodily comportment and self-identity may become all the more restricted. For example, rape survivors told interviewers Scheppele and Bart (1983, 71), "Fear has taken over such a large portion [of my life]"; "I'm scared of my own shadow"; "I'm always afraid someone's out for me now"; and "I'm just not in control of myself. It's horrible." It is not uncommon for a rape survivor to perceive as dangerous a whole host of situations, not just the one in which she was assaulted. The reactions of sexual-assault survivors testify to this: One woman attacked while riding her bicycle moved from her home and nailed the windows shut in her new home, and began to lock her doors while driving; another woman attacked in a cornfield developed a fear of closed spaces, particularly being in elevators with strange men; and still another woman attacked by an acquaintance would no longer do her laundry at night (Scheppele and Bart 1983, 69). In short, women who have been sexually assaulted perceive seemingly unrelated situations in the world as more dangerous following the assault experience.

Just as rape contributes to the embodiment of a certain kind of demeanor, so does an intimate partner's battering. Submissiveness and dependence are responses to such abuse. Traits associated with femininity are responses to subordination in general (Snodgrass, in Graham et al. 1994, 194). Just as political hostages try to keep their captors calm by taking responsibility for the captors' feelings and for the smooth functioning of the captor-captive relationship, women in relationships with physically abusive partners become increasingly feminine as a survival strategy (Graham et al. 1994, 195-96). In these ways, the norms of a rape culture are written into our bodies. Rape culture is naturalized through the somatization of cultural norms, provided by a variety of discourses and practices. As we shall see next, rape and self-defense laws have also solidified aggression as a manly domain.

The Acceptance of Men's Aggression in Rape and Self-Defense Laws

Traditional rape law reveals the social status of women relative to men. Specifically, women were conceived legally as white men's property. Rape was a property crime against a man. Wife beating was not at all restricted until the 1860s (Gillespie 1989, 39). Prostitutes and black women slaves were not regarded as capable of refusing sex, and therefore were not considered deserving of protection from rape the way white women were. Although women's rights activists have fought hard to change rape law and its application in court, today rape law and its application still regulate which men get to rape which women. (Chapter 5 addresses the recent work of visionary feminist lawyers and legal theorists.)

Reflecting all sorts of myths about the naturalness of rape, rape law puts victims on trial. Though no longer a formal rule, the woman's experience often informally requires independent corroboration for it to be valid evidence, while the man's does not (Estrich 1987). The law concerns itself with the man's word (did he experience it as rape?) rather than the woman's (did she experience it as rape?). If the man on trial says that he believed that the woman consented, then he cannot be convicted of rape (Dumaresq 1981, 53). This legal privileging of men's perceptions over women's justifies and perpetuates men's imperceptiveness toward women in matters of sexual congress (MacKinnon 1989). Men are rarely punished for their violence as rapists and as batterers. Only a tiny portion of men who rape or batter get convicted or even face a jury.

Rape law solidifies rape culture, male domination, and sex difference itself. Law solidifies "man" and "woman"—cultural interventions, forced identities, and constructs of perception—into features of being (MacKinnon 1989, 237). This is why the forced penetration of a man is so much worse in the eyes of the law, and in the eyes of many people, than the forced penetration of a woman. Traditional sodomy laws make this even more clear. Laws against sodomy affirm that men are not supposed to be penetrated; these laws turn even the consensual penetration of a man into an "unnatural" and punishable act. Men are not supposed to be put sexually in the position of women, their social inferiors (Dworkin 1987, 155-56).

In its delineation of who is allowed to resist rape and when and why, self-defense law captures a set of assumptions about why rape is wrong, when rape is wrong, what men's violence means, and what women's resistance to it means. Self-defense and rape laws have presumed that sex is a natural act between a man and a woman. Hence, if a man forces another man into sex, it is a much greater violation (a violation rather than an expression of "natural" passions) and thus warrants greater violence for its prevention. Case law allows the use of deadly force to prevent forcible sodomy between males (Schneider and Jordan 1978, 153-54).

Self-defense law has traditionally enabled men to defend themselves and their women against rape, and has not enabled women to defend themselves against rape and battery. Thus, until feminist legal reforms challenged the tradition, unmarried women had no protection from men's aggression in self-defense law, and married women could not defend themselves from their own husbands. A law, repealed in 1973, once permitted a husband to kill another man if he caught that man in bed with his wife. Yet a woman has never been allowed to kill her husband's lover if she found him with another woman in bed (Schneider and Jordan 1981, 14). This type of violent passionate rage is tolerated when it erupts in a man, but in a woman it causes public outrage. Consider the hysterical cries of men expressed in the media over Lorena Bobbitt's enraged severing of her husband's penis after what she alleged to be continual physical abuse including rape (Grindstaff and McCaughey 1996).

History gives us a sense of how laws regulated violence in ways that made men's wife abuse acceptable and women's *self-defensive* violence virtually impossible. Colonial lawmakers relied upon English Common Law to define the murder of a husband (for white women) or a master (for black women) as petit treason—solidifying white men's positions as "lords"—such that murdering one of them was like murdering the king on a slightly smaller scale (Jones 1980, 38). Many white women during these times were found guilty and sent to the gallows to be burned alive for committing acts of violence against men; many black women were hung (a form of execution thought worse than burning, as burning was considered more appropriate for the "natural modesty" of the female sex) without so much as a trial or a particularly big story in the newspaper (Jones 1980, 38, 207).

A woman in many states today cannot legally use lethal force to prevent a man from raping her. Even in the states in which a person is permitted to kill to prevent the commission of a violent or forcible felony, the statutes either do not specify which felonies they cover or are sometimes reinterpreted to exclude rape (Gillespie 1989, 62-63). So, for instance, when in 1959 a woman stabbed to death a man who was a tenant in her Los Angeles home and who had sexually assaulted her and threatened that he would have her that night or kill her, the judge disagreed with the defense's argument that under California law the woman was permitted to kill to resist an attempt to commit felony rape. She was convicted of manslaughter; the California Court of Appeals upheld the trial judge's ruling and the conviction (ibid., 63). Even when states formally permit the use of deadly force in self-defense against rape, a woman who kills a man trying to rape her must meet the other requirements of self-defense, proving that the threatened harm was imminent, that she was unable to retreat, and that her perception of danger was reasonable. Such a woman also faces the same troubles rape victims face in court: her credibility is undermined and many people do not believe her (ibid., 63-64).

In 1924, the Supreme Court of New Mexico ruled that rape was a felony covered by the state's statute permitting a person to kill in order to prevent its commission. As the case involved a virtuous wife and mother, Hilaria Martinez, who shot a man who twice tried to molest her while her husband was away from the house and came after her a third time, it suggested that a woman had a right to kill "in defense of chastity" (quoted in ibid., 62). Thus women's aggression was acceptable if women's essential role as nurturing mothers and virtuous property of men was being upheld.

This tolerance of ladylike women's necessary self-defensive aggression cannot work as well for black women, who have not as readily been seen as virtuous ladies deserving of men's restraint from hitting ladies. Nor could black women as easily pass for helpless damsels in distress, which made them appear more violently motivated if they killed or maimed in self-defense. If it is black men's violence that they are protecting themselves from, then police have historically had difficulty seeing black women's violence as self-defensive, construing it all as just so much black violence (Jones 1980, 336). Because the ideal of womanhood is white and heterosexual, and this ideal precludes aggression, few cases of women's self-defensive violence have seemed acceptable.

For most of U.S. history, a woman's pleading justifiable self-defense was practically unthinkable. Temporary insanity used to be the most common defense of women who killed to prevent rape, murder, or incessant beatings. These women have been committed to mental institutions sometimes for far longer periods than they would have spent in prison if convicted of a crime (Gillespie 1989, 25). Defense lawyers used a woman's background to justify the homicide, such as if the woman was ever molested or raped, or if she had "a particularly severe cultural or social reaction to sexual assault" (Schneider and Jordan 1981, 30)—as though preventing assault aggressively required a particularly severe reaction to sexual assault. The woman's defense would argue that she was driven to the breaking point by circumstances (ibid.). (More recent feminist reforms of self-defense law are discussed in chapter 5.)

In contrast, a man has not had to argue that he has a particularly severe reaction to forced anal sex in order to justify killing a man who tries to rape him. Many women have wound up with lawyers who did not believe that they acted in self-defense and who therefore encouraged them to plead guilty to a reduced charge of manslaughter or second-degree murder (Gillespie 1989, 25). Even when women have claimed self-defense in court, they faced judges and juries whose assumptions were informed by a culture that demands and normalizes feminine manners. At these many levels of the legal process, women's aggression is de-legitimized.

Women who killed their batterers before being killed themselves have also been seen as insane. For example, Roxanne Gay, who killed her extremely violent husband, the Philadelphia Eagles defensive lineman Blenda Gay, after repeated dead-end attempts to get the police to help her (the police preferred to talk football with Mr. Gay once they arrived at the house [ibid., 13]), was officially listed as paranoid schizophrenic. The male psychiatrists determined that she suffered from "delusions that her husband, her family and police were plotting to kill her" (quoted in Jones 1980, 306). We might question why a woman who was repeatedly beaten by her husband and refused help by the police would be considered irrational or deluded for thinking that such people were trying to kill her. A century ago, many men unabashedly struck their wives. Hence domestic violence is still often seen and treated as a misdemeanor (Gillespie 1989, 61). And a woman's violent refusal of such abuse, and claim to the appropriateness of her self-defensive violence, can still today seem startling and even a bit unbalanced.

Self-defense law varies from state to state, but generally it says that "a person may use deadly force to protect herself from what she reasonably perceives to be an imminent, deadly attack. However, deadly force may not be used if the defendant was the initial aggressor, provoked the attack or (in some jurisdictions) failed to retreat if she could have done so safely" (Bochnak 1981b, 43). Traditional self-defense law was constructed with ideals of masculinity in mind. For instance, there is the "true man" doctrine that exculpates a "person" from the obligation to attempt to flee first before using deadly force in self-defense, and the related "castle" doctrine, which allows a "person" to use deadly force if the assailant is already in one's own home (castle) (Gillespie 1989, 82). These rarely work for women, most of whom were in their own homes at the time they assaulted or killed in self-defense.

The No Retreat Rule, a precedent known in common law as the "true man rule," allows a man to kill even if he could have retreated to safety without using violence to defend himself (Ewing 1990, 588). As one commentator put it, "No one should be forced by a wrongdoer to the ignominy, dishonor and disgrace of a cowardly retreat" (Beale, quoted in ibid.). The "true man" doctrine exculpates the threatened person from the requirement of an attempt to retreat from the threat. The effect, if not the purpose, of self-defense law, then, has been to reward behaviors that are "manly" and punish behaviors that are not.

After an 1876 case, the Ohio Supreme Court announced that "a true man, who is without fault, is not obliged to flee from an assailant, who, by violence or surprise, seeks to take his life or do him enormous bodily harm" (quoted in Gillespie 1989, 78). It is harder to imagine that a "true woman" would not be expected to retreat and instead be allowed to take violent action. After all, a "true woman" in our cultural logic would simply take the abuse politely. Men are more likely than women to be in a fight that is mutually entered; in contrast, women are more likely to experience unilateral physical assault (ibid.). Thus the legal burden to retreat, as well as the "true man" exception to it, reinforce manly behavior in manly fights.

What counts as provocation in the law helps justify men's violence but not women's. Radford (1994, 193) notes that the defense of provocation, which makes the crime and penalty less than murder, has not helped women as much as men. The gendered double standard in the law is exemplified by the fact that infidelity and allegations about sexual (in)capacity are privileged as things that count as provocation over and above a history of abuse, threats, and violence. Men have been allowed to be angry ("passionate") but women usually can be only fearful. If a woman is fearful and angry, her self-defensive violence can be considered revenge-motivated murder. As Hart (1994, 152) points out, "passion and/or pathology have been the key historical constructs for explaining, and containing, women's aggression."

Self-defense law has presumed that women are naturally sexually available to those men defined as their social superiors. Hence, if a woman aggressively refuses a man's attempt to get sex she could very well be punished as crazy or as a murderer. Ideas about the naturalness of heterosexual intercourse—and hence the unnaturalness of both women's desire to abstain and violent enforcement of that desire—inform self-defense law and the typical outcomes of women's self-defense cases. After Inez Garcia was found guilty of murdering the man who had assisted in his friend's rape of her and who had called her to promise that both men would return to her home to do something worse, one juror remarked, "You can't kill someone for trying to give you a good time" (Schneider and Jordan 1981, 15).[10]

Garcia's case exemplifies another sexist bias in self-defense law. The imminence requirement, stating that the threat must be immediate in order to justify lethal self-defense, makes sense for men in an agreed-upon barroom brawl. But when it comes to a woman facing a man trying to rape her, she must wait long enough for the rape to ensue but not so long that she cannot still stop it from occurring. Thus a woman who harms a man trying to rape her can easily be accused of either acting when a man was merely "flirting" (that is, when the threat was not imminent) or engaging in vengeful violence (that is, when the threat had already passed) (Gillespie 1989, 74).

Feminist lawyers have emphasized the socially constructed and maintained differences that result from a sexist society in order to prevent women from being judged through the masculinist lens of existing self-defense law. For instance, because the imminence requirement fails to take into account many of women's self-defense situations, feminist lawyers explain, "The crucial point to be conveyed to the judge and jury is that, due to a variety of societally based factors, a woman may reasonably perceive imminent and lethal danger in a situation in which a man might not" (Schneider and Jordan 1978, 150). These feminists are fighting to have women's conduct judged in terms of perceptions a woman might have of a situation, gleaned from being in that situation or in a sexist society more broadly. They see the physically "de-skilled" state of women as a product of the sexist society. Hence a "reasonable woman," not a "reasonable man" or "reasonable person," might feel particularly threatened by an enraged husband.

Discourses that frame women as physically vulnerable and passive and men as active and capable of aggressive action are not limited to laws, science, media fantasies, and criminology. Codes of femininity circulate throughout public discourse, coming from cosmetics companies and scientific stories. They also appear in advice and public service messages—even in the very statements that attempt to alter the rate with which men victimize women. In the next section, I show how many rape prevention manuals render women's aggression impossible or invalid, followed by the challenge presented by more recent feminist advice.

Assumptions about Gender and Aggression in Rape Prevention Advice

Self-defense manuals of old and police rape prevention advice provide one set of public discourses which mediate "proper" and "sensible" social relations. How are gendered body-codes assumed, naturalized, reinforced, and challenged in the rape prevention advice provided to women? The discourse of self-protection borrows from other discourses, such as Christian discourses of feminine virtue and purity, patriarchal discourses of maternalism, and feminist discourses of choice and freedom. Many of the descriptions rely on rape culture's gender ideology and thereby reinforce the very constructions of gender that support rape culture, even while they try to teach the means by which, on a very practical level, women might challenge assailants. One researcher found that women's ideas about crime prevention were very similar to those in published crime prevention advice (Gardner 1990).[11] This body of advice, then, arguably captures a general sentiment in the United States, beyond the women who have read these books, about what sorts of aggression against attackers is necessary, appropriate, and possible for women.

Two self-defense manuals that came out during World War II, both written by military men, are worth examining before reviewing the self-defense books of the 1970s and 1980s, since they provide a significant contrast. U.S. women's fighting skills were encouraged in the same way that women were encouraged to join the military and work in the factories during the war. Many are familiar with the wartime image of "Rosie the Riveter." Her biceps bulging out of her blue-collar shirt, she was an image of female strength that encouraged women to work in factories, and fill positions usually reserved for men during peacetime. Women were encouraged to do unfeminine things, primarily through a massive propaganda campaign, when it would help win the war (Reskin and Padavic 1994, 51).

Major William Fairbairn's illustrated book *Hands Off!* (1942), which sold for 75 cents, and Corporal William Underwood's *Self-Defense for Women: Combato* (1944) provide a series of self-defense maneuvers for women. The Major explains, "It goes without saying that a woman should know how to protect herself. In war time—in America at war—this is doubly so. . . . The confidence you will gain from having learned how to protect yourself, from knowing that you are the master of any unpleasant situation with which you may have to deal, will immeasurably increase your efficiency and value to the war effort" (Fairbairn 1942, vii). U.S. women's aggression against men is accepted when it is needed by nationalism. This way the heterosexual virtue of women remains intact.

Without ever mentioning the words *rape* or *sexual assault*, the book explains a series of holds that men, familiar men, might get women into, such as the "waist hold" (ibid., 13-15), the "bear hug" (ibid., 10-11), and the "theater hold" (ibid., 33), which is a type of hold that men presumably attempt at the show. Corporal Underwood's (1944, 24-33) book shows defensive moves for "simple nuisances" to "serious but not deadly" (ibid., 34-76) to "deadly serious" threats (ibid., 78-93). In the first category, we find theater touches, a man who will not go home when he should, and a handshaker who will not let go when the period of polite greeting has more than expired. Women readers are instructed to grab the hand of the hapless handshaker, twist his arm around, throw him to the ground, and, finally, give a stomp to his Adam's apple or a kick behind his ear (ibid., 32-33).

The corporal notes, "The treatment shown may seem a trifle drastic for someone who is merely being 'fresh.' Perhaps it is, but this type of approach may lead to something more serious" (ibid., 32). *Hands Off!* (Fairbairn 1942, 25) recommends that a woman who finds a man shaking her hand too long pinch the grip to "take the conceit out of him." For the man who asks for a light, *Hands Off!* provides an illustration of a woman throwing a punch in his face; if a man stops on a dark road and *demands* a light, women are instructed to light the entire matchbook on fire and throw it in his face (ibid., 41). Clearly, these books teach women serious and violent defense moves even against dates.

In contrast, a significant number of crime prevention booklets and self-defense books for women of the 1970s and 1980s impute deficient physical competence to women, rarely recommend violent techniques, and expect women to limit themselves in order to achieve some "freedom" from sexual assault. Police emphasize crime prevention, which is understandable since they want less crime in the first place, but this emphasis with regard to women and rape means that they tell women to be less than free citizens. In a booklet on crime prevention for women, the U.S. Department of Justice (1977) says: "Be selective about new acquaintances; don't *invite* a forcible sexual encounter" (emphasis in original).[12] The California State Police manual, *Safety Tips for Women* (1976, 7), itself a partial reproduction of a booklet by the same name of the Washington, D.C., Metropolitan Police Department, cautions: "Don't invite trouble by going to night clubs unescorted." This manual also advises women to "avoid going out alone at night" (California State Police 1976, 7).

Women are encouraged to hesitate in an assault situation: "You should not *immediately* try to fight back. Chances are, your attacker has the advantage" (U.S. Department of Justice 1977, emphasis in original). If the attacker is armed, women are instructed not to even try to fight: "You should never resist if your attacker has a weapon" (ibid.). Women are routinely told not to resist an armed assailant, and not to arm themselves because the weapon could be taken away and used against them. And yet women are also told that their attacker, even if unarmed, probably has the advantage. Hence, women need a weapon to be able to match a man and yet cannot use a weapon because their assailant will be more skilled in the use of such technology and somehow take it from them and hurt them with it: "Don't carry a gun or any weapon. It can easily be turned against you" (ibid.).

Police manuals do not teach women how to take the advantage with an assailant, thus positioning women as incompetent and in need of protection and sequestration, and positioning men as unstoppable animals who are free to roam. Such rape prevention advice does not prevent rape by addressing itself to men, the bulk of the rapists, or by emphasizing women's ability to fight off attackers. Indeed, it is as though fighting were impossible or simply distasteful, even when a woman is being threatened. The California State Police's pamphlet says: "If you are *forced* to defend yourself, remember. . . . Scream, Scream, Scream" (1976, 10, emphasis in original). This same pamphlet explains that women do have some bodily weapons, and can use things like a rolled up newspaper to strike someone, but follows with this caveat: "CAUTION! 'Self-defense' tactics are not foolproof and should be used only as a last resort" (ibid., 11). Of course, screaming and staying in at night are not foolproof either.

Unlike the briefer manuals and pamphlets, self-defense books often begin by motivating women to learn self-defense with a rationale for its importance. Some speak of urbanization and the disintegration of the family, as though rural towns and close-knit communities were safer for women (e.g., Heyden and Tarpening 1970; Luchsinger 1977; Monkerud and Heiny 1980; Stock 1968). This can support the myth that women are attacked mainly by strangers. One spoke of women's "new" freedom and independence which "has thrust women into a sometimes brutal and hostile world" (Monkerud and Heiny 1980, 10)—as if women had simply been protected previously from a world that has been brutal and hostile to men only. Others present a frightening list of statistics to show how vulnerable women are to assault (e.g., McGurn and Kelly

1984). This promotion of a high-risk environment in order to encourage women's participation in self-defense is exemplified in *Self-Defense for Women: The West Point Way*, which urges: "Don't delay! The urban jungle is becoming more dangerous *everyday!*" (Peterson 1979, 15, emphasis in original).

These books, like police and government advice to women, commonly advise restricting women's behaviors. This is not to say that women should not be taught safety tactics that help minimize the likelihood of assault. After all, nobody wants to be assaulted, even if she could be certain that she would win the fight. But often the advice extends beyond suggestions of proper locks for doors and trusting your instincts. For instance, in *Every Woman Can* (Conroy and Ritvo 1982, 96), women are given these suggestions for dating: "Wear appropriate clothing; avoid provocative words and actions; don't go where you know you won't be comfortable; and avoid driving to isolated areas." *The Rational Woman's Guide to Self-Defense* (Conroy 1972, 7) emphasizes "avoiding danger" to the point where readers are told to fight only when their lives or health are in danger. "Dangers" to be avoided are things like "attending public functions alone and traveling alone" (ibid.). *Self-Defense for Women* (Gustuson and Masaki 1970) teaches "rules of modesty," discouraging what the authors see as the typical North American woman's tendency to use the curves of her body to attract attention from men.

Such restrictions women are suggested to place upon themselves in order to be more "free" of assault simply get women to take responsibility for men's interest in assaulting them. This implicitly takes for granted men's desire, and ability, to assault women. These recommended restrictions on women also, as Scheppele and Bart (1983) point out, encourage women to think that assault is an avoidable situation if they simply stay out of dangerous places and situations. However, women confront a risk of attack "that is not easily isolated in specific situations that can be avoided" (ibid., 65). Thus "guiding one's life by 'rules of rape avoidance' . . . is not necessarily helpful in avoiding rape" (ibid.).

The assumption that the men against whom women will have to defend themselves are strangers subtly underlies much advice to women. For instance, *The Rational Woman's Guide to Self-Defense* (Conroy 1972, 7) suggests that women avoid dangers like attending public functions alone and traveling alone, but does not include dating as a danger to avoid. *Self-Defense for Girls: A Secondary School and College Manual* (Tegner and McGrath 1967) instructs women on getting into elevators and their cars, walking alone at night, and talking on the phone, but not on dates or in the classroom. And *Every Woman Can: The Conroy Method to Safety* (Conroy and Ritvo 1982) provides a range of combative self-defense techniques but seems to suggest that they would only be used on strangers. The section in the book covering unusual cases along with tips for handling them includes the "overzealous date," which is followed by other not-so-likely scenarios such as the "vicious dog," "gang of small children," "woman beating," and finally "violent women" (ibid., 97-102).

Violence in intimate relationships is far more common than violence by strangers; thus woman beaters and overzealous dates are not simply odd nuisances or bizarre circumstances. Curiously, the many physical self-defense techniques shown in the book are not applied to the "overzealous date." In fact, women are encouraged to use verbal techniques and, if those fail, to "either go to a public area where he cannot continue to annoy you or leave him" (ibid., 97). This is a far cry from the advice given to women during World War II, when they were instructed not to negotiate with men they knew, but to "combato" them to the ground for improper dating procedure. (*Every Woman Can* does note that, in "rare circumstances," a woman's date may have "certain psychological disturbances" which would make him no longer a date but a "serious assailant, and a full-fledged counterattack to immobilize him may be necessary" [ibid.].)

The focus on the danger of strangers has the effect of solidifying in women's minds the myth that women are most in danger of psychos whose crazed attacks are difficult to spoil. This portrait of the assailant perhaps accounts for the attitude put forth by some writers that suggests that women temper their resistance. This then results in a condescending attitude best exemplified in *How to Say No to a Rapist and Survive* (Storaska 1975). In an attempt to convince women to wait for the proper moment to fight physically, and to talk their way out of the assault whenever possible, Storaska cautions,

> If he's skinny, you may smash his chest. But how are you to know he's skinny [if he grabs you from behind]—reach back and feel? And what do you think he'll be doing while you're hitting him? He'll be tearing you apart. At best, you'll crack one or two of his ribs. That's hardly incapacitating. Men can—and have—played a full game of football with injuries much worse than that. A man with cracked ribs can rape you just about as easily as a man whose ribs are perfect, and he's likely to throw in a beating for good measure, since you've been violent. (Ibid., 42)

That passage reads less like an encouraging promotion of women's self-defense and more like a stunning scare tactic, further undermining a woman's confidence in her ability to fight a man.

Storaska is notorious, at least in feminist circles, for having told women to dignify the assailant as a way to try to escape the assault. Storaska's advice makes sense to him because he thinks that "the rapist . . . is an angry, emotionally disturbed person" (ibid., 31). His advice may be appropriate for situations in which women are confronted by a crazed stranger attacking, possibly with intent to kill. The conventional wisdom of "don't fight back, it'll only get him angry," however, does not take into account the large number of rapes in which men simply dismiss or arrogantly misperceive women's desires to refrain from certain sexual activities with them. Thus it perpetuates the myth that rapists are usually psychotic strangers, and ignores the number of situations in which a man may be testing a woman's boundaries by trying first to speak with her and touch her briefly.

Storaska was not the only one to offer this type of advice to women. *The Womanly Art of Self-Defense* (Burg 1979, 12) suggests creating a distraction or trying friendly persuasion, and cautions, "Don't enrage him by suggesting that he is not capable of completing what he originally planned. Playing the role of a toughie or a heroine is strictly for the movies. In real life, don't play around with a man's pride (or anyone's pride, for that matter)." The ploys that women have been told to enact include defecating, urinating, fainting, faking a seizure, and vomiting. *Every Woman Can* (Conroy and Ritvo 1982, 96-97) suggests that women tell their "overzealous dates" that they may vomit. *Below the Belt: Unarmed Combat for Women* tells women,

> Yes, it pays to be deceptive! Be an actress if you must be. Someday, God forbid, you may *need* all of your theatrical skills to save yourself. It won't be nice to do, but your children will still have their mother. Your husband will still have his wife. And your family will not go out of their mind with grief. (Steiner 1976, 108, emphasis in original)

Convincing women that they should defend themselves because of what they are worth to other people, as in the citation above, comes up in another self-defense book. *Free to Fight Back* (Scribner 1988, 9) explains that women should "take care of what is valuable to yourself and to the Lord: you!" Targeted to Christian women, whom Scribner (ibid., 17) addresses as a group whose religious beliefs seem incompatible with acting physically in self-defense, the book explains, "Each Christian woman can stand before the Lord and believe that she has full rights and responsibilities before him. She is a whole person fully redeemed by the blood of Christ" (ibid., 8).

The advice to women is not homogeneous. Several self-defense books (e.g., Bateman 1978; Fein 1981; Grant 1989; Kaufman et al. 1980; Leung 1991; Sanford and Fetter 1979; Sliwa 1986; Smith 1986) differ from the aforementioned rape prevention advice and, sometimes, argue against that advice. Rather than demeaning women with suggestions of feeding the ego of the assailant or keeping offenders from getting angry, they want women to force offenders aggressively to recognize women's humanity, desires, and anger. This advice thus rejects the standard fiction that men assault women because of superior size, strength, or possession of penises with the objective capacity to be instruments of torture, and instead assumes men's attacks are gender-motivated.

This set of advice suggests that women take up space, rather than limit their freedom, in order to avoid gender-motivated attack. For instance, *Attitude: Commonsense Defense for Women* (Sliwa 1986, 31, 32) does not suggest that women change the way they dress, but instead tells women not to feel guilty for the way they look or take responsibility for someone who wants to take advantage of them: "If we want to look good, that's our choice. . . . Boldness is better than guilt. Say: 'Yes, I have what a man wants. But the only way he is going to get it is if I want to give it to him. If someone tries to take something from me against my will, I'm going to take measures to stop him.'"

What makes a man's attack a violation, and worth preventing, is therefore different in these books. The body is seen as a political construct, as invested with ideologies, and as such as worth defending. (The issue of how feminists construe the harm of rape is discussed at length in chapter 4.) Self-defense contests the construction of the female body as violable. In the former school of thought, a woman should do anything to avoid penetration and death. In the latter, a woman should not let a man even talk to her in a certain way, as that is part of the violation. His assault begins a fight; he must be made to see her ego, her pride, her humanity, and to know that he should not even try this with her. For example, *Attitude: Commonsense Defense for Women* suggests, "Do not romanticize the criminal. . . . [Criminals] are parasites with a distorted view of reality. It is your responsibility to set them straight by saying, 'Hey, Jack, your number's up. I know what you're thinking, but you'll never get away with it'" (ibid., 33). Here we see a completely different view of the point of self-defense. Women are to protect their own dignity, not the rapist's.

Grant's (1989) video on self-defense for women explains that women are not taught to fight, only to struggle. Although Grant also opposes the use of weapons for self-defense because they, like male protectors, are "outside the woman," she encourages women to fight and yell, noting that most women can spoil an attack verbally. She does not tell women to scream; she tells them to yell. The yelling that *In Defense of Ourselves* (Sanford and Fetter 1979) suggests incorporates bold, low sounds like, "Yaaaahhh" and "aah." *Are You a Target?* (Fein 1981, 32-33) tells women to yell loudly, something like "Yaaah!" and to "look mean and vicious" doing so. When women fight physically, they are told to do so immediately, to surprise the attacker, and take the upper hand in the fight.

This body of literature does not always suggest that women avoid using weapons for self-defense. In *Fear into Anger: A Manual of Self-Defense for Women,* Bateman (1978, 93) notes the irony of the double message women receive about weapon use: If you want to protect yourself, you will need a gun because you're so weak; on the other hand, you better not use a gun because a man will take it away and use it against you. *In Defense of Ourselves* (Sanford and Fetter 1979, 128) simply suggests that "if you use a weapon, be well-trained in its use and be willing to use it immediately." *Self-Defense: The Womanly Art of Self-Care, Intuition, and Choice* (Leung 1991, 115) suggests that women consider the commitment to learning and practicing to use the weapon, as well as the emotional and legal issues involved. That book also suggests that a woman who uses her weapon as soon as she shows it during an assault "will most likely defend herself successfully." *Attitude: Commonsense Defense for Women* (Sliwa 1986, 77) says not to rely on a gun because you might not get to it fast enough, but as for fighting armed assailants, "just because a criminal has a weapon does not mean that he has to get his way." The author suggests the woman vampirishly sink her teeth into his jugular vein, a technique that might kill him.

There are a variety of ways, then, in which women's relationship to violence has been articulated. As attempts to get women to restructure their relationship to aggression—both men's aggression and their own—these sets of advice reveal what we have taken for granted about gender and aggression, as well as what some have tried to challenge. In contemporary self-defense courses, women are learning to restructure their experiences of their bodies to fight off all kinds of attack.

Conclusion

Fantasies of sex differences are inscripted onto our bodies in demeanor, looks, shape, size, fashion codes, and aesthetic tastes. Insofar as our bodies function as signs for understanding social relationships, they display those differences, a notable distinction being aggression. Women's aggression is treated as an unnatural and distasteful transgression because aggression is a marker of sexual difference, which is made meaningful in a hierarchy of social power.

Aggression falls outside the bounds of "ladylike" behavior. This prescriptive femininity itself has generated a series of exclusions, as privileged middle-class white heterosexual women can more easily accomplish it. Most women, who cannot, can feel inadequate, wrong, bad, ugly, unlovable, sick, perverted, or selfish. Even those women who achieve femininity accrue no great rewards, given that the ideal forms of femininity mark the ideal of female subordination to men.

The ideal of femininity has normalized and thus perpetuated rape culture because, insofar as femininity excludes aggression, women are set up to be easy, and easily rationalized, targets for abuse. Even women who challenged gender, historically speaking, have been held accountable for their "unfeminine" actions. Aggression, then, is a primary axis around which prescriptive femininity, racism, compulsory heterosexuality, and male violence revolve. The next chapter describes the thrill of unlearning prescriptive femininity in a variety of self-defense courses.

2

Getting Mean
On the Scene in Self-Defense Classes

Self-defense courses make visible women's embodiment of femi-
nine helplessness and its undoing; thus, they are important sites for studying the
renegotiation of femininity and aggression. This chapter describes the self-
defense courses that I experienced as a student and observer. Self-defense
courses range from brief, inexpensive (sometimes free) classes offered through
martial arts dojos or rape crisis centers to expensive twenty-five hour courses
and martial arts rank or degree programs. Self-defense classes fall within four
broad categories: padded attacker courses; firearms courses; martial arts or mar-
tial-arts oriented self-defense courses; and fitness-oriented courses. Most of the
self-defense courses are for women only, although I discuss one self-defense
class, Krav Maga, which contained an equal number of male and female students.

Padded Attacker Courses

"Hey, Martha, I know you from the university. I was in your sociol-
ogy class," says the man casually.
"I see," I respond. "Well, I'm in a hurry to get somewhere now."
"Just wait a minute. I've always wanted to tell you how attracted to
you I was. Maybe we could get together."
"I don't think so. No." At this point I raise my hands casually to a pro-
tective position so that I can protect my face or strike his if necessary. My
legs are shoulder-width apart and pivoting so that I'm always facing him.
I quickly look around to see if anyone else is in the area.
He touches my arm, urging, "I thought you liked me."
"Don't come any closer," I say firmly. This is the intense part. If he
persists, I have to make a decision to fight. And if I make this decision, I
have to be prepared to continue fighting to the knockout.
He steps closer, trying to put an arm around me. I deliver a heel-palm

strike up his nose, and, just as his head tips back, I knee him in the groin. He doubles over momentarily, and I drop to the ground on my side, ready to kick him in the head.

He lunges for me. "Damn you, bitch! You broke my nose."

"KICK! KICK! KICK!" Several blows to his head knock him out. I get up, look around me, assess the assailant, see that he is indeed knocked out, run to safety, and shout "9-1-1"—the official end of the fight.

This was one of my fights at Model Mugging, one of a number of women's self-defense programs that teach techniques for unarmed, usually nonlethal, self-defense and involve practice against a padded attacker. Along with a dozen other women, I enrolled in the basic course of Model Mugging, knowing nothing about it. Model Mugging is perhaps the most famous, intensive, and expensive course of its kind.

My course takes place in a large martial arts dojo in an aluminum-sided garage-warehouse in Southern California. I walk into a small waiting area and office, with a television and video camera that are sometimes used to tape and watch the fights. The room is one large square of blue mats, with two big garage doors along one side. Hanging from the high ceilings are punching bags, and scattered around the mat are knee and elbow pads, padded helmets, and everyone's lunch bags and water bottles.

The women are wearing casual gym clothes and gather around the mat to stretch out and talk. The men get into their padded suits. Dressed as the muggers—with padding strapped and duct-taped everywhere and then covered with football jerseys and denim overalls, plus a large helmet with netting over the eyes (so students can strike the eyes and deliver full force blows to the head)—the men weigh around two hundred pounds. Their helmets have names on them, different from their real names, distinguishing the men in their role as muggers from the men they "really are."

Founded in 1971 by Matt Thomas, who also helped train local police SWAT teams (Peri 1990), Model Mugging, with affiliates in sixteen states and one in Quebec, Canada, has trained tens of thousands of women nationwide as well as police officers, children, men, and the physically challenged. The women's basic course costs $420 and consists of twenty-five hours of instruction, on several different days, usually spread out over a month.

Model Mugging courses are taught by women and men, the former usually teaching the skills and taking care of students' emotional needs and the latter doing the mugging and occasionally giving feedback on students' techniques. The female instructors, one Latina and the others white, all in their thirties or forties, often have counseling backgrounds and have completed instructor training in addition to all levels of the Model Mugging courses. Some have martial arts training as well. The male instructors, one Latino, one white, and one black, all in their thirties or forties, have trained in various martial arts. One male instructor who co-ran the Model Mugging program I attended was a martial arts instructor and Vietnam veteran, another was a police officer, and another a self-employed weapons instructor, bodyguard, and surveillance expert.

Padded attacker courses offer women a chance to experience full-force fighting, as these self-defense instructors believe that most successful assaults occur not because women aren't strong enough to fight men but because women facing an assailant often freeze up rather than fight. Because the "muggers" attack the students at full force and accompany their attacks with affronting verbal remarks ("compliments," threats, sexual profanity, and cries of pain), the attacks feel quite real to the students. This enables women to learn their defense techniques while their adrenaline level is high and their fine motor skills low, thus committing the skills to "bodily memory" which will automatically be triggered in the event of an attack.

Much of the class time that is not used for practicing specific striking techniques and fighting off padded attackers is used to "process" what is happening emotionally. Each class begins and ends with the students circling up and "checking in" emotionally. Some women are taking the class at a therapist's recommendation, others because they are being stalked by an ex-lover, still others because they live alone. One woman received the course as a high-school graduation gift. Some women have known about Model Mugging for years and are now finding the courage to take it. As a box of Kleenex gets passed around the circle, some women share their tearful stories of child abuse, rape, and battery. Others share their everyday fears of rape, and anger at that fear's constricting effects in their lives.

The instructors, two women and two male muggers, take time to tell us why we need to fight. "It's a concrete jungle out there," explains one of the muggers who occasionally joins the women's circle. They also encourage us to protect ourselves: "Think of how the mother animal in the wild protects her babies." If you don't have a child, instructors explain, "imagine protecting your 'child within.'" The instructors also pass out various handouts with empowering slogans like, "It's not the size of the woman in the fight, but the size of the fight in the woman," and "Women's Bill of Rights," which is a list of affirmations about having the right to say no, having the right to make a mistake, and so on.

The course includes this emotional processing and encouragement because mock assaults traumatize the women. For the same reason, the fighting starts out slowly. We learn striking techniques on punching bags first, and gradually work up to kicking the muggers. The first time we actually strike a mugger, we act out a tightly scripted scenario in slow motion. We are encouraged to give a kick or punch to the padded attacker while he remains stationary, but women never use full force at this initial stage. Some even apologize to the mugger, worried that they hurt him. Some of my classmates initially fold under the pressure of the fight, too fearful, too shocked, too horrified to continue. Some simply freeze when the mugger knocks them to the ground, others cry or feel faint. For a moment, one student reverts to a childlike mode, sobbing in the fetal position on the mat. Traumatic events, including molestation, battery, and rape, produce in people lasting changes in physiological arousal, emotion, cognition, and memory (Herman 1992, 34). Constriction—a numbing response of surrender in the face of real or imagined threat—is a primary symptom of post-traumatic stress disorder (ibid.).

The development of the will to fight, the determination to battle to the knockout, is the primary goal of the basic course. But before we can get the fight, we must stop worrying about hurting the mugger. Some even have to learn to stop smiling at the muggers during fights. Others must practice using their voice as they fight. One woman says that she was saying no for the first time. A strikingly confident athlete breaks down crying, explaining that learning to fend off assailants is a greater challenge than running a marathon or climbing a mountain.

Students eventually get "the fight" or "the fighting spirit" so that they will not freeze in response to male aggression. As each class goes by, although women do not seem eager to skirmish with their padded muggers, their confidence that they can gradually steps up. "Your ass is mine today!" one woman warns the mugger. We eventually get used to using our full body weight in our strikes and using our voices forcefully. We learn to yell the techniques we use ("KICK!" "KNEE!" "GROIN!" "EYES!") or to simply yell "NO!" as we fight. This is to ensure that we continue to breathe during the fights, that we intimidate our assailant, and that we get the attention of anyone in the area. As we practice our self-defense moves in these lifelike scenarios, the rest of the class stands on the sidelines of the huge mat and yells out the moves students can use: "KICK!" "GET HIS EYES!" "GROIN!" (See ill. 1.)

The assault scenarios progress in degree of complication, the number of ways in which we are approached (passing by on the street, getting grabbed from behind or front, starting with a conversation, in bed, etc.), and the amount of verbal abuse and threats that go with them. A major hurdle is learning to stay centered and fight while a man shouts "you fucking bitch," or gradually encroaches your boundaries while saying, "I just want to talk to you for a second, pretty lady." Indeed, when the attack was accompanied by verbal "friendliness," we all tended to wait longer before striking the assailant than during blitz attacks. Women in Model Mugging learn that matching a rapist verbally, without ever getting physical, will usually stop a rape attempt. Hence, while all of our mock assaults involve a fight to the finish, we practice verbal self-defense along the way, learning that in real life this itself is usually enough to stop an assailant. Thus we practice, over and over, defending ourselves verbally and physically, from a stiff "BACK OFF" to a knockout blow.

The fights are scrappy, and we learn to strike where we see an open target. What at first is an established fight pattern (yell "NO!" bite, elbow to the face, turn, and kick) becomes a viciously opportunistic fighting style in which the woman sees an unprotected crotch and has one hand free with which to strike it, or if not a hand then a foot or a knee, then might get to another target area by striking the eyes (eye strikes can cause the attacker to bring his hands up to his eyes, leaving his chest or groin area open for strikes), all the while yelling and breathing and going ballistic until he is knocked out. (See ill. 2.) The knockout is signaled when the padded attacker, after enough pressure has been delivered to his head, places his padded hands over his eyes and the instructor blows her whistle.

We also learn to negotiate with the assailant if we get pinned, and to distract him when we want to create an opening. For instance, a woman might say, "I'm sorry, I just got scared," only to coil up her energy, quickly retract her leg and kick his knee, bite his penis, or hurl him off her body with a hip throw.

The training atmosphere is supportive; women bond through the ordeal. This mutual support is structured into the class as well; before a new round of muggings, the class circles up, arms around one another, to get psyched for the fights. On the count of three, everyone stomps her foot and yells, "NO! NO! NO!" The women connect as they support the one fighting on the mat, yelling for the fighter and "passing hugs" down the line of students. Women often get a hug after a fight and at the end of class. The female instructors give out the students' home phone numbers as well as their own, encouraging us to call people for support during the days between classes.

More boxes of Kleenex go around our circles. Women share their fears, still others their anger at the "little everyday assaults" like harassment and intimidation. Some students find it difficult to continue the course, as they are remembering painful experiences. Others who had not been attacked before feel like the course is making them face their worst nightmares. We all let out a collective groan when we realize we have to face the mugger's crotch. As we are introduced to the defensive moves against oral copulation (as in ill. 3), one classmate turns to me quietly and vomits up the words, "This is what my father used to do to me." The circles allow women to talk about what it was like to be in the fights, assess our progress in the class, and discuss what skills we need to improve.

If the male instructors hear a student mention something she is most afraid of, they enact that personality, talk, or form of threat in their next mock assault on that woman. A Latina student said hearing threats in Spanish was particularly difficult, prompting one of the muggers to speak Spanish as he attacked her. We write down our own custom assault scenarios—our worst fears or perhaps a situation involving a fighting technique we feel least confident about—which the muggers read and then act out with us. Some women want to act out assaults they had actually experienced in the past, symbolically reclaiming the power that that person had taken away. I felt I needed the most practice making a decision to defend myself against a known assailant whose verbal gestures do not match his physical ones. My custom scenario thus involved a man I know who is threatening me implicitly but not explicitly. I had to trust my sense that I was in danger and needed to fight, despite my tendency to give weight to his words and his definition of the situation.

"Don't come any closer," I say firmly.
"I just want to talk to you," the mugger says gently while touching me.
I look around. It's just he and I. "Get away," I insist.
But he is equally insistent on getting closer: "C'mon, darlin', we're cool," he says while he comes after me and presses his body to mine.
Having realized that he is not listening to me and not backing off, I interrupt with a "NO" and a heel-palm strike to his nose.
He tries to gain control of me physically, pushing me to the ground.
I drop intentionally, with my foot cocked ready to give a side-thrust kick. "Stay back!"
He darts around for a moment, cursing.
"Go away!" I demand, repositioning my body so that I'm always facing him with a retracted leg and cocked foot.
He lunges in, and I kick his head. He stumbles, then grabs my leg. His groin is open and I come down on it with my fists like a hammer. The pain has made him release my leg, so I scoot back, retract my leg and kick his head three more times until he's knocked out.

Of course in real life the verbal self-defense alone might well be enough to scare off an assailant. But the course trains us for the worst, and the muggers often do not walk away after we have belted out the most firm words. These in-class enactments are real enough. Feeling threatened by the mugger trying to pin me down and feeling his sweat spray onto my face make me determined to fight through to the knockout as quickly as possible. After knocking out the assailant, we are trained to look for other threats. So in class, when another mugger approaches the scene, we yell fiercely at him, too, in case he's another attacker:

> I just finish knocking out one guy and, as trained, I assess the situation, making sure he's knocked out by stomping my foot near his head (if he is merely stunned, I would then grind his face into the ground), and looking around me for escape and possible threats. That's when another mugger approaches.
> "Hey are you alright?"
> "Back off!"
> "Hey I'm just trying to help, lady."
> "Stay away from me!" I run to the end of the line of students, and with a classmate's comforting arm around me, yell "9-1-1!"

Once I forgot to set a boundary with a mugger on the sideline, so he attacked me and I had to finish the fight with him too. After that, I always remembered to look around me after my fight, and to be wary of anyone offering what appears to be innocent help. One woman forgot to make sure the mugger was actually knocked out. He got up, went after her, and she had to fight him again to the knockout. Model Mugging is conducted in this sort of military fashion, which assumes that we will really learn when we are forced to face the consequences of our mistakes. And we did. By the end of the course, women know their moves, and are shouting and fighting back like a rapist's worst nightmare: "GET YOUR HANDS OFF ME YOU FUCKING ASSHOLE! STAY THE FUCK AWAY FROM ME!"

After several such rehearsals of kicking, poking, jabbing, and yelling, we all had "the fight." I felt different, tougher, and realized how little I had forcefully set boundaries with my voice in the past. By the end of the basic course, each woman has been mugged fifteen or twenty times. The women who encountered muggings that were similar to their own experience(s) of prior assaults said they felt good to win this time. Still, though, it is emotionally trying to go through these scenarios. Many of us enter the third and fourth classes dreading our next muggings. We leave exhausted, drained from such physically and emotionally intense fights.

Model Mugging News, now called *Self-Defense and Empowerment News*, is a quarterly publication about the class, containing instructor profiles and news about women and violence around the world. In the publication, women proudly share their success stories after getting attacked and defending themselves. Some of these stories are conveyed in class. The following is from *Self-Defense and Empowerment News*:

> While I was putting the last book in the drop, he grabbed my arm and ordered me to come with him and get in his car.
> I said "No."
> He began angrily calling me a "cunt, tease, and stuck-up bitch who needs to be knocked up" . . . and a lot of other things I can't remember now.
> As he loosened his grip to turn me around, I hit him square in the Adam's apple as hard as I could with my elbow.
> He staggered back, gasping. When he brought his hand down from his neck to come at me again, I noticed that his neck was already swelling and discoloring. As he lunged toward me I kicked off my heels and stood with my knees bent and both hands up in a protective stance, so that I could strike or drop to the ground if necessary. He then began telling me what he was going to do to me.
> I didn't focus on what he was saying because it was all verbal abuse. But when he said that after he was finished with me he was going to give me to his friends, I felt a sudden surge of anger. . . . I told him strongly and convincingly that I was prepared to do whatever it took to protect myself.
> He responded by calling me a "good looking piece of ass" and a "feisty bitch I'd like to break in bed," and then he said: "But I'm too tired now . . . and I don't have the time!" And with that, he left. (*Self-Defense and Empowerment News*, 6, no. 2 [Summer/Fall 1992]: 3)

Men figure in these stories as beatable, or at least vulnerable, posers of strength and brutality. Women emerge as victorious fighters. And that's how we feel as class comes to an end.

The course ends with graduation in which supporters are invited to come watch the combat portion of the last class. The muggings are videotaped and we can buy copies of the tape for twenty dollars. Afterward, the class alone shares gifts of food, poetry, and song. Students receive certificates of completion from the women instructors and roses from the men instructors.

On graduation day, I watched two muggers pull onto the mat and attack one of my female instructors, completely off guard. She stopped them both so impressively that I thought to myself—despite the fact that my chance of being attacked by more than one assailant is relatively slim—I want to know how to do that. So I went on to take the multiple assailants course, in which students learn to fight off up to five attackers, and then the weapons course, in which students learn to fight off an attacker wielding a gun, knife, or club. These advanced classes, while they involve more instructors and cost six hundred dollars each, proceed along the same lines as the first course. The primary difference is that women begin to learn to control their energy levels and strategize more during fights. Some of the women who were in my basic course took the second course because the first Model Mugging course did so much for them emotionally, helping them to feel empowered in all aspects of their lives, in addition to increasing their sense of security when alone at night or with a man on a date. Others still felt incapable of protecting themselves in a wider variety of scenarios and wanted further training. Still others wanted the physical challenge that the more advanced levels of instruction would bring.

Defending Ourselves is a San Francisco Bay area course based on a seventy-year-old police and military combative system that includes fighting with a padded attacker. Founded in 1991 by Helen Grieco and Patrick Phair, Defending Ourselves has trained over two thousand women. Grieco and Phair also offer self-defense instruction to women in battered women's shelters and in other community arenas. Grieco and Phair's Defending Ourselves introductory course is a $290 forty-hour program that takes place over twelve weeks. There are twelve students per class, and they have a student buddy system, sharing phone numbers to support one another.

Defending Ourselves offers three levels of training: (1) introductory (safety awareness, danger assessment, strategies to avoid assault, verbal assertiveness, physical self-defense, and response to attack with weapons); (2) multiple assailants (defense against multiple attackers); and (3) weapons (their use in self-defense, including bludgeon and edged weapons, sprays and devices, and firearms). The introductory course spends one third of class time in building awareness with feminist discussions about sexual violence, one third in skill building, and one third in simulated assault scenarios. It teaches some lethal techniques and involves some instruction in self-defense against an armed assailant. Defending Ourselves has students practice less with verbal abuse than Model Mugging students, and, unlike Model Mugging, does not push women to do things they are not ready for, insisting that honoring women's *nos* in the class is healing for them.

The course is taught in a large room in the Women's Community Building of San Francisco. Its hardwood floor and high ceiling recall the indoor basketball court of a high school gym. A small portion of the floor is covered with mats and hanging from one wall is a large padded dummy. Grieco, a dynamic white woman in her forties, wears her hair long and straight, and sports a T-shirt that reads, "Feminism is the radical idea that women are human beings." She has been a NOW activist since 1984 and has a masters degree in clinical psychology, with an emphasis in feminist therapy and education. Grieco offers free counseling to the women while they go through her class and sometimes spends an hour on the phone with a student processing the issues that come up during the training. In addition to doing some of the lectures for the course, Phair works as the simulated perpetrator, wearing padding under black motor cycle and equestrian crash gear made of plastics and foam, topped with a helmet.

"MAN WITH A KNIFE! SOMEBODY CALL 9-1-1! MAN WITH A KNIFE!" each trainee hollers as she dodges the charging armed attacker. The assault scenarios simulate fighting an attacker who is standing, seated, on the ground with you, or has pushed you to the ground—in the light and the dark. Here the women shriek, grabbing the attacker's head and piercing his eardrum with high-pitched screams directly into the ear. It took me a few minutes to get used to women's high-pitched voices because in Model Mugging I had learned to throw deep, stern words at the assailants. The women here scream mercilessly and scratch at the assailant's face. After knocking him out, each student runs to the safety of her cheering classmates and calls out "9-1-1." Grieco instructs women not to mention their self-defense training to police at the scene of assault, suggesting that instead they say, "He assaulted me and I want a lawyer." Grieco told me that she and Phair educate students on the law, and its gender bias in courts, with the police, and with respect to the "reasonable person" standard.

Additionally, whereas the Model Mugging muggers maintain their mugger status most of the time and never speak to the students when they are wearing their helmets, the male instructor of Defending Ourselves slips in and out of his roles as assailant and instructor by commenting on the techniques during and after fights, and gets involved with Helen in the supportive work throughout the class.

Defending Ourselves students engage in emotional processing as needed—unlike Model Mugging, they go from fight to fight without circling up to process what's going on. Grieco unapologetically points out students' mistakes, figuring that outside the classroom it might be a matter of life and death. As the final class ends, the women receive certificates immediately, take a class photograph, thank Grieco and Phair briefly, and arrange getting home. Braving the streets of San Francisco alone at night is not an expectation upon graduation; Grieco and Phair make sure everyone has a walk or ride to her parked car.

Impact, taught in several states in the United States, and SafeSkills, of Durham, North Carolina, are other padded attacker courses for women. Chimera offers a similar course but opposes the presence of a live padded attacker. Students hit pads and dummies instead, as the instructors believe that women should take self-defense in a women-only environment and should not have to relive assaults or contend with verbal abuse, since they experience that regularly in their daily lives. Chimera was created in Chicago and is spreading throughout the United States as its instructors move around the country. Another course, Blind Ambition, is specifically for blind people, who are frequent targets of violence because they seem defenseless. The blind students are taught their strengths in listening and reacting quickly. Using sounds to detect the motions and size of their opponent, played by a padded mock assailant, students practice disabling strikes to his head, throat, and groin.

Firearms Courses

Stance. Aim. Line up the sights. Finger on the trigger. Squeeze. The kick through my shoulder and back isn't so bad. How exhilarating to hear the loud explosion of the gun, to smell the gunpowder, and realize I had done this thing that had seemed so forbidden, if for no other reason than my own feminist principles.

My first gun lesson began with a call to a Southern California gun range I looked up in the *Yellow Pages*. I simply called and asked how I could learn to use a handgun. The man on the phone said that women tend to take lessons from their female instructor, Elaine (a pseudonym), and he gave me her home phone number. I called her, and she arranged to meet me at the range that week. She offered to let me use her gun, warning me not to go to the gun store by myself to purchase one. She explained that the men at the store would not treat me respectfully and that, if I'd like to purchase a gun, she offered as one of her services to accompany women to the gun dealer.

I spent three and a half hours with Elaine at the range. Instructors must be certified with the National Rifle Association to teach handgun lessons at the gun club. Elaine charges twenty dollars for all the instruction and donates this money to the club. She teaches about one woman per week in the use of a handgun for self-defense. Elaine describes herself as "the token woman" at the club, which means she does all the cooking and barbecuing when shooting competitions are held there. "But I don't mind," she says cheerfully. A married mother in her forties, she appears to be a mixture of Caucasian and African American (although she did not reveal her racial/ethnic identity). She has been a gun enthusiast ever since her husband took her to the shooting range one day when other social plans had fallen through. Now she is a competitive target shooter. She does not hunt.

Elaine says that it's scarier to teach women than men how to use handguns because women will fire five or six rounds at an attacker, while a man will stop at one or two. Her explanation for this: "All that anger comes up." She notes that it is illegal to carry a concealed weapon in California, but that many women do and it gives "a false sense of security." She says that if she were living alone, she'd have a shotgun in the front closet and a handgun in the bedroom. (But she suggests this only if a woman is sure she won't freeze up in an emergency, in which case a burglar could get to the shotgun first.)

Before I get the gun in my hand, Elaine notes the fear of guns that she observes in many of the women she instructs. A true hoplophobe myself, I have never shot or even held a gun before. Fortunately, Elaine eases my fears by explaining the safety rules of the range. Fears of being killed by random fire at the range subside as I realize what strict codes of conduct everyone observes. As we put on our eye and ear protection, Elaine assures me that the bullet by itself cannot hurt anyone, even if she were to throw it down onto the ground. I actually do need to hear that. She shows me a safe-handling technique and how to load the bullets into the revolver.

She is very calming as I get in place to shoot the gun at the target. She helps me line up the sights and reminds me to keep both eyes open (as in ill. 4). Feet apart. Shoulders relaxed. Breathe. Finger on the trigger. Squeeze. POW! I am surprised that my first shot actually makes it onto the target across the field. And that I don't drop Elaine's gun as it goes off. This is an immediate confidence-booster. Apparently, I am doing quite well for a beginner; one of my first three shots nearly hits the bull's eye. Elaine explains that "women are better marksmen" than men. This is because, in her view, men's hips are too narrow to enable good balance. Furthermore, women tend to be better shots in a tense, high adrenaline situation; according to Elaine, this is due to "hormones combined with adrenaline." I fire a few more rounds from her Lady Smith—a cute little revolver with a pearlized handle, Smith and Wesson's first "ladies" model handgun.

Next we head to the shotgun range. Elaine warns me that I'm "going to get swarmed" upon arrival. When I ask why, she says, "Because you've got something that they haven't got; in fact you've got two of them. . . . You are in a male world." While I would have assumed that the men would harass a woman because they would want to keep the gun range a "male world," Elaine clarifies that they'll want to marry me. So few women shoot that the men are anxious to meet women who share their hobby.

Ready for anything, I get to the "clubhouse," a little shack with not much more than a coffee pot, an old couch, a desk, and a telephone. One of the older men gives me a warm greeting, "Welcome to the club, Martha." The trap master, Jim, is even friendlier and I wouldn't have known the greeting to be odd, but Elaine says that this shy, awkward man never talks to anyone. The previous day, Elaine taught "a feminist" how to use the handgun she had purchased because a man was stalking her. Jim hit on her. He gives me his jacket to wear while shooting and then has to get something out of the side pocket, then wants me to hold his shotgun, and finally offers to let me shoot trap with him. Jim keeps trying to take over Elaine's instruction of me, coming up with several reasons for me to use his shotgun instead of hers. Elaine rolls her eyes, trying to keep him away from me, and reassures me that there's a rule that he can't call me, he doesn't intend it, and he's harmless. I am not so confident of this imperceptive rifleman's harmlessness, however. Jim keeps finding strange ways of fitting into my conversation with Elaine. Elaine tells me that yesterday he asked her if she'd cook for the club on Sunday (when he already knew this), just to be around her female student. He asks again today, along with other odd questions. Elaine smiles at me, rolling her eyes reassuringly.

We shoot the shotgun across a valley at a rock formation. The echo of the weapon in the wide-open space is powerful, and after shooting this big thing a couple of times I have a sense of mastery. It's not as heavy, as uncontrollable, or as difficult as I had imagined it to be. I learn to load the shotgun and do so before shooting again. After declining several offers to shoot trap with Jim, Elaine and I return to the clubhouse for a cup of coffee.

I ask Elaine if she knows of *Women and Guns*, a magazine in circulation since 1990. She says that she once subscribed, but didn't like it, as she felt it promoted a "false sense of security" and noted that every other page had an advertisement for a purse that concealed a handgun. (Although concealed handguns are illegal in California, they are legal in some states.) It makes having a gun seem glamorous, she notes, giving as an example one cover with Linda Hamilton on it. She's beautiful, muscular, famous, and this is not what women who use guns are generally like.

My second handgun lesson was not at a gun club but rather in an unsupervised outdoor area on a mountain ridge with a backdrop of wind-sculpted sandstone rocks. Locals come here to shoot their guns. Targets are set up in the distance, and you shoot toward the mountains. My instructor was Dale (a pseudonym), a white man in his thirties who, in addition to teaching these private lessons in "personal defense," is a skilled martial artist and works as a Model Mugging instructor, body guard, and surveillance operative for law enforcement officials. Dale charged me two hundred dollars for six hours of instruction, which included one hundred rounds of ammunition and the use of his handguns.

Dale and I shoot several of his revolvers and semi-automatics at steel plate targets. Dale has me shoot standing, kneeling, and even on my back, as if I had fallen over, with the gun pointing out from between my open knees (as in ill. 5). My favorite gun was a semi-automatic that had a clip holding nineteen rounds. Dale rearranges the steel plate targets while I'm not looking, says "OK," and I turn around and have to spot and shoot each target. I have to shoot down each target successfully before moving on to the next one. The advantage of steel targets over paper targets is that you know immediately when you have hit it because it falls over with a loud clanking noise. This kind of shooting with a semi-automatic is a real rush. For a second, it occurs to me that I am practicing some sort of nightmarish scene in which several people are against me and I have to shoot them all down.

Dale provides much practical advice for someone who wants to have a firearm for self-protection. For instance, he explains that I should know who my attorney would be, preferably one who defends police officers, and recommends becoming friends with someone at my local police station, because if one of the officers knows who I am, the tension and suspicion will be reduced right away if I call because I can ask for that officer and he or she would trust me a bit more. And whatever I do, I shouldn't say anything when the police arrive on the scene of a shooting. My sense of time and of the series of the events will be way off because I'll be upset, shaken, in shock. They could use what I say against me later, so I should just refuse to say anything. Dale also tells me that a person can legally shoot a single, unarmed assailant if he or she is afraid he'll get his or her gun. He says that deadly force is valid if there's more than one unarmed person, if one fears for one's life, although because I have Model Mugging multiple assailants training it's a "shady situation," and I could get into more trouble than a "weak," or untrained, woman. Interestingly, people in Paxton Quigley's firearms safety seminar (see below) assumed that being a trained woman would make the police more sympathetic.

The final hour of instruction takes place in my home. Dale comes with me to my apartment and points out hiding places and other strategies of defense that I can use there. He notices that I have a portable phone, and tells me that I could always ring the base unit with the intercom button on the handset to distract an intruder. He also shows me, using a fake knife and a fake gun that shoots plastic pellets, when to shoot if someone charges me with a knife. He shows me how to hold my gun so that someone can't come from around a corner and grab it away from me. He teaches me how to hold someone at gun point until the police arrive and demonstrates many tricks an assailant might use to hide a gun on his person, and the places I might hide one in my home.

Dale also has a theory about why women are better shots than men. While Elaine told me that it was hormonal (women are calmer) and biological (women have wider hips), Dale says that it's social—men are too restless and egotistical, while women are more patient. Meyer (1993, 91) notes that her first male instructor had a theory that the female ego is less connected to explosions and compared women's superior concentration to the steady focus required for threading needles. Paxton Quigley's friend Andrea Frank says that women excel at shooting because "we seem to learn more rapidly, because we don't have any fixed ideas, and we don't have a macho attitude on how we're supposed to shoot, like men do. Men look at cop shows and Western movies and use the stars as role models" (quoted in Quigley 1989, 22).

Paxton Quigley travels around the country offering women-only handgun safety training classes. Author of *Armed and Female* and *Not an Easy Target*, Paxton Quigley is the foremost advocate of women's handgun training and is known to have the best course for women in firearms and self-defense. A nationally recognized personal protection expert, Quigley has made many television news show appearances and is a paid representative of Smith and Wesson.

I enrolled in a class she offered in San Francisco at a gun club that sponsored her. The six-hour class costs $160. The class paid a $15 range fee and $7 for a package of fifty bullets. Quigley is a white woman who appears to be in her forties. Her petite frame is more than compensated for by her powerful posture and voice, which burst with confidence and authority.

Of the thirteen of us in the class, most are white; two are Latina; and one is Eastern European and lived mainly in Canada before recently moving to California. The youngest woman there is about twenty-eight, and the oldest probably sixty. Half of the women arrive with their own handguns. The other half will use guns, along with ear and eye protection, provided by Quigley.

Of the group who own handguns, only two have practiced shooting them before.

Before the class begins, everyone talks among themselves about crime, drive-by shootings, and the increasing dangers of the world around them. We begin class with introductions, telling the group why we are here: "My husband died and I have all his guns, and I want to learn how to use them." Says another, "I am divorced, happily, and want to learn how to protect myself and my daughter." One group of women, three sisters and their mother, are there with new guns purchased by the father as a Christmas gift. (Quigley later suggests to a few of them that they go trade in their guns for different ones that fit their hands better.) No one mentions being threatened by anyone specific. One participant is part of a team of documentarians making a video on guns they plan to pitch to PBS. The course is being filmed for their video. I ask the videographer taking the class if she'll be looking into other forms of self-defense as well. She scoffs at the suggestion, saying that umbrellas and mace do not really cut the mustard; there is no "real" self-defense, she says, other than a gun.

We sit in three rows facing front, where Paxton stands with a small chalkboard and a table full of self-protection items like Pepper Spray, as well as T-shirts and her book to sell. Before ever even seeing guns we go through a class session on self-protection. She first gives an introductory story of how she used to be against guns until her good friend was raped at home by a man who had broken in. The police didn't get there until well after the man raped her and left, even though she'd called 9-1-1 as he broke through the window. She contrasted this with a story of a woman who'd held a burglar at gun point until the police arrived, which, interestingly, was in much less time since she told the police she had a gun. Paxton emphasizes both the fear of men and the fear of guns turning into a feeling of control.

Before learning anything about firearms, Paxton lectures on awareness and avoidance strategies. She explains "The Five *T*s" and distributes a corresponding hand-out:

(1) *Target.* Usually attacks are not random, you are targeted: this may be for a minute or a month. Women are vulnerable, considered weaker—she is careful never to say that women *are* weaker—it's assumed that we'll freeze up when attacked, or that we won't have the strength to fight back. Go with any bad feelings you get, and don't risk trusting someone from whom you get bad vibes, she says. She also says to be less predictable, like leave your house and return home at different times and avoid going to the gas

station on your way home from work. "Don't be paranoid," she said. "Make it a game." Other advice she gives includes the following: If you think you're being followed while driving, make three right turns and then you know if you're being followed or not. Go to the same gas station all the time and make friends with the attendants so that if you can't make it to a police station, you can go to these guys and they'll want to help you. Also, if you're being stared at, mark the person with your eyes, let him know you've seen him so he knows he can't surprise you. Finally, don't ask for directions if you get lost. Have a portable cellular phone in your car to call and ask for directions. Take the phone in at night so that if a burglar takes the first phone off the hook or cuts the lines, you'll still be able to call 9-1-1. Don't give out your social security number. On your checks, put only your first initial, don't give a phone number (if you have to, make one up, or give a business number), and use a P.O. Box or a business address.

(2) Test. Men test women to see how they'll react, by following, staring, or trying the old "arm on shoulder," which happens most often in the office. Paxton mainly speaks of the mall, the street, and burglars. She recommends staring back while thinking, "get away from me" or worse, in your mind; or say firmly, "You're walking too close to me!" If a man asks you the time, don't stop. In fact, don't even answer. Cut off such behavior immediately or men will think you like it and take it to the next step.

(3) Threaten. If you've been tested successfully as a good victim, you can be threatened verbally, physically, or with a weapon.

(4) Touch. The touch is the assault. Forced oral sex is very common but, she explains rather nonchalantly, "you can bite it off."

(5) Take-off. This is where you sense the criminal's feelings—he may feel nervous, guilty, or confused. Here's where you can get murdered or receive other heavy-duty violence in addition to the rape. Your reading of his behavior and mood is crucial.

We then get a lesson in making the house safe. Paxton mentions that this is important because "37 percent of all rapes are in a woman's own bedroom." She doesn't break this statistic down by acquaintance versus strangers. We are advised to get a solid-core door as our bedroom door and to bolt it with a medico lock. Make a room, perhaps the bedroom, into a "safe room." Have a rope ladder if it's on the second floor (and practice going down it).

Next we learn some verbal self-defense. Paxton interviewed rapists in prison who told her that women's use of harsh language, specifically the word "fuck," might have deterred them. So we stand in a circle around Paxton and she has us practice telling her to "GET THE FUCK AWAY FROM ME!" Several of us laugh as we say it; one woman can't even get herself to say "fuck." Paxton goes back to her until she belts it out. Then we practice shouting "NO!" at her in the same way. She gets down on the ground and shows us a couple of kicks she learned in Model Mugging, and recommends that we take a Model Mugging course. She explains that she is a graduate of two of their courses, and that they are invaluable for getting women to practice being powerful, delivering blows, and yelling.

Quigley lectures on a range of nonlethal weapons and safety devices: The ten dollar mini-baton for key chains, which scares men and reminds the woman carrying it that she should be alert and ready for action; a remote car door opener for your key chain, which opens doors right before you get to your car, so you avoid fumbling; pepper spray—now legal in California, although you have to navigate your way through the bureaucracy for it, paying $17.95 and watching a videotape—which, if used in a wide-open area (never against the wind) and on the men who are not immune to it, makes assailants choke, cough, close their eyes, and go down to the ground in pain; twenty-dollar personal alarms, good for children and the elderly, which let off a very loud noise, as she demonstrated; and the Persuader and stun guns, which she doesn't recommend because you cannot use them from a distance, and you must hold them onto the attacker for three to four seconds. Before we go out to the range, women buy copies of Quigley's book *Armed and Female*, T-shirts that say "Armed and Female," and mini-batons to use as key rings.

Also before going on the range, we look over the "Justifiable Use of Lethal Force" handout. Paxton does not share any opinion about women's legal self-defense cases or their history. She simply explains that it is legal to use lethal force when three elements are satisfied:

(1) *The ability element.* She says that police don't usually ask women questions to test the "ability" element of the justifiable use of lethal force. The ability element is that "the attacker must have the power to kill or cause crippling injury, or be advantaged with a disparity of force or a disparity of skill." She explains that women don't usually have the strength or fighting skill, so the police presume the attacker had the advantage.

(2) *The opportunity element.* This is that "the attacker must be capable of employing bodily harm immediately. He must be within range." Paxton notes how quickly a man can get to you, say from way across the room.

Thus even across the room counts as "within range." Paxton explains that great bodily harm includes rape.

(3) *The jeopardy element.* "The perpetrator must be acting in such a manner that a reasonably prudent person would assume he intended to attack." Of course one cannot shoot someone who's bigger and standing across the room but does not pose a threat.

Paxton is careful to remind us that we are not learning to *kill*, but rather to *stop* an attacker. Never tell the legal establishment that you were trained to, or tried to, *kill* someone, she says; always say you tried to *stop* someone. She also explained that, in California, you can use any force to stop an attacker who enters your home and that a woman usually gets off even if she kills an unarmed attacker in such a situation. But, she warns, you can't shoot someone who's retreating. Paxton mentioned a case of "domestic violence," but it was an example of the use of mere threat (something known in the armed self-defense world as rarely successful), where a woman showed her gun from the upstairs balcony to, and threatened, the ex-lover who was stalking her. He never again violated his restraining order. (I address the legal treatment of battered women who shoot their batterers in self-defense in chapters 1 and 5.)

As we get set to go out on the range, those us of who need guns get sized for the appropriate one. One woman had brought in a semi-automatic and Quigley gave her a revolver to use. Quigley recommends revolvers since they jam less often than semi-automatics, and are easier to load and unload. Moreover, you can see the bullets and they're easier to clean.

Just as my old fears of getting struck down by random fire at a bullet-infested quasi–Old-West dude ranch start to creep up on me, Paxton reassures us about how safe the range will be for us. She trained us for the range exercises so that it would indeed be safe. On the range we go very slowly and shoot simultaneously at her command, standing in a line and aiming at paper targets of human silhouettes about seven feet away.

Quigley's voice sounds even more authoritative through her bullhorn. She commands us to load our guns, walk in front of the tables behind which we have been standing in an orderly fashion with our guns open, walk up to the shooting line, get in ready positions, aim, line up the sights, put our fingers in the trigger guards, and shoot. (See ill. 6.) The first time we simply shoot all five rounds and then stop. I have been so amped burning powder that I don't know if I shot four rounds or five.

After each shooting, we'd open the cylinders and turn them upward to empty our guns, walk back to the tables, place the guns on the table, remove our ear protection, and then go up to see "the damage" we've wreaked on our targets. Paxton walks over to each of our targets to congratulate us, giving a pat or a rub on the back. We clap for each woman after assessing her target. Then we put tape over the bullet holes on our targets and go back and do another exercise. Checking the five new holes, our improvement is noticeable.

By the end, we have emptied fifty rounds into the paper assailants, five at a time, using different shooting patterns—all five bullets at once, two to the chest and one to the head (to make sure the attacker is "stopped"), or all five at once without taking time to line up the sights. In one exercise we fire while walking toward our targets. Sometimes a student shouts obscenities while walking and shooting, exploding as much anger as gunpowder at her imaginary attacker. We all shoot well. All but four of my fifty bullets hit somewhere on paperman's head, neck, or chest.

Afterward, Paxton autographs our paper targets and says good-bye. Some pay ten dollars for a certificate with which to buy a gun. (As of April 30, 1994, California requires evidence of an exam or class to purchase a gun.) We all receive little gold revolver pins provided by Smith and Wesson. Paxton mentions at this time that she's a feminist and that women have to learn to protect themselves with guns. She states the importance of women's learning from and with other women, reminding us that in the mid-1980s she had to learn firearms in an intimidating all-male environment. Recalling my experience with Jim at the other gun club, I admittedly feel relieved to be in a women-only environment.

Martial Arts Courses

> A student at the dojo performs a kata (a prearranged set of movements against an imaginary opponent) for the sensei (Japanese for *instructor*). She has a serious and frightening look on her face, a fierceness in her eyes. Her arms slice through the air, creating, punch after punch, an audible wind.

The first martial arts self-defense course I took was a mixed-gender course in Krav Maga, the Israeli martial art. Before signing up, I called the instructor and asked if this class, advertised as "self-defense," was appropriate for women wanting to learn how to defend themselves from sexual assault. He answered that it most definitely was. For thirty-five dollars, I met with about forty others (twenty women and twenty men) two hours per week for ten weeks. We met in a room used for aerobics and dance classes on a college campus. The instructor, a clean-cut white North American about twenty years old and standing five feet and five inches tall, wore his white cotton martial arts uniform, or "gi," tied with a black belt. We wore sweats and shorts and stood in parallel rows of four facing the teacher, who stood on a slightly elevated block with a mirrored wall behind him.

After a brief warm-up and stretch, we practice routine movements at his command. He shouts out a number and we do the corresponding elbow jab. There are seven elbow jab positions. Students take turns holding up pads for each other to kick and punch. The men in my practice group express astonishment when I kick the pad they are holding much harder than they expected from a woman. By now I have learned to kick hard, but they don't know that. They see a woman and are surprised that I, as they put it, "just walked up to the pad so gracefully and then nailed it."

We practice stand-up fighting exclusively. We learn how to punch quickly, to scratch the attacker's face as we take him down, yelling "KIAI!" as we jab, and to "finish him off" while he's on the ground and we are still standing or kneeling over him. We learn to beat kidneys, grab the assailant's jacket or skin at the sides of the back while delivering a knee to the groin. We partner off and practice getting out of strangle holds and rear grabs. The instructor turns out the lights and we practice getting out of various strangle holds and grabs with partners in the dark. I look for a female partner, but the women are all paired up with other men or the friends with whom they are taking the class. Grappling with a strange man in the dark is unnerving. The line between practice assaults and real ones fades with the flourescent lights. Our techniques, however, are not intentionally practiced in a high-adrenaline situation. One man approaches me with arms stretched out, putting me in a choke hold, without directive from the teacher to do so.

These dynamics added up to an often condescending or embarrassing atmosphere. For instance, the men with whom I practiced kicking let me know that they didn't think I could do it; and the instructor called me up to the front of the class to demonstrate the technique of blocking his strikes, despite the fact that it was my first day in Krav Maga and I had just learned the blocking technique five minutes prior. Others (Searles and Follansbee 1984, 65) have made similar observations formally. Because women often find it difficult to move beyond traditional gendered expectations and to exert themselves physically when men are present without becoming embarrassed (or, as in my case, teased and put on display), a co-ed course with male instructors can prove more difficult for women (ibid., 65-66). Some male students either find it difficult to play the defeated role in self-defense scripts with women (ibid., 66) or find it all too easy and enjoyable to play the assailant role.

Krav Maga did not encourage a student's sense of self-worth or confidence in fighting ability; it assumed that we did not need to be taught when to fight and that it's OK to fight, only how to fight. This is quite typical of courses men usually offer to men. In this sense, the course was really geared toward those who already felt entitled to respect and who already believed that they could fight, that is, men. For my instructor simply treated us as though we did not have a fear of fighting, a fear of getting hurt, a lack of entitlement, or a lack of self-esteem.

Although Krav Maga's techniques are designed so that anyone, regardless of size, can stop an assailant as quickly as possible, the class received no instruction on how to end a fight—something that is particularly dangerous for women whose attackers could be intent on retaliation or continuing the fight if they are not knocked out cold (ibid., 66). Our instructor simply showed us the move—for instance, getting the assailant's head in our left hand and delivering punches to the face with our right hand—concluding his demonstration with the direction, "and finish him off." We were never told what we were supposed to do after getting our assailant into a submissive position. What did "finish him off" mean? Run? Wait for help? Tie him up and then run for help? Kill him?

We did not hear anything about the law, calling the police, or getting to a safe place. Nor were we told what to say to the police to explain our behavior. There was no emotional talk or discussion of prior assault experiences in Krav Maga, as there was in Model Mugging and, I would later learn, in the martial arts self-defense courses for women. We received no information on prevention, as Paxton Quigley gave in her firearms course. The instructor did not deal with any of the fears or stereotypes people tend to have about assault, nor did he deal with the different situations and ways in which women and men tend to get attacked. I left wondering what a women-only martial arts course would be like.

I visited Valley Women's Martial Arts, Inc., in Easthampton, Massachusetts, a private nonprofit school of self-defense and karate. Dojo owner and master sensei Janet Aalfs has been involved with the martial arts for twenty years. (See ill. 7.) She was a student of Wendy Dragonfire, the founder of the school, who was a student of Master Robert A. Trias, founder of the United States Karate Association. Black belts Beth Holt and Janet Aalfs took over the school in 1982 when Dragonfire went to the West Coast. Since Holt's departure in 1992, Aalfs has run Valley Women's herself. She has also served as president of the National

Women's Martial Arts Federation (NWMAF) for several years. This is known as a first-rate school.

As you enter the dojo, there is a large office to one side and a table and bulletin board to the other, filled with information, clippings, and the dojo's own newsletter, *The Shuri Spiral News*. Formerly a factory, this dojo is large and open with a hardwood floor, almost like an artist's loft. The walls are decorated with posters, paintings of the woman symbol, and creative work about women. A section of one wall is devoted to newspaper clippings and photographs of Valley Women students and teachers posed in strong defensive stances.

Aalfs, black belt in Shuri-ryu, an Okinawan style of karate, is a tall and lean white woman of thirty-seven. Her advanced class that I observed is comprised of seven white women in their late twenties. They are strikingly vital and wide-eyed. The women are wearing simple sweat pants and T-shirts. The advanced karate class is very self-defense-oriented, but, unlike the one-day self-defense classes that martial artists offer, involves the traditional rituals of the martial arts.

Before entering the dojo, students remove their shoes and then bow, which symbolizes respect for the learning place. The women form a circle to begin a meditation and warm-up. Janet sensei says, "Sashita," and the students kneel. They come to attention at the word *Kiotsuke*, and begin their meditation when they hear *Seiza mokuso*. The atmosphere is intimate, and I feel like an intruder. But then sensei Aalfs introduces me and explains that I'm observing the class for the research I'm doing. The first thirty minutes are very low energy. Students warm up with slow movements, feeling their body's energy and controlling every movement (as in ill. 8).

In this two-hour class, sensei Aalfs introduces "the Five Animal Frolics"— the crane, the tiger, the bear, the deer, and the monkey. The animal frolics are images that the women can call upon when they want to defend themselves. The crane is a very slow and controlled movement. The tiger movement is fierce. Students kick with crane energy and then kick with tiger energy. They practice front snap kicks, roundhouse kicks, and combinations of kicks. Then they pair up and practice self-defense scenarios. One attacks in an unpredictable fashion and the other responds as one of the animals.

The crane self-defense style is calm, subdued. The tiger self-defense is fierce and frighteningly loud. The voices of these women are astonishing: "GET OUT OF MY FACE!" one growls. The students playing assailants seem very calm, not worried that they are going to get kicked. The defenders' hands and feet brush right by their opponents' bodies, never making contact. These women are admirably strong. And they are obviously having fun doing this.

While the class starts out calm, it gradually builds and by the end the women are sweating and tired. There is no high-adrenaline state or major heart-rate increase. The monkey response is sprightly and takes the opponent by surprise. Janet invites my participation by asking me to guess which of the five animals a particular student is using. Aalfs seems like a wonderful teacher and role model, smiling and encouraging—far from the stereotypical stern martial artist pushing at or humiliating students.

Indeed, opposed to the idea that information should be disseminated from above, Aalfs has the students circle up again after their work and discuss how it went. One comments that she didn't like how everyone tended to laugh when they did the self-defense scenarios, particularly when they did the monkey. Another remarks, skeptically, that she thinks the animals help her get out of herself, so it's like the tiger or the monkey defending her rather than she who defends herself. Janet suggests that the students are not leaving their bodies by becoming the animals; instead, she explains, the animals become them.

Even in this advanced class, which emphasizes the artistic and philosophical aspects of the martial arts, Aalfs stresses how to use techniques in actual attack situations. She also teaches a women's self-defense course, at a sliding-scale fee, which combines various karate styles, assertiveness training, and a discussion of violence against women. Aalfs believes that women can best avoid harm by strengthening themselves physically, mentally, and spiritually. Her self-defense course uses role-playing to teach women how to get out of various situations, showing women how to break free when grabbed, when backed against a wall, and when pinned on the ground. Aalfs also teaches women verbal defense and inspires their mental attitude, insisting that the way you present yourself influences whether or not someone will bother you. She wants women to get over a pattern of thinking she calls "trained helplessness," which renders them unnecessarily defenseless.

Aalfs teaches self-defense to senior citizens, showing, for instance, how to use a cane for self-defense. Part of a whole network of organizational services for women, Valley Women's Martial Arts also offers self-defense classes through battered women's shelters and university women's centers.

I observed a fairly advanced women's martial arts course at KarateWomen in West Los Angeles. KarateWomen master sensei and co-owner of the dojo Maria Doest leads the class. A robust and cheerful forty-something woman of Asian, European, and Native American descent, Doest has a black belt in Okinawan karate, and has been running KarateWomen for over twenty years.

KarateWomen has a reputation among martial artists as an excellent place for women to learn karate. Active in the Pacific Association of Women Martial Artists (PAWMA), KarateWomen sponsored the 1994 annual PAWMA camp.

The atmosphere here is a bit different from that of the dojo in Easthampton. This dojo is fairly small, next to the loud and busy Venice Boulevard. Its tiny entranceway has a bathroom area, a little nook with a desk and telephone, and a bench with flyers announcing class schedules, the upcoming PAWMA camp, and a student's party. The dojo itself is one big matted square, with a shelf all around the periphery of the room displaying impressive trophies. A few posters with Japanese lettering adorn the walls, along with a display of martial arts fighting sticks, swords, and knives.

Women remove their shoes, bow, and enter the dojo. They circle up and bow toward the center of the circle. Eight white women and four women of color, between the ages of nineteen and forty-five, practice self-defense moves for the upcoming PAWMA camp. A fifteen-year-old boy practices weapons techniques with a visiting male sensei over in one corner of the room. All wear gis with varying color belts, showing the varying skill levels of the participants. Sensei Doest does not explain my presence to the students. They seem unaffected by and uninterested in my observation.

The class is loosely structured, as women in groups of two or three practice getting out of different holds and throwing their opponents to the ground. They yell a loud and deep "KIAI!" as they deliver the final (pseudo) blow— either a kick or a punch to the face of the opponent on the ground. Some practice with an assailant carrying a fake knife. A woman takes her opponent down by the throat, knowing that in a real fight she'd grab and pull on that delicate skin around the front of the assailant's neck.

The mood is remarkably spirited and chatty. Like the women doing karate in Easthampton, they look strikingly strong and vibrant. One woman knocks her assailant to the ground, and realizes she doesn't remember the final move in this scenario. Still in position, she and her downed opponent consult the pair next to them. The downed woman lets out a loud kiss toward the ground. Then the standing woman kisses her finger and brings it down to the cheek of her opponent, following instantly with the final move—a standing kick straight down to the head on which she'd just placed a kiss. "KIAI!" They move easily in and out of laughter and ferocity. Another group of women practicing mention the movie *Buffy the Vampire Slayer,* specifically a scene in which Buffy throws a man to the ground. "I loved that," one proclaims.

Sensei Doest goes around watching the women practice and giving them suggestions. She periodically explains to me, seated at the bench, what's going on. After an hour or so they begin to practice their katas, walking in a line with fists jutting out. Students bow to their instructor repeating, "yes sensei" as they hear suggestions for improving technique. Finally, from their positions in a single line, students present their moves to sensei Doest, each one taking a turn at being both victim and assailant with the next person in line.

I remarked that the atmosphere was more emotionally heavy in Model Mugging, and Doest explained, "that's 'cause you got men cursing at you there!" She thinks women get used to such verbal abuse and less angry at it. (Model Mugging's philosophy is that women learn to get angry at verbal abuse, and to fight through it.) Maria tells me that the beginners learn basic techniques, for instance how to get out of choke holds and grabs from behind, what she takes to be the most common ways men assault women. The more advanced students learn take-downs (taking the opponent to the ground). Whereas beginning level Model Mugging courses teach women to kick from the ground, martial arts courses train women to kick while standing up. (See ill. 9.) Doest teaches women to go for an attacker's groin with the edge of the hand, or with a slap-and-grab, so that if the man has his knees together, you can still induce severe pain and "get that spasm going." If he's wearing a groin protector cup, she explained, then that's even better, "you just grab the cup and scrape it forward and you've got cup-o-noodles."

Doest also teaches self-defense to blind women, showing them how to use their canes in self-defense, and to deaf women, who learn defenses against rear grabs, the sort to which deaf women are particularly vulnerable. (A couple of the students know sign language and serve as interpreters.) She shows women in wheelchairs how to do choke hold releases, which they can perform by taking advantage of the weight of their bodies' being in the chairs, pulling downward to release the choke. She teaches them nose and throat strikes, and suggests that they continue such strikes until the threat of the assailant is totally alleviated, even if this means using lethal force.

I asked if she taught the other women lethal techniques and she said yes, the strike to the throat and the heel palm to the nose are both potentially lethal moves. She said that her self-defense classes work for women who are not bigger or stronger than men. I asked her if size or strength was really the issue, pointing out that tiny men can become expert fighters through martial arts training. She responded: "For men, it's all ego; they have to get cut down in class. For women, it's all self-esteem; they have to be built up in class." She explained that a little boy will tell you he can kill someone when asked what he would do if assaulted, while a girl will reply, "I don't know."

Finally, I participated in a three-and-a-half-hour, forty-dollar workshop at KarateWomen, taught by dojo co-owner Deborah McCormick and an instructor-in-training. Only two other students were signed up for the class. Everyone was white. We were not asked to bow upon entering the dojo. We simply removed our shoes, walked in, and sat in a circle on the mat.

The class begins with an hour-long informal lecture. We are given the frightening statistics on rape. Fifty percent of rapists are dates, they say, and the overwhelming majority of rapists are acquaintances. Rape is about "violence, not sex," they explain. "He wants power over you; he wants control over you." This is ironically followed by the statement that most men do not know either what rape is or that they have raped when they have. McCormick says that rape is most of the time planned, and then, perhaps catching herself in the logical contradiction of the statements, corrects that to say that *sex* is planned. We hear the "Five *Ts*" as we did in Paxton Quigley's class.

The instructors critique femininity and comment on male socialization: Women are more polite and considerate whereas men tend to think only of themselves. For instance, one instructor explains, "women walk into a room and wonder, 'is someone sitting in this chair?' and 'am I in anyone's way?' whereas men just go plop." Self-defense, as they see it, involves women's consciously retraining their thought processes so that we react differently in an assault: Instead of feeling, "Huh! Omigod! What am I going to do? I'm helpless!" we might begin to feel the way men tend to feel: "What am I going to do to get out of this situation? What are my options?" And, just as Dale and Paxton suggested how we might account for our violent acts, these instructors explain that, if we ever fight to defend ourselves, we should say that we feared for our life, that we feared the man would kill us.

After the lecture we practice yelling "NO!" across the room to one another. Next, we do a verbal assertiveness drill by sitting in a circle and telling the person next to us to take her hand off of our knee, without smiling. Two of us manage to do this without smiling. One cracks a smile and giggles, mentioning that it feels so natural to smile, even in this situation.

We learn how to stomp on the instep of an attacker's foot, how to deliver a heel palm strike to the face (as in ill. 10) and scrape down the face with our nails (to "get evidence—skin, blood, and DNA"), and how to get out of front and rear grabs, all the while yelling "NO!" as fiercely as possible. Being in such a small group, in a fairly low-energy situation, makes yelling "NO!" awkward and most of the time we say it quietly or forget to say it altogether. We learn a side kick from the ground, how to knock someone down who is dragging you by the feet, and how to throw off with your hips someone who is sitting on top of you. We did not practice any self-defense moves in a high-adrenaline state, and everything was rather careful and controlled, except for the strikes to the groin of a stuffed pair of jeans which the instructor held behind us.

We also learn a lethal technique called the tiger claw, a quick strike of knuckles to the throat that collapses the windpipe. The instructors note that they teach this lethal technique in case we are in a situation in which we feel we have to kill someone. Besides, they explain, even if a student wants never to use a lethal technique, they teach it because they believe women feel different knowing that they could kill someone. "Men think they could kill someone, and 'know' they could kill a woman," McCormick explains, "whereas women don't think they can hurt anybody."

McCormick was right. We practiced the tiger claw more than any other move, fascinated with it. We practiced the form of the strike over and over, into the air and also just barely touching each other's necks. For the rest of the day I thought about how I had learned to kill someone with my bare hands. In Model Mugging I had felt fierce. In firearms courses I had certainly felt lethal when I was firing the gun. In all the classes I had felt powerful and strong. But nothing felt quite like knowing that my body is capable of lethal force. It felt as if I had been let in on a well-kept secret.

Self-Defense-Oriented Fitness

Michael Schwartz, the developer and instructor of Cardio Combat, at Crunch aerobics studio in Manhattan's Greenwich Village, is a lean and muscular white man, probably around thirty. Beaming with energy, he enters the aerobics room, where students stand already in place, facing him at front. The students are mainly young women in aerobics outfits, about thirty in all, paying several dollars for the hour-long class (eleven dollars for walk-ins, a little less for people who hold regular passes). A few men are staggered across the back row and look a bit awkward as the class begins to move to the raging techno beat. Instead of jazz dance steps (as in traditional aerobics) or patterned movements over a step (as in step aerobics), Michael leads the class in a series of heel-palm strikes and punches to the air, left and right, left and right, and a series of mock knees-to-the-groin and front snap kicks, left and right, left and right.

There is no work with partners (for instance, getting out of holds), nor are there any kicks from the ground (although such kicks would have made great leg abductions). There is no discussion about sexual violence, no bonding among the women, no practice in lifelike scenarios. Everyone just goes in for the workout and leaves. Still, though, twenty minutes into the class, you are absolutely intoxicated with endorphins among your comrades in sweat. This combative stance starts to feel fun, exhilarating in fact. Given that I had already learned to fight seriously in other courses before I came here, I could imagine that regular attendance in Cardio Combat would be a rather enjoyable form of exercise and would remind me of what I had learned in a more intense, serious instructional setting.

Several other courses that combine cardiovascular fitness, music, and self-defense moves are available in aerobics studios or sports and fitness centers, including Aerobox (in New York City) and Boxing for Fitness (in Southern California). These courses are offered as part of a variety of class options for women and men who hold memberships at a particular studio or sports center. While women make up the majority of aerobics instructors, I did not see a single female instructor in these self-defense-oriented fitness classes. Of the many new aerobic workouts on videotape now, Steve DeMasco's *Aerobic Self-Defense Workout* (1992) was sold on the cable television show *Home Shopping Network*. Interestingly, this video is a rather boring, slow aerobic workout. The only place a woman has in it is leading the aerobic workout and demonstrating the kicks and strikes while Steve explains everything. She doesn't even speak.

Conclusion

Whatever its problems and contradictions, the experience of self-defense training transformed me. Even the way I walk changed. I realized this when, walking alone at night, men were visibly aware of my footsteps behind them. Now my footsteps make them turn around nervously to see who's behind them. My personal experience can open a window into the world of women's self-defense, but the experiences and reflections of instructors and students in a variety of self-defense courses will enable us to thematize and analyze the process of learning to fight back.

What does it mean when women in self-defense classes confront their fears and prepare to fight back? Using interviews and informal conversations with women in self-defense classes, as well as the discussions that self-defensers have with one another in their newsletters and magazines, the next chapter describes what some of the women who have taken one or another of these forms of self-defense have to say about it. Who are the assailants women are learning to defend themselves against? How is rape accomplished, and what must a woman do to challenge a rapist? These are the questions that self-defensers negotiate, and that the next chapter analyzes. I draw out the critiques, implicit and explicit, of gendered understandings of aggression offered in self-defense instruction and show how self-defense metamorphoses the female body. I delineate the processes by which women substitute a physically competent, aggressive posture for a passive one, describe how students and instructors of self-defense understand that process, and suggest how that process could disrupt the ideological structure that rationalizes men's violence against women.

3

The Fighting Spirit

Self-Defense As Counterdiscourse

As the last chapter showed, women learn to shoot and fight in a highly charged sensorial atmosphere of supportive women, sweat, bullets, swear words, and fantasized and enacted fighting success. This often pleasurable process engages women mentally, emotionally, and physically. That's how it effectively encourages a new bodily comportment. By requiring women to act in unfeminine ways, self-defense instruction makes possible the identification of not only some of the mechanisms that create and sustain gender inequality but also a means to subvert them. Self-defense is a counterdiscourse: It represents woman, man, and aggression in new ways that oppose those we take for granted. Women's new bodily comportment affects not only their confidence with respect to thwarting assaults; it proves highly consequential for many areas of their lives.

Gender is a lived ideology—a system of ideas about men and women with which we live our lives. As lived ideology, those ideas get transformed into specific bodily practices. Socially produced sex differences are embodied and lived out as "real." They are materialized as habit and taken for granted as "second nature" (Bourdieu 1990; Butler 1990). Despite their implicit misrecognition as natural facts, these commonsense understandings of gender are rehearsed over and over; they are not natural and therefore not as stable as they may seem and often feel. As a collection of dispositions, gender is knowledge embodied through rigorous education.

Bodily assumption of the normative behavioral rules is crucial to the perpetuation of the power system, for as MacKinnon (1987, 118) argues, femininity is defined in terms of a rape culture; and therefore femininity means physical weakness and violability. It is not just that women and men are stereotyped or are playing out gender roles: "Masks become personas become people, socially, especially when they are enforced. . . . It is not just an illusion or a fantasy or a mistake. It becomes *embodied* because it is enforced" (ibid., 119).

As Butler (1990) suggests, compulsory heterosexuality is the institutional context in which this embodiment takes place. The political system structures our desires, as well as our masculine and feminine bodily dispositions. The dominant discourse produces bodies whose appearance and desires it can accept—bodies that are intelligible within the normative scheme. Cultural values are materialized at the level of the body. Compulsory heterosexuality and male domination are cultural values turned into naturalized, embodied understandings—as sure as chewing with our mouths closed and saying "please" and "thank you" are. Social sanctions are inscribed within our bodies and feel like second nature. In this way, our gendered bodies are materializations of power and, specifically, of compulsory heterosexuality and male domination.

Because gender is not really natural, it requires constant enforcement and repetition. This repetition is abruptly interrupted in women's self-defense classes. What feminists talk about interrupting—femininity—self-defensers practice interrupting: They enact the deconstruction of femininity. In the process, self-defense enables women to internalize a different kind of bodily knowledge. As such, self-defense is feminism in the flesh.

Unlearning Femininity

The full meaning of women's self-defense begins with women who are afraid of violence and of their inability to prevent it. Women enter gyms, dojos, and gun clubs hoping to learn some strategies and tricks with which to defend themselves. The first and most significant hurdle turns out to be their own femininity. They are afraid they will hurt someone, and they are fearful of getting hurt. Many are reluctant to touch a gun, as though it will explode on contact. In padded attacker and martial arts courses, rookie students often smile at their attackers and apologize after landing kicks—which they have yet to deliver at full force.

It becomes clear that women's inability to fight is a cultural matter of sexual politics, not a natural matter of hormones, brawn, or life-affirming biological programming. The feminine demeanor that comes so "naturally" to women, a collection of specific habits that otherwise may not seem problematic, is precisely what makes us terrible fighters. Suddenly we see how these habits that make us vulnerable and that aestheticize that vulnerability are encouraged in us by a sexist culture. The very things that mark us as successful feminine women make us easy victims. We do not consciously apply rules of social life; we simply live them as second nature. In fact, so ingrained are they that women have to practice and practice before they can yell "GET AWAY FROM ME" *without* smiling. These habits are not roles women are playing. They are embodied. These habits are not random, but are expressions of a gendered order, and beyond this, a gendered order in which women lose.

Contemporary Western women, unlike their male counterparts, grow up with a sense that their bodies are not theirs, that their bodies can be appropriated. This is particularly so for women who have already experienced abuse as children. Child-sexual-abuse survivors in the self-defense classes I took sometimes had to overcome a tendency to carry themselves in a particularly helpless manner. (As I suggested in chapter 1, this passivity which many claim "leads" to rape is itself a result of rape.) Some self-defense instructors have this same analysis. For instance: "It's every child's birthright to body sovereignty. In boys, we overemphasize it; in girls, we 'no,' beat, incest, and rape it out of them" (Helen Grieco, padded attacker course instructor). Others note that, regardless of personal history, women learn that they are capable of nothing other than submission to assault. In "NRA Woman's Voice," a feature in the *American Rifleman*, Elizabeth J. Swasey (1993, 18) provides a related argument about socialization:

> From birth, most women are brainwashed into thinking the only proper response to physical aggression is submission. On the playground, we're told "girls don't hit"—even if we're striking back in self-defense to flee a much larger and stronger school bully. Later, we're told women should "submit to criminal attack for fear of injury"—as if the crime itself were not injury. That's why for most women, the decision to learn to defend oneself is life-altering. It goes against what we've been taught from birth.

In chapter 1, I suggested that womanhood and aggression are not complementary. Womanhood, as it is socially defined, is precisely what women must overcome when learning to fight. I asked instructors, who had observed more students than I, to tell me the biggest hurdle that women must overcome. Their answers reflected the way femininity remains an obstacle to competent physical aggression. They reported that their students needed to overcome a fear of guns and a fear of hurting people, a proclivity to be nice, a physical hesitancy, and a disbelief in their physical power:

> Women aren't supposed to fight and aren't supposed to hit back and they're supposed to be nice and sweet, and not say no, and not do anything to tick people off. And to get women to go through that and actually fight and strike after years and years of being brought up, you know, where you're not supposed to, getting them through that "I don't want

to fight" or "I'm not supposed to fight" [is the biggest barrier that women have to get over]. And once that's broken down then everything else is pretty much easy sailing. (Male instructor, padded attacker course)

They don't want to hurt anyone. (Karate instructor)

Overcoming the attitude that firearms are exceedingly dangerous and inherently evil and ugly and macho. There are lots of negative connotations that people have about firearms. (Lyn Bates, gun instructor)

The fear of the gun. (Paxton Quigley, gun instructor)

How society portrays women. I think I would say most women have been raised to believe they are not capable not only of physically defending ourselves, but of a lot of things, and I think that is the most challenging. It's really digging through all of the mental attitude that's been developed and put there for many women since the time they were born. . . . It's probably the most difficult thing to get across in class that they are strong . . . and in most cases they will be able to defend themselves. (Padded attacker course instructor)

They rarely accept the fact that what you're dealing with is people you know, and not so much those like, "Well what if both hands are tied up and I'm in the woods and nobody else is there and this person has a knife at my throat?" I'm like, "OK, well, how did you get there?" you know? . . . Without putting it like, "You did something to cause this person to attack you," because nobody asks to be attacked. But just going backwards from that biggest, hugest, scariest thing and saying, "No, it's those little things that happen every day, and those things that happened to you as a kid and those messages that you get that you're not worth defending that allow that kind of thing to happen. . . . So it's a lot of education and it's education that in fact steers us directly toward situations where we're going to get mashed. (Janet Aalfs, karate instructor)

Young (1990, 146–47) suggests that women tend to do things "like girls" because we both lack confidence in our physical abilities and fear getting hurt. This is because we experience our bodies as fragile encumbrances rather than as tools with which to get something done. The following self-defense student I interviewed said she entered instruction very angry at experiences of continued street harassment, and she contrasted this to the demeanors of the other women in her class, remarking that it is possible and common to *speak* "like a girl":

What I saw in the women who were taking the class was really frightening to me because I felt, I mean, I came into the class because of this sexual harassment. . . . I was so pissed that I was ready to scream, I was ready to yell, to punch things and I don't know what got some of these other women into the class but they were so meek and so unable to even just yell "NO" in a way that wasn't like, when we did this exercise where we just went up to each other to say "NO, DON'T TALK TO ME LIKE THAT," . . . they couldn't even do that without smiling or looking down or something. . . . I had no trouble just wailing on them, and that was just when it kind of hit me, that wow, this is really a bigger problem for even other people than it is for me, saying "no" and not sounding like a girl. (Rape crisis center self-defense course student)

A different student told me that she felt uneasy learning how to hurt someone:

They taught us a lot of stuff that they practice with, "Now, you don't think you'll be able to do this, but believe me you can." And that was kind of scary learning how to gouge people's eyes out or break bones or whatever. I remember feeling kind of like, oh I don't know if I can do that kind of thing. It's just not my philosophy of life. (Rape crisis center self-defense course student)

Another simply stigmatized combative sports as too masculine, which intimidated her:

At first I thought boxers were disgusting, bloody, yucky men. But then I realized that you wear padded gear and everyone who enters the ring wants to be there. Also, it's good to be able to take a punch. We think we'll be overwhelmed, but we can handle it. (Padded attacker course and boxing student)

Another student admitted that initially she was embarrassed to act physically powerful:

I remember having a lot of embarrassment about my physical power. The coach demands and brings it out of you. In the gym it's encouraged to be as powerful as you can be. You're working to get more and more power physically. And there's also a mental power and emotional power that you develop. You may have four rounds to go and you can't just break down and leave the ring. It's realizing what you have and becoming less and less embarrassed about it, and it's permitted and it's desired. (Boxer and boxing instructor)

Women learn that girls are the objects, not the agents, of aggression through fears and experiences of abuse as well as through routine childhood socialization. Girls have Barbie, a fashion plate, and boys have G.I. Joe, a fighter. Girls have "dolls" and boys have "action figures." Another way women learn that the world of action and daring is not open to them is through popular movies. Some instructors pointed out that women routinely appear physically incompetent in films:

> It's like you see these movies where these women are beating on some guy's chest and it's like, "Oh let me go," and of course it doesn't do anything because what does beating on someone's chest do? But I'm like, you know, in that same little scene, you could imagine instead of all this energy—bomp bomp bomp bomp bomp—one little poke to the eye and he's out, you know? (Janet Aalfs, karate instructor)

No wonder women cannot imagine that they might overpower a man. Another instructor linked her students' fears of losing a fight to the images of women in our culture:

> Through television and film and movies and books, and stuff like that, we're always shown the woman tries to hurt the guy and he just laughs at her. Or he takes the gun from her. And so our power is taken away every night on television, because there's at least three shows that show a woman raped, murdered, or hurt in some way. At least three shows a night, so we are constantly seeing women being bombarded with all these horrible things that happen so we always imagine, "what would I do if this happened? I don't know." Because we're always scared of getting in those situations but we never see them getting out of them, so we never picture ourselves getting out of them. Men are always shown how to get out of situations everyday, from the time they're little boys until the time they're grown men. Every movie out there is like Rambo taking on fifty guys, Chuck Norris—you know, all these guys. . . . We have a lot of heroes, we have no *she*roes. (Karate instructor)

Feminine hesitancy and perceptions of women's incompetence are part and parcel of rape culture because they help men win verbal and physical fights with women. Even those who insist on men's incomparable brawn cannot deny that women's sight, hearing, hands, and reflexes are every bit as competent as men's. Differences in size and strength become irrelevant to two people who are armed. This is what makes the female fear of firearms so ironic, and revealing. One need not be big or strong to shoot a gun. And yet many women are as doubtful of their ability to handle and use a firearm effectively as they are of their ability to kick and hit potently. Women have learned a discomfort around power that could exert force over another person. This education is clearly not a result of the putative fact of women's physical weakness. The very ease with which women take to firearms renders the many associations between masculinity and guns all the more suspect. Women are afraid to fight for the same reasons they are afraid of guns—in either case, women's size or strength is far less relevant than the social investment in a female body that does not exert coercive force.

The theoretical model of lived, embodied power inequalities is not totally determinative, however. Women's self-defense is a reprogramming regimen for the body. Here, women—regardless of their conscious political beliefs about gender—rehearse a new script for bodily comportment. The body, then, is not simply the locus of patriarchal power, ideology, or brutality; it is a potential locus of resistance. In self-defense classes, women make their aggression, and the femininity that prevents it, conscious. They develop a new self-image, a new understanding of what a female body can do, and thus break out of the expectations under which they have acted and that have cemented themselves at the level of the body. In this way, a feminine habitus is supplanted by a fighting habitus.

The Lore of Self-Defense

What is the lore of women's emerging physical empowerment? What are the stories and images used to construct frames for women's aggression against men's? What are the means by which self-defense instructors help women discard their feminine selves and take on a new assertiveness? In what follows, I suggest that, to turn women into fighters, women's self-defense courses provide stories that make fighting OK, provide an emotionally supportive atmosphere, suggest a new relationship to the media, and enlist the mind, emotions, and body in combination.

Originally I had been skeptical of self-defense instruction that did not stress the fact that the overwhelming majority of women are victimized by acquaintances, dates, boyfriends, husbands, and other family members. I saw several self-defense courses de-emphasize, at least initially, the fact that a woman will most likely use these techniques on a man she knows and maybe even loves. But every instructor I questioned about this said the same thing: That a woman should be taught to defend herself against anyone who threatens harm, regardless of her relationship to him. Furthermore, it seemed quite clear that they knew the statistics. One instructor told me, "I've tried to demystify the whole stranger-danger thing. That's not the person—they're already prepared for that danger. So the real assailant is the trusted, perhaps loved, partner or acquaintance or relation—relative" (rape crisis center self-defense course instructor).

One instructor revealed the strategy of allowing women to imagine they were fighting a stranger: "We start off dealing with the stranger because it's a lot easier psychologically. It's harder to think about defending yourself against someone you care for or trust. But the patterns of attack are similar in stranger and acquaintance rape" (Chimera instructor).

It became clear that instructors try anything that they think will work to get women to learn some fighting skills. In other words, political or theoretical consistency is not their first priority. They attempt to appeal to habits that already sound sensible to most women. For example, one instructor frames self-defense as a body project much like eating healthfully and other means by which people prevent death and disease, while another likens it to proper auto maintenance:

> We want to enable women to be self-possessed and mature. We buckle our seat belts, we get our breasts examined, we try to eat healthy, but the tragedy is women aren't prepared [that way] for violence. The more education you have the more choices women have. (Helen Grieco, padded attacker course instructor)

> A woman unaware of the dangers out there is just the same as driving with bad brakes or no motor oil. (Athena Lee, gun instructor, quoted in Hodges 1993, 6C)

In her self-defense video, *Lisa Sliwa's Common Sense Defense* (1985), Sliwa speaks to women who she thinks might be concerned with remaining feminine, as she demonstrates how to thwart a potential threat by pressing a finger into the nook at the base of the throat: "And remember, we're talking about doing things that don't even require you to break a fingernail." Instructors try whatever it takes to get women to value themselves. Revealingly, though, women are sometimes more motivated to care for their own safety when doing so will help someone else. As one instructor said:

> We talk a lot about our importance and taking care of ourselves, and that nobody is going to take care of us. Also if she is hurt that is also impacting others who care about her, and that often clicks in for them, because women have been raised to be the caretakers. That makes them angry in a different way. (Chimera instructor)

Instructors try to frame women's aggressiveness in ways that they think will resonate with the women in their classes.

The ways in which the women talk about themselves reveal a number of cultural assumptions about womanhood and violence that the instructors try to address as they attempt to reframe women's aggression as appropriate. While a larger discourse about "nature" instills in women a sense of inevitable helplessness, nature stories are employed by instructors to justify women's use of force in self-defense. For example, one instructor told us to think of ourselves as the mother animal protecting her cubs. A student in this class told us that she thought of her fighting self as "Oso"—the Spanish word for bear, in the masculine—protecting the cubs. By the end of the course, she had changed the word to the feminine, *Osa*, which for her marked an important transition in her self-perception. Though she still envisioned fighting to save her cubs, she could now imagine fighting as a female. A woman I interviewed echoed this discourse, but extended the right of protection to herself:

> Just being my animal self and going like, "FUCK YOU!" You know, "GET THE HELL OUT OF HERE!" Like a mother does to an infant, it's like nobody can touch my child, and they talk about this animal where you don't think twice. You wouldn't negotiate with somebody who's going to harm your child so the same would go for you. (Padded attacker course student)

Women's aversion to seeing their defensive violence as legitimate, notably when *their own* bodily boundaries might be encroached, is combated by referring to the protection of *others*. Therapeutic discourse helps some women who want to discuss themselves as fierce. Occasionally a self-defenser speaks not of protecting herself but of protecting her "child within." The therapeutic trope of the "child within," an innocent being whom the adult must protect, or who never deserved the bad things to happen and that still feels the pain of abuse, might work for some women by providing them with a mythic innocent child to protect. Women must either imagine that they are defending someone else or redefine themselves as worth defending.

Other women frame their self-defense as a right of citizenship. The following student explained her sense of entitlement to own a gun and use it for self-defense if necessary in terms of other decisions she feels women have the right to make about their bodies:

> My strong feeling is the right of people to decide . . . a proven, capable citizen should be allowed to choose, whether it's, you know, your birth—I mean I feel very strongly you're in charge of your own body— whether you want children, whether you want to die, whether you want to have a gun. I mean this is a personal decision, all those things, and I don't believe anybody has the right to dictate that to you as long as you are a good citizen and mentally capable. (Gun student)

An instructor put it simply: "There's nothing morally objectionable about defending myself. I'm a good citizen for doing so" (Helen Grieco, padded attacker course instructor).

Coming to value oneself is a major part of unlearning femininity, which is in part defined by the absence of an authoritative sense of the legitimacy of one's own needs and desires. For this reason, Model Mugging passes around a ten-point list, "Every Woman's Bill of Rights,"[1] which reads:

> (1) The right to be treated with respect; (2) The right to have and express your own feelings; (3) The right to be listened to and taken seriously; (4) The right to set your own priorities; (5) The right to say "no" without feeling guilty; (6) The right to ask for what you want; (7) The right to get what you pay for; (8) The right to ask for information from professionals; (9) The right to make mistakes; and (10) The right to choose not to assert myself.

Instructors do not merely teach women to fight. They teach women that they are important, that they are worth fighting for. As one self-defenser wrote in her dojo's newsletter: "It's rarely simply a kick to the knee that we teach, but rather the world-shifting insight of the power to hurt rather than be hurt, the RIGHT NOT TO BE HURT" (*The Shuri-Spiral News*, February 1993, 6).

Indeed, instructors see it as a central task to resocialize women to be more confident. To this end, the instructors provide an important role model. Janet Aalfs, the karate instructor, mentioned that she modeled strength for her students. One rape crisis center self-defense course student explained that her role models included her loud-talking grandmother, her instructor, "physically assertive people," and the women in movies "where they're really tough." As much as women's sense of feminine comportment is generated by media images, women seek models of self-defense in imagistic discourse. That same student elaborated: "Linda Hamilton in *Terminator 2*; I loved that movie. I just loved the scenes of her, and at the end, her with her guns and her muscley arms and stuff; I just think she's totally cool."

Women's inability to imagine themselves fighting back effectively is in part media-generated. This becomes obvious in self-defense classes. For example, in a self-defense course on armed assailants, women are provided with a display of weapons (screwdrivers, knives, swords, clubs, etc.), which the women understood in terms of films in which a man murdered a woman with the weapon: "This is the Jason [from the movie *Halloween*] knife—[plunging the knife downward while mimicking the film's sound effects] eee, eee, eee, eee." None of us thought of movies in which one of the weapons was used by a female character. At the same class, as students learned to disarm and knock out assailants who held knives to their throats, one woman noted that she had not realized that this was a possible assault situation (i.e., one in which the first attacking move is a knife at the throat) because she had not seen a woman attacked this particular way in any movies.

Self-defensers use images of women in various ways to understand the relationship between women and aggression—hence the significance of the emergent aggressive woman in visual media. Many self-defensers seem to have a new appreciation for images of female toughness and take pleasure in watching female movie characters who are allowed to have and use weapons, disable attackers, and exert control. Self-defensers talk about the latest movies in which a woman fights. Not all women wholeheartedly embrace the new images of women, however. Some distance themselves a bit from the hype surrounding women's engagement with violence. One student spoke of *Thelma and Louise* this way: "I just enjoyed the movie; I thought it was kind of a fun adventure" (gun student). Another woman told me that she would prefer to see images in which men and women are cooperating equals. Having read a lot of science fiction, she laments that the main characters are usually men and, when there are women, "They're Amazons, which doesn't appeal to me because they are exaggerated and it's not a balance. It's too opposite, or the other end of the pendulum" (padded attacker course and boxing student).

The following instructor does not oppose the violent adversarial nature of certain films, but does wish there were scenes of women's legitimate self-defensive violence:

> I had a problem with *Thelma and Louise*. It was a very strong movie and I think the reason why men can come back on us is because the man didn't lunge at her, she just went off and shot the guy. If he had so much as just stepped and reached for her and then she shot him, then the whole of what happened would have fit in a better context for women. (Karate instructor)

In that film, Louise's shot at Harlon is not fired in self-defense. Although some moviegoers may have enjoyed identifying with a violent act that was at least ambiguous if not downright suspect, this instructor is clearly invested in heroizing women's legitimate use of violence in the appropriate circumstances.

One student I spoke with said she does not appreciate any images of violence:

> I don't like the violence period, whether it's men or women. It is kind of a novelty and it's interesting to see women kicking the shit out of other

people and what I appreciate about it is often in the movie the women are using violence for some reason. You can tell that they've built it up inside them, all this bullshit has been laid on them. A lot of it is sexist and a lot of it is just really bullshit and they finally explode into violence as opposed to violence being their first solution to every problem, which is often what a lot of other violent images are in movies. . . . But I'm always the person who feels bad for the bad guy who gets shot in the movie, even though I'm going "yeah, kick his ass!" But I'm also going, "Ouch, that kind of hurt," or "What about his wife?" (Rape crisis center self-defense course student)

Self-defensers also discussed films in which a woman did not get out of an attack. Self-defense training makes women more critical of the typical representations of women, as a gun student explained: "My look at the entertainment has changed a little bit. I feel super-strong. I feel like I have a lot of knowledge, and it feels really good. So we'll go to the movies and I'll be really mad when they portray a woman as helpless" (gun student). One instructor suggested that we rewrite the script in which a woman does not fight back, as we were supposed to do when we dreamt that we did not win a fight: "We always tell women when they're watching a movie to retell the story to have the woman defend herself. Or a lot of women have dreams while they're taking the class and we tell them to retell the story when they wake up" (Chimera instructor). In beginning to think to themselves how the female character in a scene might have prevailed over an attacker, as well as in deciding about what sorts of images they prefer to see, women form a more invested and critical relationship to dominant images of femininity.

Just as images of women who do not fight affect our perceived abilities and bodily comportments, so do images of women who fight. One instructor noticed that *Thelma and Louise* motivated women to learn to use firearms: "I think *Thelma and Louise* was probably a turning point in women's consciousnesses in the United States. There were a lot of women who took my class after *Thelma and Louise* and said that they took the class because they saw this movie" (Paxton Quigley, gun instructor). Despite the fact that *Thelma and Louise* was not a film about women's self-defense and contained no scene of justifiable violence, images of women's violence, whatever their cinematic context, might help women experience and deploy their bodies along the lines of differently fantasized self-definitions. If women already feel vulnerable to men precisely because they do not see images of women prevailing over men, and in fact routinely see the opposite, images of women fighting can produce a new body-consciousness complementary to women's self-defense training.

In addition to encouraging women's critical engagement with popular images of the female body, instructors attempt to undo women's belief that they cannot fight by sharing stories of women's successful fights. Sharing women's stories of triumph and survival are central to self-defense culture, and important for students because success stories are rarely reported in the media, thus perpetuating women's lack of confidence. Instructors explained:

We don't hear those kind of stories in the newspapers, and if we did we'd have a whole different view of what's possible, so we have to support each other. And that's like the main purpose of the workshops that I do besides, you know, giving some . . . practical information about "What would you do if this happened or that happened?" But a lot is about hearing each other's stories and knowing that whether we have formal education or not, in terms of self-defense, that we have a lot of wit. (Janet Aalfs, karate instructor)

[Women's success stories are] the big root of what we teach, because those aren't shared. We read about the violent attacks, not the four out of five women who successfully get away. Women need to have an example. (Chimera instructor)

These success stories help instill a sense of confidence and a broader, less androcentric perspective of what counts as self-defense. For instance, self-defense is not necessarily a formulaic set of tightly controlled moves, for instance a cool Clint Eastwood "make my day" shot or a Bruce Lee karate chop, kick, and spin. It is a set of strategies employed that might begin with tricking or distracting an attacker, include only verbal self-defense and then running away, involve flailing and going ballistic, or may even include, in a gang attack for example, a strategic decision to submit to the first man in order to create an opportunity to escape. Sharing women's success stories helps redefine what counts as fighting, and thus enables women to discard the self-defeating conceptual framework that defines fighting as those things men tend to do better than women. As one instructor put it, "An eye is an eye and a throat is a throat and we've all got 'em" (Helen Grieco, padded attacker course instructor). Another instructor explained,

We don't want to have a brawl but for the woman to get out of the situation as fast as possible, and that don't have to do with the woman's strength or the man's strength but with the anatomy of the body. . . . For instance, a man's kneecap. There's not a lot of muscle there and it breaks easily. If a woman can lift her leg to walk up a stair, she can break his knee. Same with the eyes or throat. It's very easy to go into those areas.

Striking any of those areas, it's going to disable him because he can't see
or breathe or run and that gives a woman a chance to get to safety.
(Chimera instructor)

Sharing success stories reminds women that there are many ways to fight an
attacker and that women have the wit, will, and strength with which to do it.
Hence women often share with the class their own triumphs that occur while
taking their self-defense course. During the month I was taking a padded
attacker course, I yelled fiercely at a man on the street who was sexually harassing me. Never before had I turned around and verbally confronted a harasser.
In that same month, another student was confronted by a man in the parking
lot at her workplace. He faced her with his pants down, masturbating. So forceful and piercing was her clamor that the man had to release his penis to put his
hands over his ears. The class applauded. Sharing success stories provides
women with alternative possibilities for action. This helps alter beliefs and, ultimately, bodies.

The success stories self-defensers read about can be a bit more sensationalis-
tic. Like the success stories in the NRA publication *American Rifleman*, those in
Women and Guns are upbeat and triumphant. They do not interview the
woman about her trauma, regret at taking a life, or dismay at being the target
of attack in the first place. Masaad Ayoob, the renowned firearms instructor and
founder of the Lethal Force Institute, has criticized the NRA's glamorized
reporting of self-defense success stories. In an interview for the *Chicago Tribune*,
Ayoob declared his anger at the heroizing images in the *American Rifleman's*
"armed civilians" hall of fame, insisting that protecting oneself with a gun
should be something gun owners hope never to face, and reminds them that
such shooters may very well have to face a criminal trial which, at best, can wipe
them out financially and, at worst, land them behind bars (Mashberg 1994).

Whatever their cost in terms of portraying the difficulties of taking someone's
life, or the consequences within the criminal justice system, even sensationalis-
tic success stories allow women to imagine that, despite years of advice and
images that have made them believe and feel otherwise, they might win a fight.
Far from simply a "false sense of security," such an affirmative belief in one's own
capacities enhances one's abilities. Bandura (1977) has shown that observing
someone model behavior not only affects one's ability to imitate and learn it but
that expecting and believing that one has the capabilities actually influences performance. This is the significance of challenging the rape myth that men are so
dangerous and women are so vulnerable to them. That myth actually becomes
a soma-reality. Imagining a new scenario makes a new soma-reality possible.

At Model Mugging and Defending Ourselves, the group cheers each female fighter on to victory. A karate instructor noted that women's egos need not be torn down (the way some think men's should be in the martial arts). Rather, women need to be praised relentlessly. Quigley pats her students on the back saying, "good job," while the rest of the women clap for the shooter. This is a celebration of women's strength and victory, of fighting and winning, of KOs and killings. By extension, it is also a celebration of women's entitlement, of living, surviving, and thriving. The sharing of success stories and the group support are combined with a modeling on the part of the instructors of a new womanhood. These factors create an overall atmosphere in self-defense courses in which, paradoxical as it may seem, women get nurtured into aggressivity.

Bodily Memory

The coaching is only the beginning: women have to enact the aggressive posture. Self-defense provides a knowledge at the bodily level that is distinct from that at the intellectual level. Self-defense, then, requires much more than a theoretical understanding of body or voice. Women must inscribe it into their bodily schema. The sharing of success stories, the modeling of strength on the part of the instructors, the renegotiation of media images of women, and the encouraging atmosphere of women's self-defense courses help women discard their feminine hesitancy and physical incompetence and imagine new possibilities for action. But it is the intense physicality of self-defense courses, exemplified by mock attacks, that accomplishes this. In the language of Model Mugging, women "get the fight" and it becomes a "bodily memory."

Committing the fighting techniques to bodily memory requires practicing assertiveness. Quigley first instructs women to take on an assertive posture in daily life. She suggests that women mark a man with their eyes, avoid answering men who ask what time it is, and not worry about being polite to them. Quigley's technique of having each student yell obscenities at her command gets students to practice being rude. Practicing shouting "NO!" forcefully and stating firmly, without smiling, "Take your hand off my knee" help women begin to unlearn the enslaving feminine demeanor that prevents them from fighting effectively. Women are coached throughout their training. For instance, as women practice defensive moves on the mat, padded attacker courses remind them, "He's in your space!" "Set your boundary!" and "He has no right!" Women receive encouragement from instructors and classmates as they actually enact a new posture. The significance of practicing assertiveness is clear: If rapists rely on a script of femininity to overpower women, then women must begin to rehearse a new script. But unlike a traditional script that an actor reads, women's scripts are written into their bodies, and the physical nature of the instruction begins to write a new story of womanhood.

Women's self-defense courses do not teach artistic, stylized techniques. They focus on practical techniques that any woman can use to disable an attacker and give her time to get away as quickly as possible. In one class, the instructor constantly repeated, "This is not Jean Claude Van Damme." Indeed, this is practicing assertiveness under realistic conditions of fear and attack. Teaching women under high-stress, high-adrenaline conditions approximates the emotional and physical state under which women would have to defend themselves. One instructor explains that teaching women to fight under conditions of terror reinforces in them techniques that will work under those conditions, because they lose fine motor control and only have gross motor control. She thus teaches specific techniques that do not require fine motor control. This is scrappy fighting for safety: "It's not male, masculinist, Rambo stuff. You might even have a bowel movement" (Helen Grieco, padded attacker instructor). Fighting in a high-adrenaline state also enables students to commit the fighting techniques to bodily memory, so that women's first response in a real situation will be to fight.

But before committing fighting techniques to bodily memory, women have to exorcize the bodily memories that a sexist culture has lodged in them. Learning self-defense parallels learning to drive a car on the opposite side of the road in a foreign country. Anyone who has done this, for instance an American driving in Great Britain or vice versa, knows how conscious one's actions behind the wheel suddenly become. The turning, signaling, and looking that were second nature become strained, stressful, and perplexing gestures. In much the same way, acquiring an aggressive response system takes purposeful reflection and mindful motions.

For this reason, classes begin with very slow and purposeful movements, usually in a very strict order or routine. Women have to think about how to hit, shoot, kick, and yell. Gaining confidence in physical abilities and overcoming a fear of getting hurt are two primary objectives of self-defense instruction for women. Many women realize that they become paralyzed at the sight of a gun or an assailant. Students learn that they must use their voices for effective self-defense; many realize that they are not accustomed to talking firmly, much less yelling. Although some women find this fairly easy, most, even those who feel relatively secure in their physical strength, find it difficult:

I have a pretty strong body and I've always been very confident that I can kick ass. . . . The scary part in the course was the verbal stuff. When I had to use my voice to tell them "Get away," I would smile a lot. . . . The power of the course was definitely the voice and the shifting position, like startling the assailant by taking the initiative. You turn the tables. . . . I [said] "Don't" [meekly] like it was never totally my power. . . . But I felt the shift. (Padded attacker course student)

Still others felt that they were verbally assertive but lacked the physical skills to fight. As women start out aiming a gun toward a target, or giving a kick to a punching bag or to a stationary padded attacker, they often apologize or let out nervous laughter.

After hours of practice employing very specific stances, aims, punches, and kicks, self-defensers eventually learn to make decisions about how to move their bodies as they encounter specific situations. In Model Mugging, for example, we initially know what kind of attack we are going to encounter (e.g., walk-by assailant, rear-grab, or forced oral copulation while being pinned on the ground). In gun classes, we are initially told exactly what kinds of shots to fire and where to fire them.

As we become more experienced and the moves become more "natural" for us, we become better able to think of appropriate techniques in the moment— what Model Mugging instructors called "seeing your openings." We begin to apply moves spontaneously from a repertoire of techniques. The mock attackers become more and more spontaneous as well, forcing us to think and act quickly, spotting open targets (a knee, an eye, a groin, a face) and deciding on appropriate moves, in the moment under peril. This "assessing" and "split attention" is especially necessary for students in the multiple assailants padded attacker course. In martial arts classes, students begin to fight against unanticipated types and levels of attack. In firearms classes, students eventually speed up the pace and spontaneity with which they shoot. The feminine gestures gradually go by the wayside as women practice conscious control of their responses ("I'm not going to smile this time"). As women adjust to using their bodies in new ways, their confidence and readiness to fight bloom.

In learning how to stop attackers in their tracks, self-defensers learn that rape is a process not an inevitability. It becomes clear that rape is "a scripted interaction in which one person auditions for the role of rapist and strives to maneuver another person into the role of victim" (Marcus 1992, 391). Self-defensers learn how to deploy their bodies, including their voices, in ways that surprise and overpower the assailant, disabling him or simply allowing the self-defenser to escape to safety. Crucial to self-defense instruction is the demystification of rape culture's myths about fighting back. Women not only learn that they are much stronger than they thought, but also that men are more vulnerable than they thought. One student put it this way:

> I think they were trying to educate and train people to know that they can fight back. . . . Even a weak, light, small person can do things like, you know, crush someone's kneecap or gouge out their eyes or Adam's apple or whatever. I mean she [the instructor] taught how to kill someone! She stressed that a lot, like with the Adam's apple technique. And I personally thought that was cool; I was struck by that. (Rape crisis center self-defense course student)

Knowing you can take a punch is almost as significant as knowing you can deliver one. A student elaborated:

> Women don't get to learn they're physical; what they can do physically, and it's kind of neat to learn that you can actually—one time [in boxing class], I got hit by a woman and I actually got whiplash, this like pain shot down all the way down my arm and I was scared, I thought something horrible had happened, and it turned out I had whiplash. And another time a woman hit me and my feet actually went off the mat, you know I went right up in the air. The surprising thing was I was OK in about thirty seconds. I was fine. . . . There was kind of a power in being actually able to take a punch. . . . And even being able to give it, giving a really good strong punch, is kind of a neat thing. (Padded attacker course and boxing student)

The experience of being hit in boxing classes made this same student more sure that she could prevail in an attack even if struck, despite the fact that students did not get hit during the mock assaults in her padded attacker courses:

> [The padded attacker] will pretend he's going to hit you and then he'll hit the mat next to you or something. Well, you kind of figure that if he really hit you, you'd be out of it; but it might not be true, maybe you could take the punch and still fight, even if it did daze you. (Padded attacker course and boxing student)

Thus women learn that fighting is not as impossible as they had imagined. Women lose fights with men not because of physical size but because they have developed a demeanor that makes them unable to resist attacks effectively. This sentiment is represented on the T-shirts worn by some of the Model Mugging instructors and passed out on a Xeroxed flyer that says, "It's not the size of the woman in the fight, but the size of the fight in the woman."

As self-defensers become more aware of the many ways in which men try to manipulate women into a situation of vulnerability, the continuum of sexual violence is thrown into sharp relief. Some students start to realize how few entitlements men grant them:

> I didn't understand how quite politically exciting or powerful it was until I went [to self-defense class]. And like I get it, it's like, "Ooooh my God—Right!" As women we get to receive a whole bunch of attention that we don't want—or that we learn that we want, something like that. (Padded attacker course student)

Needless to say, self-defense training helps women set boundaries early on so that they do not wind up in wickedly vulnerable situations that would require more advanced skills to get out of.

The realization of your ability to fend off men's advances and attacks comes through the bodily activity of rehearsing powerful responses to assault. The resulting changes in bodily comportment occur quickly for self-defensers. The consciousness raising (if I can refer to the bodily, emotional transformation that takes place here as consciousness raising) happens fast because of the do-or-die, emergency, and visceral nature of the training. Much as military soldiers learn their moves precisely because high-stress training conditions force them to suffer a physical consequence for a mistake, self-defense trainees undergo a series of intense, often terrifying, bodily experiences that force them to respond to simulated crises. In padded attacker courses, for instance, students who fail to deliver a knockout blow, or fail to check to be sure they knocked out their attacker, are inevitably assailed again. Such a training regime forces women into a new set of abilities.

By the end of the padded attacker course we simply stand, walk, or lie down, not knowing what kind of assailant we will encounter (he might be someone you know aggressively coming on to you, a screaming psycho running at you, a man behind you who grabs you just when his friend distracts you by asking you the time). Thus we begin to practice looking for our target areas and performing moves that seem appropriate for the situation. If we get pinned, we reassess, perhaps feign cooperation, and then begin to fight again when we have an opportunity (such as when the assailant puts his weapon down or leans his body in a way that enables a quick leg retraction and side thrust kick to his head or groin). Ideally there is no pause between deciding and doing. In martial arts courses, specific techniques and routines evolve into spontaneous responses to surprise approaches and grabs from a sparring partner. Boxing incorporates practiced gestures with thinking as well:

There's a lot of emotional stuff that's in the sparring. When the sparring is happening, you have to use your mind; it's cerebral, and at the same time you have to execute. It's like a chess game—what you want to do, how you're going to execute it, how to trick them. It's constantly out-witting the person, and that's fun in and of itself. It's a game. It's not about hitting them as hard as you can or trying to take them out. That's not it. It's about trying to out-do them, being a smart fighter. . . . I can never rely on just force, so I have to out-think them, anticipate what they're going to do before they do it and do something that throws them off balance and take advantage of that. (Boxer and boxing instructor)

In firearms courses, shooting quickly at steel plate targets, the locations of which you do not know until ready to fire, shooting while walking toward your target, and shooting after having fallen onto the ground (firing the gun between your knees) also increase the spontaneity of the action and incorporate mind with physical technique. In her firearms safety course for women at Lethal Force Institute in Concord, New Hampshire, Lyn Bates trains women to shoot under stressful conditions, so they get used to the feeling. Women discover that they can shoot effectively under those conditions. Bates brings in a "garbage mouth" to shout obscenities and threats to students who must, at the instruc-tor's command, shoot at their targets. This gives students the sense of trauma that they might have while shooting, incorporating their fighting techniques into that sensibility you have when you are afraid. In her classes, she also employs the lower intensity "spaz drill," started by shooting instructor Masaad Ayoob, which is where

> you have people aiming at a target, two arms straight out, and you clutch the gun as hard as you can so your hands start to shake, or the instructor will squeeze your hands to make them shake, and then you have them shoot like that, to prove to the students that even then they can shoot like that and shoot accurately. (Lyn Bates, gun instructor)

Since "it is not easy to shoot well under pressure, and shooting under pres-sure is what you must be trained and prepared to do" (Quigley 1989, 196), Quigley recommends combat shooting or action shooting as a way to "learn to use a handgun safely and effectively under time constraints and in stress situations, which will prepare you to save your life and your family's life, should the need arise" (ibid., 23). Bates also recommends competitive shoot-ing (of any kind) to produce that sense of intensity while shooting. Some firearms courses have targets that move toward the shooter, who must fire a certain number of shots before the target reaches her. This can be arranged as a competition among the students, intensifying the stress under which students fire.

In the same way that women in padded attacker courses learn that their determination to fight and their surprise of their assailant will give them the advantage in the fight, firearms students learn that their training in threat management can minimize the immediate paralysis that they would be likely to feel if attacked. This involves for each knowing the layout of her house, having a "safe room," and getting immediately into a position of tactical advantage. Dale shows his students the places in their homes from which they might shoot and helps them develop a strategy for home defense with a firearm. Women learn that they must keep their cool. This does not mean denying fear or anger, but channeling them. Gun instructors say that this kind of self-control is the advantage the self-defenser will have over her attacker. As Quigley (ibid., 247) states, "Never forget: tactics beat marksmanship."

The high-adrenaline state is achieved in the mock assaults of padded attacker courses, during competitions and tests in the martial arts, and during the "garbage mouth" and the "spaz drill" in firearms courses (recall that I was full of juice in Quigley's class just firing five rounds at a paper target). The feelings of fear and degradation with which an assailant hopes to immobilize a woman get turned into part of the feelings a self-defenser has while, and associates with, fighting. This kind of control over, or incorporation of, one's feelings in fights becomes part of the self-defense scenario. In this way, self-defensers are taught to bring their minds and bodies into emotive, mean fighting machines:

> There's something about boxing that is so raw and so emotional. And you can't escape if you're in the ring. You've already committed, you're already in there. So it forces you to confront things you might be able to avoid otherwise. It's a catalyst really; I mean I don't want to be Miss Therapist or anything, but that's what I've noticed. (Boxer and boxing instructor)

In order to get women to merge the mental with the physical, instructors explain the importance of "staying in your body." In the martial arts, students are taught to find their "ki," a mental power that centers and energizes them, increasing their strength, resolve, and control. Instructors stress students' making their emotions work for them in the fight. Instructors do not tell women to stop being afraid; they tell them to use their fear by turning it into anger or energy. Fear is what gives women the boost of adrenaline they use to fight powerfully. Determination to stop the attacker also provides this boost. While some women get more angry about sexual violence after taking a self-defense course, other self-defense students learn to rechannel the anger they already had. For this woman, rechanneling her anger was a crucial part of her training:

> I'm getting in touch with just more being pissed, being angry. Not shying away from that. . . . I think I'm getting more and more to the point where I don't just want to cry. I mean, in general, I think people cry instead of act it out in what would certainly be a safer place or whatever, but just as a woman, I'm tired of that outlet. . . . I think I've always been pissed, all the time; I think I get really pissed at everything, at the world, and I don't know what to do with it except get depressed. (Rape crisis center self-defense course student)

Students are told to assess situations, and are supposed to think clearly and "coil up" their energy when they are pinned. Karate teaches a variety of response techniques—the five animal frolics for example—which demand different types of emotional-physical energy levels. In these ways, learning to fight involves a coordination of thinking, feeling, and acting.

It is the assumption that a form of self-defense fails to engage a combination of body-mind-spirit that accounts for its derision by advocates of some other form of self-defense. One instructor remarked that her biggest problem with some self-defense courses is an overemphasis on the physical without the mental and emotional:

> There are people who don't quite understand what they are doing when they teach . . . and I think part of it is that instructors don't offer what I call a balance—mental and emotional aspect of human beings combined with the physical skills—because self-defense isn't always physically defending yourself. And you really need to make the choice to take care of yourself any way you can. And, for me, the physical defense is always a last resort. (Padded attacker course instructor)

Some martial artists think that guns provide a false security and fail to empower women in the long term (e.g., Wong 1993, A-15). Yet some gun instructors have said that martial arts may be as much self-delusion as self-defense, insofar as they emphasize the spiritual over the practical, the art of the kata over the science of attack (e.g., Strain 1992). Of course, martial arts courses for women do focus on realistic strategies that can be used even in an elevator, and gun instructors do emphasize the role of the mind in firearms use. Most self-defense instructors seem to agree that the way to habituate women's bodies to a new set of beliefs—beliefs in their own strength and self-worth—is through a combination of physical moves and emotional expressions.

1. A padded attacker course student kicks the assailant's face as her instructor monitors the technique. *Photo by Karen Krogh.*

2. A padded attacker course student lands a kick to the padded attacker's face. She'll continue to fight until she delivers a knockout blow. *Photo by Karen Krogh.*

3. This defensive move against forced oral copulation takes advantage of the woman's free legs and hips, which she draws up, locks around the assailant's shoulders, and then yanks downward, hurling the assailant onto his back and leaving his crotch an open target for striking. *Photo by Karen Krogh.*

4. A firearms instructor shows a student proper positioning, how to line up the sights, and shoot the target with a Colt .45. *Photo by Garry Bryant.*

5. Shooting between the knees while supine is a useful defensive technique if one has fallen to the ground. *Photo by Nancy Floyd.*

6. Paxton Quigley's students shoot paper targets in a kneeling position on the range at her firearms course for women. *Photo by Nancy Floyd.*

7. Janet Aalfs, black belt in Shuri-Ryu, an Okinawan style of karate, kicks an imaginary opponent at her dojo, Valley Women's Martial Arts, Inc. *Photo by Plumcakes.*

8. Black belt instructor Janis Totty, at Valley Women's Martial Arts, Inc., demonstrates the snake form in the Shuri-Ryu style of Okinawan karate. *Photo by Janet Aalfs.*

9. Three martial artists belt out forceful roars as they demonstrate supreme flexibility, balance, and strength in kicking. Martial arts courses teach women many kicks to perform from an upright position. *Photo by Beth Silvis.*

10. A young student in martial arts gives a heel-palm strike to a practice pad. This strike is intended to land the hard heel of the palm at the bottom of an assailant's nose. *Photo by Janet Aalfs.*

The belief that a combination of training, physical strength, and emotional strength is required for good self-defense explains why so many self-defense instructors advocate a variety of methods of self-defense training. Bates and Quigley have both taken Model Mugging courses, and recommend them in addition to firearms courses. Although *Women and Guns* refers to the "armed sisterhood," which possesses the means by which they might "truly take back the night" (quoted in Wolf 1993, 218), the firearms instructors I spoke with by and large favor a variety of self-defense techniques for women.

For instance, the week I interviewed her, Bates had been speaking with a Model Mugging class about self-defense. Weapons instructors recommended a number of other forms of self-defense training. Lyn Bates offers an assault prevention lecture course which, as she put it, "introduces the notions of self-defense, why self-defense is justified, what the range of options of self-defense is, what the continuum of force is, and why no one method of self-defense is good for every point along the continuum."

By the same token, martial arts and padded attacker course instructors emphasize women's ability to fight with and without weapons, explaining that when women are given weapons it is as if they could not fight without them:

> I always think physical self-defense is only the first line of self-defense, and then picking up a weapon is your second. Look at the military: They always train them in hand-to-hand combat, then they teach them how to use a gun and a hand grenade, a tank and a plane and you know, and whatever. But your first line of defense is the physical self-defense. But [for] women, they always go, "Here's mace," or "Here's a key chain," or "Here's this," or "Here's a whistle," or "Honey, the gun's in the drawer and the bullets are over there," or whatever. . . . But they never think of women as like, their first line of self-defense is physical because like, "Women can't hurt anyone," "Women are weak," "Women are not strong." But women are like *the* best fighters. We have always been excellent fighters. We are more agile, we have a lot more strength—in different ways than men do. And that's what we [instructors] do. We show women where their strengths are and where their weaknesses are in attacks. (Karate instructor)

Another instructor sees many a student who was given a weapon by a man in her life. (She's aware of this precisely because some of these students have requested that she get rid of the weapon for them.)

> I'm usually concerned when a loved one or family member will go out and buy [some kind of weapon] for them thinking, well, if they have it inside of them, they can just pull it out and use it. They decide that for

the other person when they give it to them and forget their [the other person's] concerns. (Padded attacker course instructor)

Paxton Quigley also recommends both hand-to-hand training and firearms training for self-defense:

One, once you know how to use your body, and use your body as a weapon, you know that your body has a certain amount of power. But then you're going the next step because, technologically speaking, a gun is more powerful than the body. And once you've mastered the power of your body, and the power of the gun, you have reached ultimate empowerment.

Clearly, then, all sorts of instructors believe in the benefits of a variety of defense strategies, and all can incorporate emotion, muscle, voice, and will to fight into their pedagogical strategy. The bodily memory makes these skills stick. This is "the fight" or "power" women achieve in self-defense training. This set of dispositions is called "the fighting spirit," not incidentally. After all, the new bodily comportment itself captures a new will, a will to fight. Here, we see the ways in which rehearsing a new bodily comportment actually encompasses the realm of the cognitive.

Model Mugging instructors tell stories of women who, thanks to bodily memory, stopped assailants years after having taken self-defense. There was the sixty-something woman who knocked a man out cold within one minute of his assault of her. She had taken the basic course five years earlier. Then there was the woman who, knocked unconscious in an accident, kicked a paramedic (whose hands were making their way up her leg, checking it for possible broken bones), sending him sailing clear across the room. She wrote the paramedic a letter of apology. As these stories illustrate, our fighting gestures become as automatic as our feminine gestures had been.

The Significance of Physicality and Pleasure to Training

The sensorial nature of the activity presents the stakes of self-defense—you can smell them and feel them as the adrenaline rushes through your body. Fighting or shooting while some big smelly, swearing, sweat-dripping thug is going after you or yelling at you makes you tangibly, organically invested in the scene. Despite the unpleasantness of these attack simulations, there is a certain pleasure in the aggression, which stems from the fast pace, the heightened adrenaline state, and the physical and emotional consequences of fighting. Women train not only to ensure physical survival; they train for dignity, to survive socially as people with a certain sense of entitlement (which assailants try to deny them). In this way, the increased sense of value a woman has for herself is etched onto the body through a series of aggressive words and gestures, an explosion of gun powder, or maybe even a series of punches and kicks to music.

The physicality of the practice, the emotional character of the venture, and the sensorial character of the atmosphere solidify in women a new body. One student explained: "Having someone [the padded attacker] physically assault you, or having that man [the padded attacker] lay on top of you, like this is what it would be like, like they put you right in it. So, like, you're there, and it's not just hypothetical" (padded attacker course student). One instructor said that the physicality of self-defense training is what makes the difference over all sorts of traditional consciousness raising: "I spent *years* in rallies, feminist therapy, etc., and when I get a woman in her body for forty hours and she has a kinesthetic experience of her power, that's a major difference" (Helen Grieco, padded attacker course instructor). In his interviews with women who took Model Mugging, John Gaddis (1990) also heard this theme:

> I'm a lot more sensitive to my boundaries—this began during the train-
> ing, and I preface this with saying prior to the training I had studied
> boundaries, and disorders of boundaries, through therapy, psychology
> school, AA, Adult Children of Alcoholics, etc., and I had done a little bit
> of "boundary work"; but in Model Mugging I did the real work—I
> became hyperaware of my boundaries. (Padded attacker course student,
> in ibid., 166-67)

A woman I spoke with explained: "Whereas therapy may take weeks, to talk about it, this just brings it up immediately. . . . I go into these really intellectual things, whereas the body just needs to go 'whoa, like what are you doing? It's not OK.' It's a nice clean feeling" (padded attacker course student). Self-defensers do not just think about assertiveness; they practice it. That the practice engages the body, the mind, and the emotions is critical. For femininity is embodied, sensual, and habitual; this is how it gets disembodied and replaced with the fighting spirit. The fighting spirit is a new body, a new idea, and a new feeling.

The energy of the fighting spirit is extremely intense. In karate, being around the women who are so committed and self-possessed, visible through their piercing eyes focused on the physical tasks before them, audible through their grunts, shouts, and feet stomping, olfactory through the smell of sweat and dust so characteristic of gyms and dojos. You can feel the determination in their grip, and taste it when it's your turn to eat the mat. On the range the smells and sounds are different—gun powder, sometimes the great outdoors, the startling sound of gunfire and the clanking of steel plate targets—but the overall atmosphere is much the same: a stirring sensorial one that engages the body. Even the fitness self-defense courses, with the sweaty, scantily clad bodies and the intense vibration of the speakers blaring music and of your feet bouncing up and down on the hard wood floor, make for a sensory experience that instills a sensibility about using self-defense, melding mind and muscle. These maniacal moments, inspired by an endorphin rush, make self-defense fun to practice and an all-encompassing experience in which you are no longer thinking clearly or deliberately moving your body, but simply stepping, kicking, punching, or shooting in harmony with the music, the energy of others, or the instructor's commands.

Women find that mastering the challenges of getting out of holds and handling weapons that heretofore would have left them baffled and feeling helpless gives them a sense of pride, accomplishment, and bodily mastery. This itself can turn into a physical "high," which makes women really "need" and enjoy the fights. For instance, after watching other women fight in Model Mugging, occasionally the instructor's assistant would mention that she "needed a mugging," to give her a sense of "release" after watching so many bouts from the sidelines. By the same token, women often leave their lessons drained of energy, because mock fights and intense shooting experiences boost the adrenaline and then leave them feeling drained. (Women sometimes say that they feel they could go home and sleep the rest of the day after a self-defense class.)

In one of my first self-defense courses, I heard a more experienced woman remark that she really enjoyed the sparring that took place in the mock attacks. I was stunned. Can we, should we, actually enjoy mock combat? A boxing instructor told me that whether a woman takes up boxing for the great upper-body workout, for some self-defense training, or for the one-on-one combat, the sparring is what captures the hearts of all. She explained:

> When they get their punches down and all the foot work, then we start sparring, that's actually the most fun for all types of them. . . . The feeling is, when you were a kid, did you ever have friends you could horse around with? It's that feeling—a fun way to see how powerful you are. (Boxer and boxing instructor)

The pleasurable character of combative bodily practices no doubt reflects the pleasurable character of becoming a new kind of woman. Self-defensers' new body-selves are celebrated throughout the course, and solidified at the conclusion of many self-defense courses. The transformation from nice girl into mean woman is ritually marked in many self-defense courses with graduation rituals. For example, Model Mugging students are presented with roses, which symbolize the new women they become: beautiful, but with thorns for protection.

On the last day in padded attacker courses, women invite friends and family members to watch their fights and cheer them on. Often former students also attend—and are pulled out of the audience by the muggers for a spontaneous fight. Plenty of hugs, food, and, sometimes, mementos go around. In Paxton Quigley's course, several students left with "Armed and Female" T-shirts and tiny handgun brooches. Students also took home the targets they shot, autographed by Quigley, and went out for drinks. The target may seem like an insignificant ritual marker. But I'm sure I wasn't the only one who actually put the bullet-torn target up on the wall. It symbolized my own passage from feminine incompetence—much as my first pair of high heels marked my passage into it.

The joy of witnessing the transformation is what instructors routinely told me was the most rewarding part of teaching. Self-defense instructors are not simply helping women avoid future assaults. Self-defensers are not only taking back the night; they are taking back their bodies. If women as a group are rendered powerless by the pervasiveness of sexual violence, then self-defense instructors are "deprogramming" women into a new bodily sensibility that does not fit so well with male domination. An instructor explained that self-defense will spill over into areas besides sexual assault:

> If women learn to physically defend themselves they are more likely going to defend themselves in other areas—take a stand in their work, with their competitors, in their family life. And I've seen it and I've heard it so I know that it's very much a part of standing up, taking care of themselves and all that. (Padded attacker course instructor)

The changes might be described as becoming a "better woman," "more of a woman," or "more myself," as one karate instructor explained:

> Being really excited to see people become more themselves—which is really what this whole thing is about—that's what it's been about for me. It's realizing that I was not completely myself, and I will never be completely myself, but that feeling more and more like, Oh I'm doing what I want to do, I'm taking up space in the world, like you know, what more could you want, right? (Janet Aalfs, karate instructor)

To get the fighting spirit, self-defensers learn a new set of reflexes that encompass attitude, will, spirit, body, and technique. The change is quite literally metamorphic. What was once ingrained and felt so natural, femininity, is displaced by a new learned-and-ingrained bodily disposition. The end result is like finally getting used to driving a car on the *other* side of the road. Self-defensers internalize a new bodily disposition, but not from a natural state of passivity and helplessness.

For the "nice girl" is itself a bodily disposition previously internalized and, until self-defense, mostly taken for granted as natural. Thus it is not that self-defense inscribes a set of "unnatural" rules onto the naturally docile bodies of women. Nor is it that patriarchal culture has enforced a set of rules onto the bodies of women and self-defensers finally free themselves of any rules, disciplines, or ideologies. Nor is it that women in self-defense are unleashing a naturally aggressive instinct.

Self-defensers replace an old embodied code with a new one—a more pleasurable one and a differently consequential one. In the context of self-defense, imitation becomes mimesis. That is, conscious acts of female aggression (imitation) become new aspects of who the women are, such that, much as they did not think of the feminine dispositions they had when they arrived to their first self-defense class as imitative, they no longer think of themselves as imitating anything in acting aggressively (Bourdieu 1990, 73). By the end, self-defensers have effected an art of living, based on a new aesthetics of existence.

Consequences of Metamorphosis

Students mention that the emotional part of self-defense is so much more than the physical, not only because they realize how often men assert their privilege in everyday situations (which do not involve a sexual assault and a response of physical self-defense), but also because they develop a new habitus, with a new set of values that get projected out from this disposition. In this way, the physical and the emotional impact of self-defense training are inseparable. Women's socialized feminine bodies that had been living the experience of womanhood change. Self-defense constitutes a habituating order that installs itself right into the daily lives of the students. The consequence is a new way of being in the world.

The following women's statements tell something about the significance of both the fear of violence in women's lives and learning how to fight back. For their sense of confidence and security in general has been altered, which has implications for their lives whether or not someone ever assaults them:

Before I felt equal and now I feel better. I used to feel I had more bound-aries—I'm a woman so I have to go into the education field. I married a big, macho man. You know what I mean? I never really thought of it before. I feel stronger. I feel like the knowledge I have makes me feel stronger. I feel like I can defend myself if I need to. I feel safe by myself now. I'm not afraid to be in my house alone. I don't feel like a wimp any-more. I don't really ever feel afraid anymore. The last thing I want to do is go to an ATM at night, but I don't really feel afraid. (Gun student)

I think it kind of goes into other areas of my life. [Like what?] Like talk-ing more confidently in general. I mean I don't *always* talk confidently but I'm aware when I don't. (Rape crisis center self-defense course stu-dent)

Hopefully I'll never have that happen, using it in self-defense. But I feel a little more confident physically and also a little more aware about how to handle situations without having to do something physical. . . . I always kind of felt strong, because I have a bit of a sports background. And now it's a little more mental confidence. (Karate student)

Women learn a new set of assertive responses to various forms of intimida-tion, threat, and harassment that fall along the continuum of sexual violence. Self-defensers sometimes remark on the "little assaults" they respond to with "little defenses." One instructor explained,

The physical aspect is such a little part of what self-defense is. We women are always defending ourselves all the time, just the little slurs on the street, the looks, the stares, interacting with a boss or teacher that's not taking you seriously. That's all self-defense. That's the harder part of self-defense. (Chimera instructor)

One woman who took a class offered by her local rape crisis center (which included practice of verbal defense skills and explanations, but not practice, of physical defense) found the verbal assertiveness the most important aspect of self-defense training:

I'm much more aware of, I mean, I grew up in New York, and I just, I can't remember a time when I wasn't harassed on the street on almost a daily occurrence. . . . It is my main experience of harassment directed against me and my main experience of being so incredibly frustrated. . . . Verbally I think I'm even more inclined to say no. You know, not even address the comment, but just turn and yell "NO!" or whatever, some-thing. And the feeling that I had in that class with just saying that was really something positive, really empowering and, yeah, I think I'm more likely to do that. . . . Physically I'm not sure. (Rape crisis center self-defense course student)

Some women remarked that their increased self-confidence is a psychological effect of their training and concomitant sense of strength, distinct from the utility of their fighting techniques for specific threats. For instance, a boxer explained that she thinks boxing is not really the best form of self-defense, but feels confident nevertheless:

> The feeling I have now is different from what I had before. It feels like a sense of power but it's really about confidence. I don't feel afraid anywhere I go, even if it's in a bad neighborhood. And it may be foolish because someone could pull a gun or something. But I just don't have that fear anymore. Identifying yourself as a fighter and as somebody of strength. (Boxer and boxing instructor)

A rape crisis center self-defense course student, who explained that she was less certain about the physical aspect of self-defense than about the verbal, still feels increased confidence:

> I think that I'm more confident. That I do feel a little more threatened but I also feel tougher and so when I get onto the subway, you know, I look around, I make eye contact with people, I have my back to the wall, and I just—that's, you know, kind of common, it was what I always knew from when I was little, but I do think I'm more confident about it. (Rape crisis center self-defense course student)

These statements should not be dismissed as some naive "false sense of security." Research has shown that a confident demeanor is a deterrent to attack, and a woman's belief that she can fight, along with the concomitant willingness to put up a fight, are central components to thwarting attacks successfully in the vast majority of situations.

A student from another rape crisis center course (in which no actual physical fighting was practiced) explained,

> What was most valuable to me out of the whole class was not so much the actual physical knowledge of where to place your kick or how to throw a punch, because actually I've mostly forgotten that because I haven't practiced. But what was valuable was the awareness that I got out of it that I could do this. . . . Things that they told us like any kind of resistance is usually going to scare off most attackers. . . if you yell and you seem tough and ready to fight then you know, most of your attackers will not continue. . . . Just the idea that it is better to be loud and out

there and saying "NO, GET AWAY FROM ME" than to just be kind of all "don't hurt me, eek" kind of thing. (Rape crisis center course student)

Another woman expressed a similar sense of psychological relief or comfort from her training, which results in greater social maneuverability:

It frees me up to not have to think about [defending myself and safety] all the time. . . . In general I'm more confident and more able to do more or less what I want to, go where I want to. . . . Like being alone with a man I don't know very well. (Karate student, in Turaj 1993, 58)

That statement also provides one answer to the question of whether preparing oneself for violence amounts to putting on a pair of goggles that make every man look like a potentially violent monster. When a woman learns that she is not inherently vulnerable and men are not inherently Herculean, her sense of vulnerability and, along with it, her ideas about men change dramatically. Men become less threatening, not more so. Many self-defensers also became more comfortable going to anxiety-provoking areas, and became more physically oriented in general (Gaddis 1990, 97-99).

Learning to fight back also simply feels liberating and pleasurable:

It felt great to kick the shit out of a six-foot two-inch guy [serving as padded attacker for the class]. (Padded attacker course student)

For me, it was incredible. It really made me feel good, and so much less powerless. I mean it really gave me a perspective that I don't think I'd ever had before. . . . I felt like I learned a lot and I really felt different. (Rape crisis center self-defense course student)

The increased confidence and pleasure in the use of one's physical strength cause many women to develop more athletic interests after taking some form of self-defense. One woman commented that she got more involved with other sports after she began to box:

I think I've gotten more involved in sports. I've never ever in my life been involved in sports. I hated sports, I was absolutely worthless at them. I've taken an interest in baseball. I feel like recreationally I could play sports, like if people were playing volleyball, whereas before I didn't like to because I just sucked. (Boxing student)

A self-defense course is the first time many women fully experience their bodies as active agents. Young (1990, 147) suggests that women experience their bodies as things at the same time that they experience their bodies as a means for the enactment of their aims. Indeed, the experience of routine sexual objectification and the constant threat of sexual assault encourage women to feel that their bodies are not their own.

Women in self-defense classes often realize that they have learned to withhold full bodily commitment to things, like fighting or yelling. Several instructors said that overcoming the fear of hurting someone was a primary obstacle they must help their students overcome. For some women, the transition from an acted-upon, looked-at body to an active, forceful body is painfully difficult. One woman in Model Mugging began to cry while watching the videotape of her powerful fight against the padded attacker, explaining that she knew she'd had a good fight, but all she could focus on was how fat she looked. Her painful struggle illustrates the enormous power of women's sense of themselves as objects, and the difficulty of struggling to transform that into an experience of themselves as actors. But the transformation does take place, a transformation in embodiment that may explain why self-defense enhances self-confidence and even helps some women overcome eating disorders.

But as Young (ibid., 155) points out, a woman is damned if she does and damned if she doesn't. A woman's distance from her body and physical hesitancy may come from seeing herself as a sex object for others. And yet, she must keep herself "closed in" because to use her body freely is to "invite" sexual objectification (not to mention claims of crassness). Thus keeping in your enclosed space is a defense against being leered at, touched, and accused of inviting rape. Through self-defense instruction, women lose a certain bodily comportment of femininity—of watching that their breasts are not exposed as they bend over, of keeping their legs crossed, acting demure, and looking down. A boxing student remarked on this: "I feel stronger, my confidence is up, I feel like I look better. I carry myself better. Before I walked around with hunched-over shoulders, looking at the ground, just not real secure in myself. Now I just feel really good" (boxing student). Self-defense teaches women to make eye contact. When women "mark" other people with their eyes, they are not developing a paranoid public demeanor. Men do not generally avert their eyes. If women have learned to avoid eye contact with men, it is because of the fear that making eye contact would be misconstrued as a sexual invitation. Gone is the treatment of men as brutes that women are responsible for controlling through a series of "modest" gestures. Women have a line of defense beyond controlling the body in ways that avoid objectification or sexual "invitation."

Perhaps this is why some self-defensers note a change in their body images and styles of dress. Gaddis (1990) found that women's sense of physical and emotional self-acceptance increased as a result of their involvement with self-defense. One student explained,

> I've been exposing myself more in many ways, sharing my feelings, sharing my thoughts, my experiences, sharing my body in terms of dressing more femininely or more revealingly [instead of hiding my body] . . . before Model Mugging, unless I felt my body was absolutely perfect I wouldn't be seen in public in a bikini. Now I feel able to lay out in the sun and actually felt good about myself in a little bikini—I even bought myself a new one to celebrate the new me. (Padded attacker course student, in ibid., 94)

Another woman said that she used to go out of her way to avoid appearing in public in her exercise clothes, but now, for instance, will stop at the market on her way home from the gym if it's more convenient to do so. In providing a sense that one need not present oneself in ways that either please or temper men, self-defense allows women to take less responsibility than they had previously for a man's interest in raping them.

Another self-defenser noted a change in her dress style:

> I'm not sure if this is related to boxing, but since I've started boxing—I used to dress in combat boots and flannel shirts and lately I've been dressing more sophisticated, stuff more tailored, I think it's kind of ironic that since I've started boxing my wardrobe has changed like this. [What do you make of the change?] I feel there's a real feminine side to me and real masculine side to me. The boxing shows my masculine side, and before the clothing showed my masculine side. (Boxing student)

While this student still associates toughness with masculinity, her experience with self-defense seems to allow her a greater range in self-expression. Her ability to fight, which she deems her "masculine side," may be a more central component of her self-conception than her clothing. Another woman I interviewed said she wears more dresses now that she has had self-defense training. Her explanation reveals the way her self-defense training seems more authentic to her than the clothing she had worn to look tough. She said she had worn tough clothing as "a front" because she felt vulnerable but actually did not know how to fight. She feels more latitude now that she actually has confidence that she can fight.

In contrast, the style renegotiations of other self-defensers ran in the other direction. One student bought a pair of Doc Marten brand orthopedic boots that are styled after combat boots, while a second self-defenser had a new feeling about the boots she already owned:

> They're big heavy boots, I could really hurt somebody bad with those boots. Given that so much of the self-defense is kicking, and they're laced boots that don't come off, they're very heavy. Definitely [self-defense] had something to do with my desire to buy those particular boots. (Padded attacker course student)

> Sometimes when I wear my boots I feel like I can kick ass. (Padded attacker course student)

Whether these women adopted this style because of a commitment to defend themselves or because of a new aesthetic that seemed to merge with that ability, they just might change what it means to be a "knockout." This is perhaps the first time in North American history where women are making fashion choices based on an entirely different aesthetic: stopping power, damage power. It's now comfortable, functional, and perhaps even attractive (at least bearable) to keep the size and shape of the foot intact, rather than squeeze it into a tiny pump to make it look smaller, with an elevated heel to make the leg look thinner and forceful walking impossible. Women's fashions have inhibited their movements, making a manly bodily comportment impossible, and making male protection necessary, at least symbolically. Thinking of what one's feet can do in a particular pair of shoes, rather than what one's legs look like in them, seems to be a step forward.

But self-defense offers more than a new bodily comportment or combative aesthetic. Women credit their self-defense courses for all kinds of changes they make in their lives—like getting divorced, starting their own businesses, going back to school, confronting an abuser, and getting over an eating disorder. It was common to hear women say things like: "The physical part of self-defense is only 'this' much [pinching thumb and forefinger almost together] and the emotional part is 'T H I S' much [stretching arms out wide]." One instructor remarked on the transformation, which she sees routinely in her students after their completion of her course, and its extension into many aspects of their lives:

> [The transformation] is very swift and it's very exciting but I know that it continues. They move on; they end unhealthy relationships; they quit their jobs; they go back to school. They jump out of planes! They climb mountains; they start new businesses. I mean they just reach a place within themselves that they can do more than they have and they unleash that chain or the wall, or however you want to label it with that person, to pursue other things in life. . . . I've had students walk in here maybe six months later and I don't even recognize her because she's so proud of her appearance and her body. (Padded attacker course instructor)

A student put it this way: "Fighting would've been the farthest thing from my mind and my identity; now I consider myself a fighter. You can't really be a woman unless you have that strength" (padded attacker course student). This karate student explained that many aspects of her life had changed, including her dreams at night:

> My dreams over time have changed from being always stopped and hiding and people trying to kill me and rape me to where right in the dream I would say "I know karate." And I would either stop them from doing it right there or wake up just as I was about to and then other times I'd be fighting back. And I know that what was happening was a real shift like in my understanding of who I am in the world and what I can do. (Karate student, in Turaj 1993, 61)

One of the most striking transformations I found reported by women who took self-defense was a greater sense of courage around men in everyday situations. I heard many stories of women who noticed that they were less willing to put up with everyday intimidation, insults, and abuse. Given that the threat of sexual violence gives force to men's intimidation and harassment of women, and women's fear of that violence lies behind their capitulation to men's insults, it should hardly be surprising that self-defense training has this result.

A nurse who took three padded attacker courses and began boxing after that, described the transformation in her relationships with men at her workplace:

> I didn't realize until after I took Model Mugging that when I was around the doctors I felt like I didn't exist. I felt like I was this little mouse running around in between all these big, important men and that they didn't even recognize my existence, that I didn't even have a right to expect them to recognize who I was, and that they were obviously far superior to me. Once I took Model Mugging—it wasn't like I thought all the doctors were going to beat me up—but somehow it gave me a sense of I have a right to be here, I do exist, you have to recognize me, I have a right to challenge you, and I have a right to tell you what I want. And it kind of made me feel equal to the doctors. (Padded attacker course and boxing student)

Other students' comments suggest that they too stand up to men more often as a result of their self-defense training:

> I am no longer as afraid to voice my opinions to men, or anyone, but especially to men. (Padded attacker course student)

Model Mugging certainly stopped [my boyfriend] from forcing sex on me all the time. After the Model Mugging I didn't let him do that to me anymore. (Padded attacker course student)

Somehow I got over the fear of men. Maybe that was Model Mugging *and* therapy. Certain men intimidated me. Men stare at lunch and it dawned on me that I was scared. And then it dawned on me, I was no longer intimidated. (Padded attacker course student)

It actually helped me deal with people, and I'm not timid and scared of people. (Padded attacker course student)

I'm less timid. (Padded attacker course student)

My observations are confirmed by those of Gaddis (1990). One woman he interviewed explained her increased sense of entitlement to boundaries:

I'm prone to say something a lot more quickly when people infringe on me. For example at work I'm usually not a demonstrative person. I have a male friend who I occasionally allow to hug me, providing he first ask my permission. Recently, he tried to hug me without my permission and I backed off, put up my hand and said "No." In the past I would have given in, to not create a scene or embarrass the other person. . . . I used to be so concerned about taking care of the boundaries of others, to the detriment of my own. (Padded attacker course student, in ibid., 155)

This boxing student explained that her actual fighting brought back painful memories of abuse, rendering her physically helpless during a match, ultimately leading to a more healed, assured state:

I was in an abusive relationship for three years, and it kind of brought that up—when I spar with my trainer it kind of brought all that up again. Fortunately I have an understanding trainer. [Was it therapeutic?] Yes. I think for a long time I didn't think it really affected me as much as it did. I thought that since I had gotten out of the relationship I had kind of gotten over it. This one night we were having a particularly intense sparring match and all of a sudden I just had this flash of my old boyfriend coming at me and feeling helpless and not being able to defend myself. My trainer had me cornered and I wasn't fighting and I started crying. My trainer helped me face my fear and helped me realize I could defend myself. It just really changed my mindset that I don't have to be helpless and intimidated by somebody but that I could defend myself. . . . [Do you feel that if you were in another situation, in which there was abuse in an interpersonal relationship, your response would be different now, as a result of your training?] Yes, but I don't think it would be my first response to bust out with a right hook. The boxing has helped reinforce my self-confidence to know that I could leave that situation. (Boxing student)

Thus the combat in self-defense classes can actually help assault survivors still struggling to come to terms with the powerlessness they once felt. In this way, there is a distinct therapeutic aspect to some forms of self-defense. Women, particularly survivors of child sexual abuse, often take padded attacker forms of self-defense for therapeutic purposes. One woman from a Model Mugging class said,

> After much discussion with my therapist, I decided to sign up for MM. It seemed like a great way for me to learn very important self defense skills, bond with women, and improve my self image. Most importantly, it seemed like a way to get at buried anger toward my stepfather who sexually abused me, and toward my mother, who played a major role in my abuse. During the five weeks of the program, many new memories of my abuse surfaced. And though it was very painful, the tremendous support I received from the group of women, and both the male and female instructors was extremely helpful. My life has indeed changed and improved. (*Self-Defense and Empowerment News*, 6, no. 1 [Winter/Spring 1992]: 7)

Self-defense training can also help survivors of rape and abuse by providing a cathartic release when women fight through scenes similar to those they were subjected to in the past. As one woman in *Model Mugging News* explained, taking the multiple assailants course helped her deal with a real gang rape she had experienced twenty-four years earlier, while in high school, about which she had never spoken:

> It wasn't easy. We designed scenarios based on the assault and I relived the past. Only this time it was different. Much different. This time I won. And I realized that I didn't deserve it. While I may have used poor judgment in the past, I didn't deserve to be punished, hurt, raped. No one in my class betrayed me. They filled me with love and support. I found out that I was not the only one with demons to slay, and I was grateful for the opportunity to support my classmates in return. (*Model Mugging News* 4, no. 1 [Spring 1990]: 4)

In this way, survivors experience going through assault scenarios, and winning this time, as healing. Reenacting one's trauma in a carefully controlled environment when one is ready to do so, as the above self-defenser described, can be an important step toward coping with the symptoms associated with post-traumatic stress disorder (Herman 1992). Of course, no student should be forced to relive any scene she does not wish to. One self-defense school rejects reenactments across the board.

Precisely because a significant number of self-defensers (like many women in the population at large) are child-sexual-abuse survivors, a Chimera instructor stresses the importance of women-only environments without a live mock assailant:

> We do not use a padded attacker. We believe that women experience that kind of assault daily. We practice on kicking pads. We feel that it's as useful for women to be in a totally supportive environment only with women and practice full-out on pads and it's not necessary to relive a situation. . . . We don't use a man in the class for anything because we want the women to feel safe. It's really an intense experience so we want an environment that's as safe as possible so that women can grow as much as possible. (Chimera instructor)

Model Mugging tends to push students into practicing every scenario, reasoning that "the real assailant isn't going to go away because you have a cold today." But Defending Ourselves, Grieco explained, stresses allowing a woman to choose not to participate in a particular exercise if she does not feel like it, as a way to practice "honoring women's *nos*" which in itself "is healing."

Of course not all women are affected the same way by self-defense training. Two explained to me that they felt self-defense enhanced the assertiveness they already displayed:

> I never went through this sort of epiphany experience that a lot of people seem to, like, "Oh my God this class opened up all these doors"; it bleeded over into all other aspects of their life where they were suddenly assertive and it really affected all of their decision-making processes. I mean for me it was very much more compartmentalized. This was a defense class that I took, and this is where I learned that behavior and that's where I applied it. It didn't, I mean I guess I'm already more assertive than a lot of people I know [laughs] so I already started at a different level. "Bossy" maybe is another word [for me]! (Padded attacker course student)

> I don't know if it like totally affected me, I know like some of my friends who took the class were much more affected by it than I was, in terms of having been a little bit more meek before they started. But I was always kind of loud and pushy so it didn't [affect me] as much. (Rape crisis center self-defense course student)

Clearly all women do not have the same experiences or embodied subjectivities, but noticeable patterns emerge that indicate how self-defense helps women develop a different relationship with their bodies, the various manifestations of female degradation, and a culture that celebrates their vulnerability to abuse. Although my data does not group experiences learning self-defense by "types" of women, and no national records are available to tell us exactly how many women of specific racial/ethnic groups have sought self-defense training, some self-defense instructors have suggested the specific challenges common among women of distinct subjugated racial/ethnic groups. Of course, women in any given racial/ethnic group are diverse, but nevertheless some instructors have written about some general patterns they have observed.

One self-defense instructor noticed that African American women in her self-defense classes were usually more psychologically prepared to channel their fear into anger and defend themselves, and needed to learn physical skills more than the psychological ones (Searles and Berger 1987, 72). Bart and O'Brien (1985) found that contemporary black women are more likely to resist, and stop, attacks than white women. Advised by their families to fight back when attacked, a result of the "street smarts" required of less-privileged groups in society, some black women might have an easier time than other women mastering the "mental" aspects of self-defense. In contrast, Native American women often need most help with the mental aspects of self-defense. Often feeling that outsiders control their destinies, Native American women may experience assault as yet another instance in a life over which they have no control, making the mental self-worth component of self-defense particularly important (DuShane, in Sanford and Fetter 1979, 164-65).

Chicanas, Asian American women, and white women often face both physical and mental challenges learning self-defense. Unlike white women, however, Chicanas may be more likely to fear that the pride and physical strength involved in learning self-defense makes them "man-haters," taking them outside their own cultural frame of reference from within the context of racism (Benavídez, in ibid., 162-63). Asian American women must learn self-defense in the context of stereotypical North American media portrayals of themselves as always sexually available to white men, particularly soldiers, or as damsels in distress in Bruce Lee films (although martial arts films for Chinese-speaking audiences tend to portray men and women as equally strong in the martial arts) (Wong, in ibid., 156-59). While the challenges of self-defense for women differentially positioned within a racist social structure vary, self-defense that stresses both physical skills and a confident, entitled attitude clearly benefits all women.

Becoming a Gender Transgression

As I have already suggested, women's refusal of a status of helpless, sexually available objects can be disconcerting. To become a self-defenser is to become a gender transgression. Self-defensers thus have to contend with a series of reactions to their training, from being seen as a "tough cookie" to serving as a role model for other women. I heard the same joke from men over and over, that went something like this: "I'd better watch my step around you or you'll beat me up!" Men will not be protectors in the same way, and both men and women realize this. Some women told me that some men in their lives did not support their involvement in self-defense. In the following, boxers explain a mixture of reactions:

> As far as men, you get a lot of jokes like, "watch out, she's going to beat you up" and other men it's like, "heeeyyy!"—you know, it's a turn-on kind of thing. With the men, at least the ones that aren't in any kind of boxing or martial arts, they tend to humor you—like "oh how cute, she can punch." [Like a condescending attitude?] Yes, a definite sense of condescension. Like you're a little Barbie doll in boxing gear. That seems to be an instant issue like, "wow, you could beat me up?" Like that's going to come up. The ones in martial arts or boxing, they just see you as a comrade: "You box? Oh cool." (Boxer and boxing instructor)

Another boxer concurred, for the most part:

> Guys in the gym are accepting, except for the immature, young ones, which are not the ones I would want to spend time with anyway, if they're like that. I had suspected that the men at the boxing gym might resent the presence of women, but they actually seem quite glad that women are there. Except the young, immature guys from the university. (Padded attacker course and boxing student)

Most men outside the boxing gym, however, do not know how to react to her. She explained,

> Some of the male doctors at work joke with me, and I don't know how to react to them. For instance, one pretends to square up to me for a fight or will jokingly punch me. But I want to be feminine, but what is that and how do I integrate it with my self-defense? I don't want to be related to as *only my self-defense skills.* (Padded attacker course and boxing student)

Even if a woman feels like she is still a full person with a variety of interests, opinions, hobbies, and so on, after self-defense training, others may focus on, and elevate the centrality of, the aspect of who she is that makes her deviant.

One woman explained that she has been impressed with how nice everyone was in the "totally man's world" of guns:

> You're in a totally man's world. You know, everybody in their fatigues and hats and guns . . . and they're just so nice, they really are very, you know, sometimes they're a little patronizing, but they're just really nice and very helpful. . . . [What do you mean by patronizing?] When I bought the second gun he calls you "dear" and he's sort of "Well that's OK," [that she didn't know how to clean the gun] you know, I mean, patronizing is the word but it's in a nice way; it's not a nasty patronizing; I don't mind that, you know. (Gun student)

Thus while this student made it clear that she does not have negative experiences with the male shooters she has run across (in fact, she distinguished her experiences from those of women in "other professions or circumstances of the all-male world" in which "you hear real complaints, how they really are nasty"), she also told of a certain amount of condescension that she must manage when interacting with them. At the time of our interview, this woman was about to embark upon her first trip to the gun club unescorted by a man, to show a widowed friend how to shoot her late husband's Colt .32. Here is what she anticipated:

> [The gun instructor] said, "Don't come up here alone," you know, "Come up here with a friend," and I thought that was interesting and I've heard that a couple of times. . . . But I haven't tried that and I wouldn't feel comfortable doing that, going alone. I probably could and then I'd see. . . . I am going to have to teach her on Saturday, and Saturday afternoon I guess is a time where all the men go so that'll be sort of a learning experience. I'll see what it's like and I'll see if we run into any segregation type thing or any problems [laughs], but I don't anticipate it because most of the men really are pretty nice if you just ask them nicely, I mean, you know, even apologize and say, don't try and flaunt the fact that you're, you know, a woman with a gun. (Gun student)

Another gun student, because of some "ugly" experiences at the gun range, came to see the assumption that men have a greater aptitude for shooting as part of the problem of rape culture:

> Sometimes at the range I've had some pretty ugly experiences there. I had a 10 mm., big caliber gun that not many people shoot, and one man said, "What is a little lady like you going to do with a big gun like that?" Since when does self-protection have gender lines? Maybe we wouldn't have

such a screwed up rape culture if women could take care of themselves. (Gun student)

That same student was heartened when she felt encouraged by a man at the range. She encountered him one day after taking a combat class, which she took after Paxton Quigley's firearms course for women, she said, "put a bug in me" for more training:

> After my second, hardest combat class, I remember putting myself in the car; it was a rainy day, and some gentleman—I was the only girl—came up to me and said, "You did extremely well out there today. Keep up the good work." And I almost had to choke back from crying. I'm shooting as well as these guys. If for any reason I was in a threatening situation, I could take care of myself. You feel kind of scared *and* good about yourself. Like a mixed emotion. (Gun student)

The following self-defenser said that she fears being isolated and alienated by men who might label her a lesbian as a result of her participation in self-defense. This dread of isolation is especially great due to her prior history of being overweight and having "the issues surrounding it," which for her included not dating at all:

> I hesitate telling people that I box—and I'm embarrassed to even say this—because I'm afraid I'll be labeled a lesbian. It already happens to me. And I have nothing against gays; it is just that I am not gay and I'm afraid I'll get known as or labeled a lesbian and then men will dislike me. (Padded attacker course and boxing student)

This next student, who identified as gay, perhaps has less reason to fear alienation from men. She explained that her involvement in karate has made her somewhat of a role model:

> [Outside karate] they were quite impressed. People have this thing in their minds and ask, are you a black belt yet? . . . It's a little mysterious and also powerful. Both my sisters want to be able to do this. (Karate student)

A gun student explained how people react to her:

> A little bit amazed. I'm not a little, petite girl. I've never been a quiet, shy person. I've always been kind of loud and obnoxious. But people were amazed that that was part of me. "Do you hunt?" "Are you going to kill animals?" I'd say, "No, I'm just into the sport of it." People were shocked. (Gun student)

Although that gun student's female friends were influenced, even if initially surprised, by her involvement, some self-defensers seem to have a sense that women, those against violence, might react negatively to their activities. For example,

> I've noticed that there seems to be an assumption that you're a violent person, and that's bothersome. And I don't feel like that at all. I mean I enjoy [boxing] as a sport, and I'm not a violent person. They think of boxing as a violent sport, and I guess from an outsider's point of view it is, but to me it's just a sport. And I think I could actually be healthier than people who don't do this. I vent; I get out my anger and frustrations in a healthy way. I'm not about to blow, because I'm constantly processing it. Of course there's more than one way to process things. (Boxer and boxing instructor)

The self-defensers sometimes speak to a kind of skeptical feminist audience when they discuss how they think they are perceived. This instructor's statement frames her views of self-defense as an issue of citizenship, and in terms popular among feminists who value women's nurturing roles: "There's nothing morally objectionable about defending myself. I'm a good citizen for doing so. This is connected with nurturance in a way that feminists who are concerned with nurturance ignore. It's another part of our human potential" (Helen Grieco, padded attacker course instructor).

Conclusion

Self-defense makes clear that gender reality is a matter of performance. I learned in my observations of self-defense classes that women's helpless bodily comportment in part comes from actual experiences and fears of being attacked. Women do not merely, over time, develop an aesthetic preference for a feminine demeanor; we are not simply seduced into it. It is forced upon us; we are taught that we will not live, eat, or be loved without it. We are punished for challenging it. Even if we "accidentally" have the wrong physical demeanor, there are costs.

Gender is thus constructed through corporeal acts. A feminine comportment serves to materialize the body as a female body, a gendered body. Our bodies are the signs of our historically and culturally delimited identificatory possibilities. Of course, sexual assault itself (and consensual heterosexual sex, for that matter) is such a corporeal act which can make one "feel like a man" or "feel like a woman." Butler (1990, 139) states: "The body is not a 'being,' but a variable boundary, a surface whose permeability is politically regulated, a signifying practice within a cultural field of gender hierarchy and compulsory heterosexuality."

In an actual assault situation, when the self-defenser confounds the script of helpless female victim and unstoppable male attacker, she is refusing the sex class status that acts of rape and woman abuse impose. This is the political—and feminist—importance of refusing sexual assault. Self-defense enables us to see gender ideology or power operating not just at the level of ideas, social interaction, and relationships (as though the effects of ideology are limited to one's beliefs, roles, or psychology) but at the level of the body as well. The body-self is transformed through rehearsals of aggression, which solidify a new embodied ideal, not because a woman becomes conscious of her political situation and then changes her behavior. This is the political, and feminist, importance of learning self-defense, beyond its ability to enforce women's refusal of men's attacks.

When women perform a decidedly unfeminine script, as in self-defense classes, they are challenging gender reality. When women learn to get mean, they realize that feminine niceness is a historical effect, not a natural given of womanhood. Feminists have long been contesting the idea that gender differences are natural. What is revealed so clearly in self-defense classes is the level at which gender is incorporated into the body. Even some feminists have considered the male body naturally suitable for raping the violable female body.

Some women might think that self-defense makes them unnaturally capable, hence leaving gender undeconstructed. But evidence against this is that self-defensers say things like, "I'm becoming more myself," and "You can't really be a woman unless you have that strength." This suggests to me that self-defensers are trying to naturalize fighting, to argue that there is nothing unnatural about their abilities. By the same token, though, I do not see women's cultivation of aggression as an essentialist unfolding—as though the possibilities or fighter identities were there and simply repressed due to female socialization (a narrative that Jackson [1993, 125] suggests characterizes self-defense instruction). Self-defense instructors do not release a more real, albeit dormant, instinct. They impose a new behavior, much as women's old behavior, for instance an inability to kick hard, was also at some point culturally imposed.

Men and women learn to inhabit their bodies in a gendered political system, embodying the ethos of rape culture. Yet self-defense enables us "to imagine the female body as subject to change, as a potential object of fear and agent of violence" (Marcus 1992, 400). The rapist and his victim are not in some primal predator-prey relationship; those are precisely the terms of the event that the act of self-defense rejects. The embodied ethos of rape culture is radically transformed in self-defense instruction not only because women consciously adopt and make habit new gestures and voices, but because their lives change after their involvement. They expand; they are less afraid of men; they are ready to claim new territory.

It is worth emphasizing that while women are glad they learn self-defense, they still wish they did not have to. For some women, it seemed too conciliatory to learn to use violence, given that it seems like a "male mode" of interaction and because it should be men's responsibility to stop assaulting women:

> I remember being really pissed like, why the hell should we have to do this? You know, God damn it, you guys don't even get it. . . . It concerns just how vulnerable we are systematically. Why should we? Why is that the case? But then the course goes, don't just ask why, let me teach you some things that are realistic and you can apply. So, yeah, I was like a warrior for women, you know? (Padded attacker course student)

> I think a world without guns is the ideal world, absolutely. If I had my druthers I'd have every weapon sucked into a giant vacuum and destroyed, you know, I mean that's of course, you know, the way I feel. . . . I mean these kids all killing each other and all the destruction is terrible. But in the world we live in, you know, and since the guns are so widespread, we've got to deal with the world we're in. (Gun student)

> I'm still one of those people who says, you know, the world shouldn't be like this, and we shouldn't have to know how to do this. Just because men use violence, there's no reason we should use violence because the solution is for men not to be violent in the first place. . . . Why is it my responsibility to learn how to defend myself from some asshole? Shouldn't it be their responsibility not to attack me? (Rape crisis center self-defense course student)

A former self-defense instructor told me that the friction over women's "becoming like men" forced her to give up teaching:

> That's why I stopped doing it [teaching self-defense]. Because I'm not really a political person. People assumed I was and had a position on this. I don't have all the information and I don't have strong opinions. I don't think women *can* become like men. I'm all for women fighting back. I just have this faith or this trust that a woman is not going to go out and maliciously hurt someone unless she has been beaten down. . . . I'm this pro-peacenik but I'm going to stop the violence before it comes to me. (Rape crisis center self-defense course instructor)

Of course we all want to live in a world in which disputes are resolved without violence, and in which violence does not enable the domination of one over another. With a fear of immediate threats, what is a principled feminist to do?

I have argued that self-defense embodies a set of feminist ethics about women's entitlement to make their own sexual choices and challenges the naturalized association between masculinity and violence. But despite its radical potential to challenge rape culture, self-defense and feminist politics remain distant. I asked self-defense students if they saw their practices as connected to the women's movement in any ways, usually only to face blank stares, fumbling comments like "well yeah sure," or intimidated confessions such as "my consciousness is not totally raised." The connection between self-defense and feminism was commonly framed in terms of women's getting to do more things or feeling more empowered. Only one student framed her involvement with self-defense as a way of enacting feminism. She identified herself as a feminist and explained:

> All of the advances—sexual freedoms, birth control—mean nothing if we cannot protect our own bodies. If I opened my mouth too much, I get punished. Punishment is being beaten or raped. So all the other gains women can make are smoke. So my commitment to feminism and to other women is to self-defense. It's like feminism on the physical level. (Padded attacker course student)

Although several self-defense instructors I met see themselves in the context of the women's movement and identify themselves as feminists, some— whether or not they consider themselves feminists—feel frustrated with or simply distant from feminism proper. To them, the women's movement is too hoity-toity to embrace the work of self-defense. For example, in her book on unarmed self-defense techniques, *Attitude: Commonsense Defense for Women*, Lisa Sliwa (1986, 30) says,

> The women's movement exists mostly in the minds of some East Coast ivory-tower intellectuals whose main function is to give one another awards every year at lavish banquets. They are out of touch with the most urgent problem confronting girls and women today: how to deal with the increasing violence committed against women.

The following martial artist contrasted self-defense training with social services "that just patch up the damage of violence against women after it's been done (e.g., rape crisis centers and battered women's shelters)." She explained in her dojo's newsletter:

I see teaching self-defense . . . as a very concrete way of teaching/encouraging resistance, a place to begin discussions of forms of oppression and possibilities for resistance, and so on. In this way, I don't think of what we do as a social service (although I have no problem with presenting ourselves as a social service to get grants—as long as there aren't big strings attached). Social services are necessary to preserve the status quo. Providing services that enable people to survive or even escape violence and oppression is a very different thing from stirring up the kind of consciousness and action that leads people to fight against oppression, and I hope we are doing the latter. . . . What we are doing is not a service; it is a (at least potentially) very disruptive form of education. (*The Shuri-Spiral News*, January 1993)

The need to do something to prevent violence, indeed to see violence as preventable, involves a more radical outlook than that which seems to characterize feminist crisis centers for victimized women. Such services may be necessary, but self-defensers claim that they are not enough—and may even preserve the status quo by confirming the association of men with unstoppable aggression and women with inescapable victimhood. In much the same spirit, the gun instructor Lyn Bates told me that looking to long-term solutions should not be the only feminist strategy to end violence against women:

The women's movement is doing women a tremendous disservice by overlooking the fact that there are a number of ways to protect yourself. [How are they overlooking this fact, specifically?] They tend to be on the side of looking to long-term solutions—what can we do to society to keep people from wanting to commit violence? I like to give the analogy to AIDS: the short-term solution is sex education and condoms; the long-term solution is research to find treatment or a cure. No sane person would ever argue that all the eggs should go into one basket. The same thing is true of violence and crime. . . . There are people who are being attacked right now and they need tools and training right now to deal with that situation. Because they can't wait for the educational reform and the welfare reform and all the other reforms to change the situation. The problems I have with that *Ms.* magazine article [May/June 1994] is that it says to women, there's nothing you can do in the short run. In the short run there's something wrong with you, immoral and dangerous and bad if you learn to use a gun, and that simply is not true. But an awful lot of women buy into that because they hear it from sources that they respect.

Here feminism is so antiviolence, or at least antigun, that it frightens some women away from training in self-defense.

Paxton Quigley makes clear that feminists against guns just don't get it:

I think there should be certainly more philosophical discussions among feminists, especially Eastern feminists [feminists on the East Coast of the United States], about the use of handguns. For some reason, Eastern feminists tend to be antigun, and I think a lot of that has to do with the fact that they haven't been around guns, and they don't understand what a gun can do to a woman psychologically. I think that they're missing a link in understanding total feminism.

As for the feminists who think that it is Quigley who is missing a feminist link, she said,

I don't think those women who've criticized me really have any understanding of what I try to say and do. There are a lot of antihandgun women that I've asked to be in my class and not even pay to do it. Not one of them has taken my class. Perhaps they don't want to know, perhaps they're fearful that I might even change them. I don't mind being criticized, but at least take my seminar so that you can come from a place of knowledge rather than a place of hearsay or assumption.

Thus it seems less that self-defensers dismiss feminism than that feminists disregard self-defense. The next chapter presents the uneasiness feminists might have about women's self-defense, uneasiness that I suggest is based on a set of assumptions about violence and the body. I indicate some ways that women's increasing engagement with self-defense can prompt feminists to refigure those central assumptions in feminist philosophy and politics and embrace self-defense as an important feminist project.

4

Changing Our Minds about Our Bodies

What Can Feminism Learn from Self-Defense?

Women's experiences in self-defense courses show that bodies are inscribed in particular ways that perpetuate gender inequality. The new "mean" bodies that self-defensers develop reveal that reinscription is possible. Grosz (1994, xiii) insists that bodies can be "lived and represented in quite different terms, terms that may grant women the capacity for independence and autonomy, which thus far have been attributed only to men." Changing the body incorporates and projects new knowledge about women and a new sense of self. Social identity cannot be distinguished from the lived body; the lived body is how self-identity is actualized.

If one's self-image cannot be distinguished from the living of this body as a whole, then it should not be surprising if changes in the body effect changes in the structure and fabric of the self (Diprose 1994, 117). The disciplined reorganization of one's responses to aggressive men breaks through a habit of feminine manners in which the female body perpetually repeats a repertoire of socially desirable, feminine acts. Just as the body and hence the self can change through an injury, disease, or pregnancy (ibid.), self-defensers, in forming new bodily habits, change what it means to be a woman.

I anticipate that some might be skeptical of the feminist potential of a movement in which womanhood still seems so important, in which shooting is "fun" and "sexy," in which physical combat is pleasurable, and in which women embrace rather than forgo the "manly" practices feminists have criticized. Feminists have looked critically at women's engagement with popular culture, particularly when some corporation stands to profit from it, when it is lauded as good for women, and when it is celebrated as empowering by many who lack feminist commitments. This is the strength of feminist analyses that challenged, for instance, claims that the sexual revolution benefited women (e.g., Jeffreys 1990). So it is understandable and necessary that feminist critics do not easily accept new cultural trends that purport to liberate women. As much as we should take these feminist critics seriously, we must also take seriously the many women whose pleasures seem to lie in the popular activity of self-defense.

My purpose here is to suggest a critical and feminist way of experiencing and enjoying women's self-defense. I arrived at this analysis not only by taking self-defense and talking to other participants but also through my position as a feminist theoretical interpreter. As I propose a way of understanding self-defense, I consider what feminism can learn from self-defense culture. This chapter presents some feminist hesitations about women's cultivation of aggression, identifies the political and philosophical legacies behind those hesitations, and suggests some ways in which feminists might reconsider those philosophical assumptions and resultant scruples.

The discourse of gender—feminist or not—is part of the ongoing struggle to establish an ordering of human bodies and affairs. Appealing to the agency of women involves an attempt to become part of the set of voices and interests trying to shape the system of identity, normative order, and power. For instance, if women say that "it's sexy" to shoot a gun, then it could be, as Lorber (1993, 574, following Mangan and Park 1987) cynically assumes in the context of women's sports, that women manage the "status dilemma" of engaging in unfeminine activities by redefining the activity or its result as feminine or womanly. However, I think we might say that women are not so much devoted to appearing womanly as they are to allowing greater room for what can count culturally as "womanly." Rather than naively contradicting themselves, they are suggesting that women can be simultaneously nurturing and aggressive, sexy and respectable. When a woman says that self-defense makes her "really" a woman, more of a woman, or sexier, what does that tell us about gendered identities? What are the utopian aspects of this notion of womanhood?

If feminism's focus on the body led in the 1970s to an intense antirape campaign, it also led to the offering of some self-defense courses for women as a feminist practice. But, as Shannon Jackson (1993, 111) notes, since then

> feminists have questioned some of the assumptions which fueled their initial act of resistance, forcing them to examine the extent to which racism, classism, capitalism, and homophobia structured their rhetoric and goals and inadvertently perpetuated patriarchal values. This process of self-examination has necessarily disrupted efforts to forge unambiguous and decisive prescriptions for political action.

Although I share this concern to connect gender oppression with other forms of oppression, and to be aware of contradictory locations within a power structure, I think that abandoning an emphasis on self-defense within feminist politics is not merely grounded in the innocent desire to avoid perpetuating oppression and actually causes more harm than it avoids, particularly when it comes to perpetuating heterosexist and racist definitions of womanhood.

Two major assumptions, manifested in several different forms of skepticism about women's aggression, particularly women's armed self-defense, prevent feminists from embracing self-defense as a central anti–sexual assault strategy: the assumption that any form of violence is "masculinist" and therefore does not genuinely transform society; and the assumption that transforming the body cannot lead to feminist transformation, at the individual much less the societal level. Self-defense presents a compelling case for feminists to question these assumptions.

Two commentators (Jackson 1993; Lentz 1993) actually reject those assumptions but remain skeptical of women's self-defense on the grounds that self-defense culture holds those very beliefs. I contend that self-defense is not in danger of perpetuating the philosophical and political problems associated with either the assumption that all violence is masculinist or the assumption that body projects cannot lead to feminist transformation. This is not to say that self-defense is perfect. I suggest that overcoming the problems in feminism and in self-defense requires a more explicit merger of the two and, ultimately, a philosophy of the ethical significance of women's self-defense.

Gun Use and Gun Control As "Women's Issues"

A good deal of the intensity of feeling about women's self-defense is linked to concerns about armed violence specifically. This may be in part because many underestimate the damage trained women can do without firearms. Still, positioned as the most "male," the most deadly, and the most taboo for women, guns are the most controversial form of self-defense. Guns are "male," in this logic, and therefore oppressive; hence resistance to them should be "female." If guns are sold to women, it could only be to corrupt women with masculinity or a "male" political agenda, making the world a more violent and more sexist place. Self-defense culture proves some of those anxieties to be ill founded and prompts a reevaluation of the set of assumptions informing those fears.

The idea that guns represent male culture and male violence against women makes many cynical about the National Rifle Association (NRA) even when it appears to be attempting to do women some good. For example, Karen

Lehrman, in *The New Republic* (1992, 45), writes: "All this women's lib stuff, though, can't obscure the gun lobby's real agenda—exploiting women's fears of rape. And it's this rhetoric, ironically, that's most in sync with today's feminists." According to antigun folks, women are being "seduced by the NRA's ads" (Rosen 1993, 466) and "targeted by an industry that wants us to join the vigilante crowd" (ibid., 464). Women who shoot are construed as pawns of men—as though women who disagree with certain feminists had simply become naively engrossed in a plot against themselves.

But it's a dirty trick to view the women who interpret the Second Amendment in ways similar to or compatible with *Women and Guns* or the NRA as victims of patriarchal double-dealing. In this way, feminist opponents of guns make *their* opposition a gender issue—as if women who use guns were not thinking for themselves. Lehrman (1992, 45) quotes the NRA booklet "It Can Happen to You" as it suggests, "There is no way of telling a criminal predator by the way he looks. . . . He might be a potential suitor. He might work in a nearby office." Lehrman (ibid.) scolds gun manufacturers for using "feminist code words" as a "marketing strategy." She is so committed to the idea that guns could not be in women's interests that the fact that "the anti–date rape crowd couldn't have said it any better" (ibid.) is only further evidence for her that the NRA is manipulating women.

Critics assume that if the NRA increases its female membership, they must be exploiting women to make money. But that the NRA has never positioned itself as a feminist organization does not mean that feminists cannot make it more accountable to women by educating its members. For instance, if the average male NRA member thinks his wife or daughter will use her gun to shoot strangers then he could be in for a surprise. Claims that women are taking up arms because they have bought into NRA rhetoric obscure the capacities of women to reinterpret specific orthodoxies. Moreover, such claims ignore the fact that guns are one part of a whole host of self-defense activities increasingly popular among women.

We cannot blame or credit NRA advertisements for the entire self-defense movement. Women are increasingly seeking self-defense in many nonlethal forms as well. These programs also gear themselves to women and want to increase their enrollment. Even if the interests of the NRA and the anti–sexual assault movement do not converge, and even if the NRA is manipulating women, the end result may work to women's benefit. Even if the tools are questionable, even if the ideologies are not the same, women might take advantage of the NRA to achieve their ends. Women might also have a distinct contribution to make to firearms culture. For instance, in 1988 Marion Hammer, now NRA president, created Eddie Eagle, the award-winning gun safety program for children.

Organized feminism has turned gun control into a women's issue in part as a response to the NRA's connection of women and firearms. In the 1990s the NRA began an extensive advertising campaign in women's magazines suggesting that women could "choose to refuse to be a victim." They tried in 1988, but the women's magazines refused to run the ads (Maines 1992). As soon as the NRA framed self-defensive pistol packing as a women's issue, Adelle Simmons of the John D. and Catherine T. MacArthur Foundation and Marjorie Benton contacted Betty Friedan with their idea to identify gun control as a women's issue of the 1990s (Rosen 1993, 464). These women organized against "random gun violence" and "drive-by shootings" (ibid.), not rape and woman battering.

For armed self-defense culture, however, opposing random gun violence and supporting women's armed self-defense are not incompatible projects. Quigley (1989) makes clear that guns should be used only by adults who use them safely and lawfully. Her answer to accidental shootings is careful deliberation about whether or not to own a firearm, discussion with one's children about them, safe-handling courses, and practice sessions. The intense fear of guns so common among North American women makes them more likely to take a course to learn to handle them properly. Men might have a false confidence about how to use and handle firearms safely. This is not to say that every female gun owner is careful. But gun instructors believe that an organized culture of shooting institutionalizes professional safe-handling instruction and activities for continued practice shooting, making accidents less likely to occur. For those who are worried that women will acquire a gun and end up on the wrong end of it, the women's armed self-defense movement encourages the training necessary to prevent that circumstance.

In fact, females for firearms see those kinds of worry as a form of paternalism, since, as gun instructor Lyn Bates put it, "the number of cases [of women using guns irresponsibly] are infinitesimal and shrinking with proper training." Still, some may fear that firearms for self-protection will injure children, and hence see women's advocacy of armed self-defense as irresponsible—perhaps particularly so, since mothers are still held more responsible than fathers for their children's welfare. Self-defensers who use weapons note the importance of teaching women safe ways to store guns in their homes. Also, they might point out that the fatal firearms accident rate per capita maintained an all-time low from 1986 to 1993, 0.6 for every 100,000 people in the United States (1,521 occurrences). This is an 82 percent decrease since 1904, when the rate was an all-time high of 3.4 (National Safety Council 1995, 44-45).[1] The National Safety Council (1995, 809) estimates that in 1994 among children under five specifically, the accidental deaths from firearms numbered 50. The accidental deaths from liquid or solid poison[2] numbered 30, from fires 700, from drowning 600, and from choking 180 (ibid., 8-9)—some of the very dangers from which we trust women to protect their children. Among all U.S. children under age fifteen in 1994, the National Safety Council estimates that the number of accidental deaths from firearms was 200, from liquid or solid poison 40, from fires 1,000, from drowning 1,000, and from choking 220 (ibid.).

But feminists for gun control often cite the study that appeared in the *New England Journal of Medicine* to reinforce their point that guns are used more in random accidents than for self-defense. The study concluded that guns kept in homes in King County, Washington, were involved in the death of household members eighteen times more often than in the death of strangers (Kellerman and Reay 1986). This study unwittingly replicated an already seriously criticized study which made similar conclusions in 1975 (Kleck 1991, 127-29). The primary problem with both studies, which should be obvious to feminists who have attempted to dismantle the myth of the stranger assailant, is that they presume that the killing of a member of the household must be accidental rather than self-defensive. Women's self-defensive shootings of their abusers could be counted as evidence of the beneficial effects of gun ownership. Even if the numbers could be determined accurately, a greater number of accidental (or home) gun deaths than self-defensive (or stranger) gun deaths cannot indicate that guns are necessarily used less often in self-defense. This is because not all self-defensive gun uses result in death or even shooting. Assailants wounded by gunshots survive 85 percent of the time (ibid., 116) and the number of attacks that a gun stops without ever being fired is a significant portion: under 40 percent of defensive gun uses actually involve the defender's shooting (ibid., 123-24; Rand 1994).

Though many claim that it is too easy for a U.S. citizen to get a gun, there are those who say that women have a relatively hard time getting guns for self-protection and the legal permits to carry them when their lives have been threatened. One instructor told me about a woman who went to the police department of a major city to get a firearms license and was told, "We don't give permits to broads here." When former editor of *Women and Guns* Sonny Jones set out to purchase a gun some years ago, the man running the gun shop told her, "Lady, you don't need a gun. What you need is a man" (quoted in Draper 1993, 302). Jones also knows that salesmen often try to sell women a .22 or .25 caliber gun: "They're called mouse guns. A woman doesn't want a gun that looks cute. She wants a gun that looks like a gun" (quoted in Maines 1992, 22). Also, the "cooling off" period required in some states before the purchase of a firearm can be a severe disadvantage to, say, a woman who's being stalked by a violent former partner in violation of his restraining order. This is not to say that the regulation of firearms is necessarily bad, but that the dangerous situations in which women might find themselves are not always the result of someone's quick and easy access to a firearm.

Of course guns do not provide automatic security against vulnerability. Owning a gun takes a lot of work, expense, and time. And guns are only useful against certain types of assault, primarily those in a woman's own home or, in states that allow citizens to carry concealed weapons, in parking lots and other such places. Further, they are useful only in states that permit the use of lethal force to stop an assailant from raping or in cases where the woman believes that the assailant might also attempt to kill her. They do not usually protect women from office assault, from roadside assault, from date rape, and so on. This is all the more reason female shooters should be part of an overall women's self-defense movement. Alienating armed women will not encourage wide-ranging self-defense strategies. The gun instructors I spoke with advocate eclectic self-defense tactics. A gun is not the only method of self-defense, but simply part of an overall personal protection strategy. If a gun is a woman's first choice of self-defense instruction, for whatever reason, she is likely to develop a sense of entitlement to avoid victimization which just might spill over into other areas, even if her armed self-defense course does not include such training.

Guns should be a social issue and concern. Both women for "domestic disarmament" (Rosen 1993, 464) and women who arm themselves are fighting for the same thing: freedom from fear and violence. The battle between anti- and pro-gun feminists is waged in a way that gets both groups accused of being too feminine *and* too much like men; being strong minded *and* weak willed; and being self-determining *and* brainwashed by a male-constructed ethic. The level of one's womanhood or of one's feminism is the trump card played by both sides in the debate. A particular set of assumptions within feminism helped frame the debate in these terms.

Many feminists no doubt more readily accept unarmed self-defense, possibly due to the faulty assumption either that a woman's armed self-defense necessarily results in a fatality while a woman's unarmed self-defense necessarily does not, or that a woman's training in firearms does not yield the empowerment effects of training in hand-to-hand combat. But the line separating the acceptable forms of self-defense from the unacceptable fades as feminists acknowledge the presence of weapons in the martial arts, the potential to kill with a knuckle jab to the throat or a heel-palm strike up and down the nose, and that guns used in self-defense do not lead to anyone's death in most cases (Kleck 1991). We are left with a general skepticism which, while often directed at women's use of firearms specifically, leaves a large number of feminists suspicious, apathetic, or dismissive of self-defense more generally. This sentiment stems from a set of assumptions connected, however unconsciously, with a series of traditions within feminism.

The Legacy of Cultural Feminism

Women's espousal of nonviolence *as women* leans on a cultural feminist agenda. A branch of the women's movement in the early 1970s and part of women's activism for a century, cultural feminism insists upon women's distinctiveness and the political importance of that distinctiveness (Echols 1989).[3] Cultural feminists appeal to women's life conditions—such as worrying about one's children during war—to get women to take a more consciously pacifist stand (e.g., Morgan 1989). Contemporary cultural feminists do not necessarily believe in some natural gendered order, in which men are programmed to wage war and women are programmed to clean up after them—although their nineteenth-century counterparts did believe this (Donovan 1992, 62). Instead, cultural feminists rally women politically around things women already "know" by virtue of the conditions of their oppression, specifically an ethics of caring.

Cultural feminists do not write men off so much as they look to women's lifestyle habits, instead of men's, as normative guides for action and social organization. In other words, power has created what we know to be masculinity, not vice versa; similarly, subjugation has created what we know to be femininity, not vice versa. Cultural feminists have not dismissed men's potential to achieve with women a "partnership model society" instead of a "dominator model society" (Eisler 1987). Indeed, they encourage nonviolence not only in terms of its status as "female culture" but in terms of its potential to lead to some sort of androgyny. For instance, Bromley (1982, 154-55) states,

> The history of the "male way" of countering violence with violence points directly to the grave. The nonviolent "female way" of life-giving, nurturing, protecting the young and cooperative labor has pointed to life, all through human existence. . . .
>
> We have all seen evidence of the stirrings of energy in the women's movement. May this energy supply vastly increase, so we may create the means whereby male aggression will be controlled and women's poten-

tial nonviolent power be enhanced, leading to more androgynous, creative individuals.

Bromley desires androgyny, but her description of men's aggression as something that must be *controlled* and women's nonviolent power as something that should be *enhanced* suggests that they are already existing qualities, tendencies that feminists might solidify even while working against them. Those cultural feminist views come dangerously close to the idea that there is a naturally existing "feminine principle" that compliments and balances out the "masculine principle."

Cultural feminists do not criticize femininity but rather its negative valuation. In her 1973 article "Mother Right: A New Feminist Theory," Jane Alpert declared that averting nuclear war and ecological disaster would take a society-wide rejection of the masculine way and a recognition of the feminine way:

> Could it not be that just at the moment that masculinity has brought us to the brink of nuclear destruction or ecological suicide, women are beginning to rise in response to the Mother's call to save Her planet and create instead the next stage of evolution? Can our revolution mean anything else than the reversion of social and economic control to Her representatives among Womankind, and the resumption of Her worship on the face of the Earth? (Alpert 1973, 94)

Attempts to increase women's political participation and elevate their political status on the grounds that women have better, or special, insights have a long history. For instance, while men tried to use women's status as delicate to justify their inability to vote (as though the vapors in the voting booth would bowl women over), some women countered by saying that women's moral superiority over men should be expressed through voting.

Making guns (or the violence done with them) something women should control actually reinforces their social position as peaceful and nurturing lifesavers. This social position is affirmed by antigun folks themselves: "But it is the women, from grassroots neighborhood groups to the PTA to NOW, who are the best organized constituency in American civil society. As Eleanor Roosevelt used to say when a problem seemed intractable, 'Let the women do it'" (Rosen 1993, 465). As another antigun activist put it: "The possibility that excited me the most is that gun control might become another area in this century where women act as our national conscience" (quoted in ibid., 466). This sentiment stems from an assumption that women should temper male vice, not participate in it.

But North American feminism's legacy of positioning women as morally superior pacifists, the custodians of all life (Donovan 1992, 31-57), can only provide limited gains. Although it seems important to value "women's culture" and the contributions women have made, even while politically subordinated, to the overall good of the community (instead of evaluating women with a male-centered standard), such a framework simultaneously relegates women to virtues that help sustain their subordination. Specifically, the ideology of women's nurturance, giving freely and expecting nothing from others, has confined women to relationships that are unsatisfying and even abusive. Further, the logic used to legitimize women's voting rights failed to support the advancement of women of color—for they were not considered delicate or morally superior by the white men deciding whether or not to grant the vote. Moreover, that logic still could not legitimize any woman's entrance into other important male-dominated spheres.

Cultural feminism tends to set up a falsely universal "woman." Its Goddesses, disempowered angels, and protesting mothers mostly reflect the historical conditions of white women in particular. The "feminine grace" that women were supposed to maintain by staying out of public politics was a grace reserved only for privileged, heterosexual white women. Women of color were not granted that grace in our racist society; they commonly had to do work outside of their own homes, often in the homes of those virtuous white ladies. This ideology, then, even when turned around to support women's rights, still left out women of color (Davis 1983). Sojourner Truth's famous speech in favor of voting rights for blacks and women throws into sharp relief the racist double standard for femininity. She countered the argument that women would succumb to the vapors in a voting booth by reminding people that black women are expected to do back-breaking work, beseeching, "And aren't I a woman?" (White 1985). While white women were expected to need help getting into carriages, black women barely counted as women at all.

Cultural feminism continues not only racist assumptions, but heterosexist ones as well. Lesbian feminist culture in the 1970s upheld the cultural feminist notion that women's relationships escaped male-defined norms such as hierarchy and violence. However, as I noted in chapter 1, and as numerous lesbian feminists have noted since the 1970s, the designation of women as nonviolent is often couched in an ideology of heterosexual virtue and has functioned as an obstacle to women's freedom (Allen 1986, 35). Women fighting heterosexism must break from the construction of womanhood as the peaceful ally of male violence.

A number of right-wing women actually support war with the very same heterosexist ideology—supporting war supports their men and their families, and upholds men's status as protectors of women and children (which explains why right wing-women oppose women in the fighting ranks of the military). Since there is a nationalist investment in heterosexual femininity, supporting gender difference does not necessarily oppose war. Cultural feminists may not agree with most of the views of right-wing women, indeed they reject all violence, including rape and nationalist violence against innocent countries. But their rejection of all violence leaves no room for women's self-defensive violence.

Whether as political strategy or theory of gendered differences in aggression, the "separate styles" approach central to the cultural feminist project might well be abandoned. Anne Campbell (1993, 55-56) upholds the separate-styles position: "For men, to be at the mercy of another person, whether physically or symbolically, is to be denied respect; and without respect there can be no self-esteem. Thus men aggress to prove to others (and so to themselves) that they merit respect. . . . The anger they feel is at the impertinence of another person's attempt to devalue or humiliate them. Unlike women's anger, it is about redressing social standing, not about catharsis." I have shown that the self-defense movement reveals that if there are gendered patterns in aggression, it is that many women feel less entitled to respect and to reinforcing that respect than most men; if there is any ethical issue to address, it is not the pros and cons of an expressive versus an instrumental style of violence—as if women aggressed only when so furious they exploded and men only when denied respect—but the gendered patterns in entitlement to self-respect, and the very real conflicts of interests men and women sometimes display.

We should address the conflict between a man's sense that a woman's refusal of sex is an offense to his social standing and a woman's sense that a man's attempt to force her into sex is an offense to her social standing. We share a cultural legacy in which it was deemed reasonable and legal for a man to kill an unfaithful wife and her lover if he caught them in the act. This same culture has suggested that a woman's killing someone to save her own life in her own home, if the person she kills is her partner or ex-partner (and it often is), is immoral and unreasonable. Feminism is about women's right to feel the same kind of mastery over their social environments as men, and the same right to defend threats to pride, dignity, and that environment.

Many have challenged the power-averse approach in feminism with regard to sexual relations, emphasizing difference among women's sexual styles and the impossibility of having "power-free" sexuality. But worries about aggression carry on cultural feminism's power-averse legacy. Cultural feminists might say they are not averse to power per se, but rather to "power over" in favor of "power with." What in principle seems like a great idea, however, winds up ignoring the real-life conflicts. What counts as "power with" to one person feels like "power over" to another. This dynamic is fairly clear when we consider women's violent self-defense. First, it is a case of using violence against violence. Many people would not have a problem with anyone's right to do this. But when we consider that the male assailant might not experience a woman's violence against him as justifiable self-defense, especially if he does not even understand his own actions as aggressive or "power over," we can see how there are competing definitions of reality, competing visions over what counts as appropriate interaction in public and private.

The Wake of the Sex Wars

The construction of women as sexually passive and men as sexually dangerous is another, related legacy of cultural feminism. First-wave feminism a century ago not only embraced women's special moral virtues but also positioned men's sexuality as belligerent and competitive (Echols 1989). In focusing on the dangerous aspects of men's sexuality—whether or not it is now conceptualized as socially constructed—contemporary feminists have perpetuated an association between masculine sexuality and pleasure on the one hand, and feminine sexuality and danger on the other. Radical feminists in the anti–sexual assault movement have continued this to some extent, while some "pro-sex" feminists have challenged this association, arguing that women can take pleasure in sexuality, and even in the dangerous things that are supposed to be unpleasurable. Both radical and cultural feminists of the 1970s attempted to make their sexual practices conform to their vision of a power-free world. Some even suggested that sex with men was bound to be hierarchical, and envisioned lesbianism as a personal model of equality and cooperation (ibid.). This perspective, however, wrongly construed women's heterosexual experiences as always terrifying and lesbian experiences as wholesome.

For women, sexuality has been both repressive and dangerous as well as pleasurable and exciting. Too much focus on women's sexual victimization ignores women's experience with sexual agency and, some suggest, increases the sexual terror in which women live (Vance 1989, 1). By the late 1970s, some feminists began to embrace forms of sexual expression that had been deemed forms of "false consciousness," for instance, sadomasochistic sex or bisexuality (Echols 1989, 291). The anticensorship or pro-sex feminists tried to gain support for feminism not by denying differences among women, but by emphasizing them. Thus the pro-sex feminists have urged women to speak as powerfully in favor of sexual pleasure as they do against sexual danger. In doing so, women might break through stereotypes of women as naturally passive, essentially different from men in erotic styles and preferences, and thus challenge some of the very myths that perpetuate sexual violence.

Kirsten Marthe Lentz (1993) links the debates about women with guns to the sex wars and specifically feminist debates about pornography. In these debates, the meaning of womanhood shifted. Anti-antiporn or pro-sex feminists challenged the victimized subject of the antiporn group, and favored the pleasure-in-danger rather than the pleasure-versus-danger framework. Lentz (ibid., 396) notes that both discourses explore masculine vice (porn/guns and violence) and both discourses establish a pleasurable "outlaw" status for women: The rebel has agency in the form of sexual (porn) power or lethal (guns) power. But ultimately Lentz (ibid., 395) criticizes women's armed self-defense because, she insists, it is too similar to cultural feminism and antiporn sentiment (which she, however erroneously, equates):

> The only major departure in the representational system of *Women &
> Guns* from the cultural feminist, anti-porn discourse would be the repre-
> sentation of *women*. While the anti-porn discourse presents women as
> thoroughly dominated victims, the rhetoric of *Women & Guns* most cer-
> tainly does not. . . . Her gun makes her a non-victim.

I suggest that this is no minor departure.

Lentz (ibid.) is skeptical of women's armed self-defense because she thinks it shares the hidden discursive commitments of an antiporn, antisex feminism (which she assumes construed men as inherently dangerous and women as inherently vulnerable). Antiporn feminists were primarily criticized for putting women in the position of victims of dangerous men. The appropriation of "male" violence makes women's gun use very different from antiporn feminism, at least as it has been construed by its opposition. Cultural feminists and antiporn feminists (Lentz collapses these two positions) were criticized for representing women as good, wholesome, sexually innocent, and on this basis politically insightful.

But perhaps Lentz is more concerned that the positioning of rape among self-defensers makes them more like the asexual victims of antiporn discourse. Women's armed self-defense rhetoric, as Lentz reads it through *Women and Guns* magazine and Quigley's *Armed and Female*, turns rape into the ultimate terrible crime one must prevent from occurring. In this way, self-defense might depoliticize rape and sexuality, "producing new articulations of the problem of women as victims and men as rapists/victimizers" (ibid.). But self-defense need not depoliticize rape. In fact, unlike much of the anti–sexual assault movement proper, the self-defense movement denaturalizes rape without naturalizing sex. By treating men's coercive violence as interactional strategies that need not succeed, self-defense undermines the notion of men as physically indestructible and women as vulnerable—a central component of the naturalized sex binarism. Rather than assuming that the female body is a sexualized violable inner space, self-defense aggressively refuses an attacker's attempt to make female bodies into things to be taken (Marcus 1992). Moreover, self-defense practices need not desexualize women. By harnessing women's aggressive desire to be treated with respect in matters of sexuality and sexual congresses, self-defense construes women as sexual agents in the fullest sense.

In the popular imagination, as well as in much feminist rhetoric, women are construed as either consenting to or refusing sex—but not as active sexual agents: "The feminine part is to consent or to refuse (to be taken) rather than to desire or will (to take)" (Rooney 1983, 1273). Feminists have long posed the question, How free can a woman's consent to sex be if the man might have simply raped her had she refused? In other words, how free can a *yes* be if *no* would not have been respected? When women in self-defense classes learn to speak their sexual desires, assert *nos* forcefully and prepare to defend them aggressively, they are also taking themselves seriously as sexual beings.

Self-defense makes possible the view of women not as passive but instead as active desiring subjects. This helps remove women from the impossible place of innocence in which they can only forcefully claim their victimhood, when victimized, via a notion of female asexual innocence. Self-defense allows women to be pro-sex and antirape simultaneously. Thus Lentz's (1993) cynicism about women's armed self-defense as an antiporn, antisex feminism is, in my view, unwarranted.

Embracing women's sexual agency breaks down the oppositional associations between white women and women of color, associations that have sustained each other for the maintenance of white women's privilege. White women cease to be the sexually protected and prized ones, and women of color, whose status in the racist imagination as sexually disrespectable helps to solidify white women's status (in much the same way that women's status as physically incompetent helps to solidify men's status as physically powerful), cease to be the social "others" of white women.

Antiviolence feminists who are cynical about women's gun use or violence more generally seem wedded to a *purity* of their own—a moral, political and theoretical purity that comes from refusing to own a gun and being willing to harm one's attacker. This kind of purity has its own problems, namely the perpetuation of an elitist and racist bias in feminism. Veena Cabreros-Sud (1995) suggests that it is white women who benefit from feminism's stance of political and theoretical purity. The racism endemic to the construction of womanhood as pure and passive, and to the concomitant reluctance to embrace violent resistance, is obvious to Cabreros-Sud (ibid., 44), who finds that, upon recounting some of her "choice violent moments," most white feminists

> are appalled, morally repelled by this unbecoming behavior. One even giggled, holding her breast bone ever so lightly and saying she is a non-violent type, blah blah blah. The messages are, on the surface, (1) I'm educated and you're not, (2) I'm upper class and you're not, and (3) I'm a feminist and you're not (since her brand of feminism is equated with nonviolent moon-to-uterus symbiosis).

I have already suggested that white women, not women of color, have benefited from feminism's moral purity stance. Still, it is possible that women of color cannot afford to engage in the "impurity" of self-defense politics, as it could exacerbate the very associations they have fought against, namely the associations between people of color and violence and impurity (hooks 1992, 160). On the other hand, Cabreros-Sud (1995, 46) worries more about the fear of embracing violent resistance on the part of "the ivory tower debutantes," positioning herself affirmingly in the category of "the alternately poor, colored, Third World, loud, violent, nasty girls."

Thus, even if self-defense training feels particularly subversive for white women whose race privilege and gender subordination have historically been based on their status as sexually pure and weak, self-defense politics might be more accountable to women of color than cultural feminism's antiviolence. When women are represented as, or encouraged to be, very different from men, gender becomes falsely construed as the only form of oppression. Instead of a politics that presumes that women should keep away from everything men do, self-defense blurs the boundaries of masculine and feminine. In so doing, self-defense deconstructs the essentialized and racist notion of "womanhood."

Embracing women's lack of innocence might make white women take more responsibility for the ways in which they oppress women and men of color, and make heterosexual women of any race take more responsibility for the ways in which they perpetuate discrimination against gays and lesbians. As Jane Flax (1990, 181–82) points out, "We need to avoid seeing women as totally innocent, acted upon beings. Such a view prevents us from seeing the areas of life in which women have had an effect, are not totally determined by the will of the other, and the ways in which some women have and do exert power over others." Cabreros-Sud (1995, 45) states that the form of feminism that we might call "innocence feminism" implies "that one's own collaboration with mass-approved violence—i.e., institutional racism, First World nationalism, and apathetic complacency—doesn't count." Thus, the disposition of feminine purity cultivated among white women, and the concomitant political stance of pacifism, might be dismantled for a better, more strongly antiracist feminism that doesn't let white women off the hook for the atrocities they've supported.

Of course, this itself attempts to cleanse feminism of a set of impurities with which, say, cultural feminists against guns are willing to live. In the former case, expunging gender categories as a way to deal with the problem of violence (risking that violence will remain) is preferred over a cultural feminist use of these categories to get rid of violence (risking that gender and race inequalities will remain). The question may come down to which strategy seems to reduce the violence we already face. For many, the issue amounts to a mathematical equation: Violence plus violence equals more violence.

Increasing Violence

Closely related to the worry that women's indulgence in masculine vices will hinder, not help, the transformation of society is the fear that all these images and practices of women's aggression, especially women's gun ownership, will simply make the world an even more violent place. This sentiment is echoed in debates about women taking up combat positions in the military. For instance, Milt Levin (1990, B11) wrote to the *Los Angeles Times* declaring that training women for combat actually helps condition us to accept war as a way of life: "Sending women, the future mothers of our country, to war is criminal. Sending women into combat is uncivilized and insane. Let's keep our women feminine, genteel, kind and lovable." Like cultural feminist arguments, worries that the world will get more violent position women as the group who is responsible for world peace and moral order.

Some people think equal opportunities for good as well as for vices will create more female serial killers and dead husbands. No statistical evidence to date supports this concern. A closer ratio of women to men commit spousal homicide (although women more often than men kill spouses in self-defense) in the United States than in Canada or Great Britain (Wilson and Daly 1992). This might be regarded as evidence that the diminution of traditional sex roles leads women to murder with almost as great a frequency as men. But if this were true, the ratio of women to men nonspousal familial murderers would be just as high, which is not the case (ibid., 194-96). The greater availability of guns in the United States might be regarded as a cause of the greater sex ratio of spousal homicide. However, research reveals that the relatively small gap in husband and wife victims in the United States predates the contemporary prevalence of gun killings (ibid., 193). Further, the sex ratio of spousal homicide is not greater for shootings than for other homicides; in fact, it is lower, revealing that "gun use is still predominantly the province of men and that women's lethality relative to that of men is actually greater when cases involving guns are excluded" (ibid., 193). Others think that women's style of killing may come to resemble men's, but this is also speculation unsupported by any statistical data.

It would be dangerous and simplistic to assign feminism responsibility for female murderers. Worries that women's self-defense will only make the world a more violent place ignore (or take for granted as natural) the men's violence that women's self-defensive violence could prevent. Besides, women's ability to violently defend themselves might not increase men's violence but deter it by instilling in men a fear of immediate negative consequences.

Some might fear that women's increased empowerment through self-defense will spur men to step up the level of violence or the number of weapons with which they assault women, creating not a deterrent effect on men's violence but a "backlash" against women who are encroaching on men's privilege. I have attempted to convey a subtler picture of power relations and of masculinity than that which underlies this suggestion. In chapter 1, I argued that rape does not necessarily proceed by way of violent or oppressive intention. I argued that not all men who rape "intend" to gain power over women with their actions, although their actions accomplish just that. The conspiratorial view that men are intentionally trying to control women is too simplistic. Men assault women because women are easy targets, and they often get away with it because of the gender ideology that construes women as sexually passive and pacifist.

For the men who rape their dates with carefully constructed fanciful notions of their dates' consent—the imperceptive rapists who do not think that they are doing anything wrong—knowing that women are likely to stop them aggressively is not likely to have a deterrent effect. In this case, though, a woman's ability to defend herself from such a man is still likely to stop him from completing the attack, thus interrupting the very imperceptiveness with which he attacked. Felson's (1996, 444) research indicates that one's perception of the physical power of one's opponent does not affect one's likelihood to engage in an armed attack, although it does affect the likelihood that one would engage in an unarmed attack. This suggests that we might see men attack women less, not more often or more often with weapons.

One social program showed that women's readiness to fight back deters assailants; it trained female citizens of Orlando, Florida, in the use of firearms and publicized this training widely. The program was studied for its effect on crime. As Kleck (1991, 134) reports, between 1966 and 1967, the Orlando Police Department gave 2,500 women defensive handgun training. The rape rate decreased by 88 percent in 1967, compared to 1966, a decrease far larger than in any previous one-year period. (The rape rate was constant in the rest of Florida and the United States.) Still, crime may well have been displaced onto areas outside Orlando, where women were still known to be sitting ducks. While five years after the program the rape rate was 13 percent below the pre-program level in Orlando, it had increased 300 percent in the immediate area around Orlando (Kates 1989, 12). This suggests that the deterrent effect of women's self-defense is substantial, but would have to be taken up in every city to actually deter assailants altogether.

On another level, it is possible that if men see women as capable of fighting, then those men whose restraint is simply based on manly fight etiquette, which suggests that a proper fighter not pick on a weaker target (Campbell 1993, 60-61), may no longer have reason to see women as inappropriate targets for violence. But then, if the self-defense movement subverts the idea that there is a "weaker sex" and in so doing makes a woman seem as likely a target for aggression, it makes her as unlikely a target for aggression for the same reason. If this occurred, we might still live in a violent world, but one in which we would have to debate how to control specific types of violence rather than policing the borders of manhood and womanhood.

Aggression As Unvaryingly Dangerous

Another reason leading feminists to dismiss women's aggressive self-defense as ineffective masculinist influence has to do with the way feminists have structured aggression itself. Cultural feminists have been power-averse and have sought practices that oppose "male" ways of doing things. If aggression is seen as corrupt and unvaryingly dangerous, then women's cultivation of it must be ignoble.

In her advice to battered women based on her study of several hundred of them, Bowker (1986, 28) notes that counterviolence, or threats of it, did work to reduce men's violence when the husbands were convinced that their wives were serious. For instance, when the women would point out that they could kill their husbands while they were sleeping, and the husbands genuinely feared the homicidal threats, "the threats shocked them into realizing the seriousness of their own behavior, or they came to 'respect' their wives more for having fought back" (ibid.). But rather than present this as evidence that women should (effectively, strongly) fight back, she continues on a cautionary note: "Gaining your husband's respect by engaging in behavior that is valued in the world of macho men *lowers you to his moral level instead of raising him to your moral level*" (ibid., my emphasis). Bowker reminds women that her study showed that *ineffective* resistance did not work to stop men's violence and cautions them not to take chances that would result in even more severe beatings. However, the author does not point out what kinds of counterviolence tactics do work or what kinds of strategies women can successfully employ. Nor does the author acknowledge that her study is skewed by its focus on women who stayed in violent relationships instead of exiting (by whatever means).[4]

In order to draw public attention to the oppression of women, which is not always located on the body, feminists described nonbodily forms of oppression as "violent." Thus feminist politics have construed *violence* to mean *oppressive* or *diminishing*—hence some feminists' claims that leers and patronizing jokes are cases of violence, and hence feminist trepidation about women's participation in violent sports such as rugby, even though the effects of the violence on individual participants and on society may not be degrading or oppressive (Liddle 1989, 766). Such a framework has backed feminists into a corner: It leaves out the possibility of legitimate or nonoppressive violence, notably women's self-defensive violence (ibid.), and subtly requires damaged, violated bodies to substantiate claims that women are oppressed. The moral meaning assigned to various violent acts must be questioned, so that women who kill to protect their own jeopardized lives are not considered bad but in fact exercising their right to self-defense. Women who defend themselves would, of course, prefer not to need to. Women are oppressed because they are targeted for abuse, whether or not they successfully fend it off.

When it comes to women engaging in combat, some feminists, like many others, have a problem. After all, how will the feminist critique of masculinity or patriarchy survive if women actually start to identify with the very pleasures we have defined as the problem? If self-defense is taken up with seriousness, as a necessary evil, then it might be tolerable to feminists. But if self-defense spills over into new arenas, like competitive combat shooting or amateur boxing, then women are finding something pleasurable in combat. What makes some feminists uneasy is *the pleasurable nature of the combat*. Violence is always bad, so women should not enjoy it and feminists should not advocate it. If women were learning combat but did not enjoy it, then it might be tolerable to feminists. Feminists are skeptical of popular pleasures, and women's fun might mean women getting duped. This is connected with an assumption that our political work should be serious; if it's pleasurable then we are not taking violence seriously, and/or we are more likely to be co-opted. "Getting mean" is fun; in class, some self-defensers even "need a mugging."

While some feminists disputed women's exclusion from domains defined as male, such as sports, and helped create laws (such as Title IX) that would increase gender equality in those areas, others simultaneously critiqued the enjoyment of those competitive sports as "masculinist." Some argue that sports should be open to women and that women joining these sports are not "becoming (just like) men," because women play sports for the feelings of physical competence, playfulness, and pleasures of developing bodily skills. But if women enjoy a sport for the same reasons that feminists and masculinity theorists (e.g., Messner 1990) have chastised men for enjoying sports (i.e., the pleasure of domination and combat), then, some might fear, a critique of masculinity will not be sustained.

However, women might not engage in martial arts, self-defense, or firearms ownership the way men have. Although sports have emphasized masculinity, and thus have been competitive, aggressive, enemy-oriented, and so on, women may find camaraderie, physical self-love, fun, and cooperation as much as the other things. As one gun student told me, women will not necessarily perpetuate the system as is. A boxing instructor told me that she enjoys the aggressive combat of boxing but rejects the stereotype that boxing is violent or implies that one is a violent (i.e., exceptionally masculinized) person.

Women's self-defense has an impact similar to women's sports, but it is potentially more radical. While female athletes are physical, self-defense draws women, many of whom are not athletic, because of a problem connected with male domination. Women's self-defense could downplay feminist leanings as easily as women's athletic programs have in order to gain respectability (Searles and Berger 1987, 78). Yet women's self-defense training poses more of a threat than women's athletics because it cannot as easily be framed as an activity that involves physical and natural skills (Clarke and Clarke 1982, 63).

Simply advocating "nonviolence" is pointless, especially for feminists. Feminists who advocate a woman's right to legal abortions are accused routinely of violence by those who consider abortion murder. What matters is how we define the action and the context. The use of violence implies boundaries. Simone de Beauvoir (1952, 369–70) wrote that "violence is the authentic proof of each one's loyalty to himself, to his will. . . . It is a profound frustration not to be able to register one's feelings upon the face of the world." Lakeland and Wolf (1980, 13) write: "We must reclaim for ourselves all human potentials, including those unduly established as masculine, that is, those monopolized by men in order to enslave us more thoroughly. . . . For instance, violence: it's up to us to choose its form and its goals."

If women abdicate violence without being capable of it anyhow, it makes less of an impact than if that abdication were a real choice. Stiehm (1982, 376) notes that "much 'successful nonviolence' is related to having (1) a potential for violence to renounce or (2) having someone else use or threaten force for one." Having the capacity for violence does not mean one will act manipulatively or violently. Just as male martial arts experts are often known to be as gentle, polite, and discerning in matters of conflict on the streets as they are rough and ruthless in the dojo, women with the capacity for violence are not likely to start attacking innocents, picking fights, or verbally abusing.

If women's self-defense helps women gain some of the protective powers that men and the state have monopolized, thereby removing women from the class of "the protected" (ibid.), then women of color, who have been the victims of violence not only by men but by the police (e.g., harassment, threats of deportation, trivialization of their complaints, and assault) (Matthews 1994, 151), might be at least as liberated by a framework that dissociates men and the state from the class of "protectors" and "defenders." After all, even if white women begin to realize (experientially or through the claims of feminists) that the men who are supposed to be protecting them are frequently the ones assailing them, white women are still relatively likely to believe that the police will help them in a time of crisis (ibid.). Further, self-defense weakens the heterosexist assumption that man and woman are a natural pair that functions together in a protector-protected relationship.

If aggression is seen as a chaotic force that rips the social fabric (Gilmore 1987) then women—the ones assigned by tradition to maintain the harmony of relationships and the dignity of society—who are aggressive appear as an extremely dangerous and perhaps even irresponsible lot. In this light, self-defense culture can clearly appreciate its potential for drama and catharsis, and even find pleasure in these dramatic interventions.[5] In thinking of aggression as sometimes appropriate, self-defensers, and anyone who advocates the use of handguns for self-defense, must carefully consider when and under what circumstances lethal force is appropriate. But we might do better to argue over what types of self-protective violence should be legal and appropriate in ways that do not position women as the ones responsible for maintaining the moral order.

Co-optation

Another area of discomfort for feminism is closely related to the assumption that violence is always oppressive and therefore bad. Feminism's revolutionary overtones, in which we imagine the postrevolutionary world as peaceful, nonviolent, harmonious, and power-free, requires us to imagine a complete change in the "masculinist" way things are done. The significant view behind established feminist politics is represented in the oft-quoted statement of Audre Lorde (1984, 112): "For the master's tools will never dismantle the master's house."

Feminists' revolutionary strategy made central concerns about how consciousness develops and how it is acted upon reality (Donovan 1992, 87). It emphasizes the integrity of the process of change, insisting that the process is part of the change: "The end cannot fully justify the means. To a surprising extent, the end *is* the means" (Steinem, quoted in ibid.). This classic social anarchist theory places primacy on the idea that not only should the postrevolutionary world be power-free and nonviolent but so too should the actual process of revolution. Some contemporary feminists, including socialist feminists, believe that women's culture, experience, and practice can provide the basis for feminist opposition to destructive patriarchal ideologies (ibid., 87–89). The assumptions of cultural feminism are also at work here—that some things are "his ways" and other things are "our ways."

Those who do not want to accuse women of being like men accuse women of being dupes of men. In this logic, if guns are "boy toys" then so are the women who use them. Those committed to a cause tend to understand those who do not agree with them as not acting consciously (e.g., Jones 1994). If anti-gun feminists who are invested in seeing guns as a gender issue, a "man problem," can simply say that women who shoot or do anything that is traditionally masculine are not engaged in conscious action, then they can explain away their ideological opponents as foolish.

Wolf (1993, 44) suggests that women who reject the feminist label find more appealing the Nike corporation's slogan, "Just Do It." Although feminists may be skeptical of the corporatization of grass-roots feminist politics, Nike has captured something appealing: Self-reliance, physicality, competition, winning, and strength. It is just this appeal that renders women's pleasurable resistance vulnerable to capitalist co-optation.

Feminism's revolutionary overtones makes the concern over co-optation particularly acute. Feminist cultural critics have suggested that even practices that seem to disrupt the conventional bodily codes of sexual difference or challenge the passivity of the female body (athletics, for instance) become recuperated by a capitalist system that profits from those progressive body projects, thereby maintaining the female body as a commodity, and a fetishized, eroticized one at that—even in a pair of Nikes.

But it is true that women's popular pleasures take place in a complex social setting of consumer capitalism, sexism, racism, and heterosexism. The recent proliferation of visual representations of tough women in advertisements for self-defense products and instruction often still eroticize women. For instance, an NRA advertisement featured a muscle-bound woman in a bikini with a gun. Tough woman images have appeared in advertisements for products not related to self-defense. For example, an advertisement for Caffeine Free Diet Coke depicts a woman boxer coolly knocking out one conceited male wanna-be victor after another. Revlon's mascara advertisement boasts "knockout lashes" and features Sugar Ray Leonard and five top female models holding fists in boxing gloves up in fighting stance.

Feminist cultural critics concerned with capitalism, co-optation, sexual objectification, and beauty standards might worry that the tough woman will simply become the new sex object, and that strength and self-defense training will contribute to a new, even stricter, beauty standard forced on women. Capitalism, as it has perpetuated women's subordination, becomes the object of feminist skepticism no matter what. Even the rewarding aspects like competition and winning (at least in the context of sports), which might help women in this culture, are scorned. The possibility of capitalist co-optation can hardly constitute a reason not to embrace self-defense. For capitalism has too long fueled women's inability to fight.

Worries about who's buying into whose value system presume that there is some social, political, or theoretical location from which women can renounce all that is masculinist, racist, or capitalist. But we cannot escape the values that have dominated our social institutions. Further, certain activities seem to reflect such values only because men currently engage in them. We have invested so much energy in critiquing the mistakes of male dominant culture that we have neglected to elaborate alternative forms of female subjectivity. Some would say that women's entrance into violence cannot be a new form of subjectivity, because it is male. Yet women's pacifism is not a new form of subjectivity; it is simply not-male in a patriarchal context that defines man as aggressive. We must have a new form of female subjectivity while still stressing a new vision of subjectivity at large (Braidotti 1994, 161).

We must also ask if women of color will benefit or lose from the new visual representations of (primarily) white female heroism. A greater diversity of women in heroic roles might enable more women to identify with the heroism. Women's emancipatory activities cannot escape the capitalist context. The racism of Hollywood, which puts white actors in most of the choice roles, does not indicate that racism is endemic to images of tough women or to women's self-defense in particular. The racism is not peculiar to women's self-defense, therefore it is not self-defense per se that is racist or that demands representation in racist ways.

State co-optation might also concern skeptics of self-defense. Attempts to change structures that obviously need to be changed could wind up reinforcing those structures. Several feminist scholars have noted the complexity of feminist activists' involvement with the state. State engagement is risky. Feminist intentions on the part of those who receive state funding does not guarantee that the work contributes to women's liberation (see, e.g., Matthews 1994; Reinelt 1995). After all, the rape crisis movement had to emphasize rape as violent in order to get state funding, a strategy that inadvertently solidified the sex-is-natural-and-good assumption. This definition transformed the feminist rape crisis movement into yet another state agency with professional demands, qualification/certification requirements, and various state controls (Matthews 1994, 149-66). The movements against rape and battery that have attracted funding and the attention of NOW have been co-opted in some ways.

Self-defense, even when developed in a capitalist context, is one practice that does not legitimate state interventions in our everyday lives. On the contrary, self-defense makes possible women's self-sufficiency in this particular regard. To some extent, the informal, grassroots character of self-defense has helped it remain a radical project (Searles and Berger 1987, 69). This makes it vulnerable in different ways, however. Specifically, Searles and Berger's (ibid.) case-history study of one self-defense organization shows that the trademark feminist principles of grassroots organizing—namely, a democratic structure, heavy reliance on the volunteered time of committed activists, and availability to as many women for as little cost as possible—caused increasing tensions and troubles for the maintenance and expansion of the organization. The financial and time commitments required to teach women's self-defense caused committed instructors to give up teaching. As a last resort, the organization changed into a private, for-profit business, causing many feminists involved to resent the certification requirements, licensing fees and agreements, and so on, and ultimately to disengage from the organization. In this light, whether or not women's self-defense should be private or government-funded is questionable.

Feminists have inadvertently pushed women, as oppressed people, to be pure victims whose awareness is clear (at least after a few standard consciousness-raising sessions) and whose actions are clean. But we can't strive for violence-free ideals when we are victimized by violence. Moreover, a nonviolent stance in feminist politics ignores the ways in which power is not simply restrictive or repressive but also productive, capable of generating new forms of pleasure and new identities and positions from which to resist the status quo (Woodhull 1988).

A notion of progress that views humanity locked onto some guided path toward collective self-realization is philosophically naive and politically short-sighted. Further, power is not centralized, existing solely as a repressive force deployed by the state or by men as a class. Power is decentralized, which means that transforming social relations will not necessarily proceed by way of revolution but by changes at the everyday mundane level (Foucault 1970). We might abandon the vision of a centralized power that will be overturned by revolutionary change and admit that history proceeds differently, where fights are never over, and violence and exclusions are inevitable. Feminists could change the rules and change what counts as deviant, and feminism could offer a different ethic—for example, one in which men's sexual violence would be marginalized instead of normalized.

We should be attuned to the ways in which opposition to violence harms women presently in danger, ignores women's pleasure in it, makes too little of men's fear of it, and plays into Victorian notions of morally superior womanhood—an ideology that justified white women's class and racial privilege, and men's privilege to vote, speak, write, and edify themselves. Many of the women I spoke with told me that they wished that we lived in a world without violence or guns. But, they would add, we do not, and they must contend with the reality in which we do live. We need to risk co-optation and risk appearing as if we supported masculinist values. Self-defense and the feminism behind it go beyond a moral position of critique and constitute a force for institutional change.

The rejection of "ideologically pure baby steps" in favor of "practical giant steps" is what Naomi Wolf calls "power feminism" (Wolf 1993, 53). Her power feminism is not an agenda, much less one like the NRA's Refuse to Be a Victim program; nor is power feminism a politics that denies women are victimized, systematically. Power feminism discards the impossible perfect-and-powerless stance in favor of making compromises to use power for social change.

While Wolf (ibid., 136) carefully distinguishes herself from popular antifeminist feminists like Katie Roiphe and Camille Paglia, she claims that one of the "real differences in power" between men and women that Roiphe should not ignore is "physical strength." Wolf (ibid., 216-20, 314-15) claims that she wants to benefit from the fear that women's increased gun use or other training might inspire in men, but she does not rock the feminist boat by going so far as to embrace women's self-defense as part of her power feminist agenda. Wolf's reluctance to organize women to fight back physically shows the extent to which the opposition to violence, without deconstructing the sexist discourse of bodies, has become a central axis around which feminist politics revolve. Still, what she suggests can help frame women's self-defense.

Physicality and Bodily Discipline

Another overarching assumption that has kept feminists from embracing self-defense as a feminist project involves the place of the body in feminism. It's not that feminists have ignored the body. Whether it's reproductive rights, beauty culture, pornography, eating disorders, alternative sexualities, or sexual violence, a large portion of feminist activism and theorizing concerns the body and its control, representation, discipline, or violation. But ironically, it is just this way of looking at the body that has rendered the body work of self-defense irrelevant and even suspect in much feminist theory and activism. Of course, it would seem that self-defense would fit right into feminists' fights for bodily autonomy and independence from male "protection." Certainly it does for some; yet under the prevailing political framework, we cannot as easily imagine the female body as an agent for social change. Further, women's body issues are so highly charged that some fear any body work that women do will inevitably lead to either an oppressive bodily discipline, a naive way of construing why and how a woman has a right to bodily integrity, or an uncritical privileging of sexuality as a natural essence that defines who we are.

If feminists have been skeptical of women's interest in strength training, or the intensive commitment and bodily mastery required to succeed in boxing or the martial arts, then it is perhaps because they fear that this kind of regime construes the body as a tool requiring intensive discipline and training (in this case, if not for beauty then for self-defense). On the basis of their reading of Foucault, some feminists may be skeptical of the discipline women subject themselves to in order to get in shape, practice martial arts, and so forth—as though all discipline subordinated them.

But Foucault claimed not that discipline is oppression to be eradicated through resistance but rather that discipline is a possible procedure of power (in Rabinow 1984, 380). Not all relations of discipline are necessarily relations of domination. There can be consensual disciplines (in ibid.). Certainly the pride

that women find in their control over finely tuned bodies can exhibit the liberal values of self-proprietorship, which many feminists criticize as masculinist,
for example in the female athletic revolution (see Twin 1979). (I argue in the
next sections that the meaning of *self-proprietorship* changes when women claim
its entitlements.) Feminists have suggested that women's physical activities,
even if seemingly empowering, still connect their self-worth to body management (Cole 1994, 16). Feminists have worked against the shaping of women's
bodies to the figurative ideal, and want to have "real" bodies.

The problem is that all "real" bodies are to some extent imaginary constructions (Gatens 1996). We all have to have some fantasized definition of the
body—there is no "real" body underneath the fantasized image of the body.
This is not to say that a woman can think herself out of breast cancer, but it is
to say that we must always have an idea of the body when we deploy it or constrain it along certain dimensions. From this vantage point, boxing and karate
are no more, and no less, disciplinary than yoga or dancing. A cultural form of
body that results through gun use or martial arts training is no less "natural" than
any other more common cultural forms of bodily comportment women might
take up (or that take up, and make up, women). As I suggested, femininity
includes the internalized bodily ethos of rape culture, while self-defense trains
women to internalize a different bodily ethos in reaction to rape culture. There
is no bodily demeanor devoid of culture. Without a disciplined body project,
one cannot be effectively subversive or conformist (Grosz 1994, 144). In other
words, systems of corporeal production per se are not oppressive, as many feminists appear to assume.

But perhaps feminists worry that self-defense as a body project does not
escape the all-too-familiar relationship women have had with their bodies
(aside from that of sex object): that of craft object (Smith 1988, 48). Women
already know that we must work at our bodies, hair, skin, and faces to be
acceptable. Many women try so much to look more like something or someone else, comparing themselves with the latest popular ideal image (ibid., 48-
49). Men's body projects seem less loaded. We tend not to question men's
motivations when they take up physical activity. Women, however, must contend with the fact that they have always viewed their bodies as objects of work.

Courses that fuse aerobics with self-defense, like Boxing for Fitness and Cardio Combat, combine a traditional motive of the body as craft object with the
body as fighting agent. The aerobics studio's description of Cardio Combat
boasts, "Elevate your heart rate to its target zone while learning how to knockout any target that enters your zone." *Glamour* magazine's photos for an article
on women's boxing do not display a female boxer but a skinny model wearing

a long black dress and boxing gloves, leaning listlessly against the ropes in the boxing ring, facing not a woman or a man but a kangaroo.

Who knows what kind of bodily sensibility will prevail for any given student? Women take aerobics for many reasons, not always to craft themselves into appealing objects for men. Aerobics is a place that women gather to do physical activity in an uplifting environment. Exercise itself is not bad or oppressive. Self-defense can transform its purpose. Self-defense reworks the body-self in a way that enables its expansion into the world rather than its constriction. My hope is that we might see self-defense as infiltrating aerobics, not the other way around. One woman I interviewed told me that she had always wanted to learn karate for self-defense but could not afford the fee. She belonged to Gold's Gym, which offered a Boxing for Fitness class. She loved it, and went on to join a boxing gym and become an instructor.

Some feminists support women's bodily transformation through self-defense but remain skeptical of women's use of firearms, partly because they assume that firearms fail to transform the body in ways that padded attacker and martial arts courses do. As I mentioned in chapter 1, Grant's (1989) instructional self-defense videotape dismisses guns as, like male protectors, "outside the woman." Yet I have suggested that even a firearm transforms women's bodily comportment, since women have been associated with an inability to master technology, and to handle guns specifically, since guns have been associated with masculine power, and since the learning process is much the same as other self-defense forms. For the body is capable of prosthetic synthesis, and the gun is a device that enables the body to transform its environment. Incorporating objects into the body's own spaces can augment its powers and capacities. Such objects, "while external, are internalized, added to, supplementing and supplemented by the 'organic body' (or what culturally passes for it), surpassing the body, not 'beyond' nature but in collusion with a 'nature' that never really lived up to its name" (Grosz 1994, 188).

Lentz (1993, 384) still suggests that the discourse of *Women and Guns* as well as Quigley's *Armed and Female* positions women as essentially vulnerable, the gun allowing women to transcend that essential vulnerability. Lentz suggests that if women naively accept their bodies as naturally passive and ineffective, then their use of a firearm will not affect their understanding or experience of their bodies. She assumes that women who undergo firearms training feel, or are positioned as, essentially vulnerable. However, Quigley was careful in her class never to describe women as innately *anything*, much less essentially vulnerable. Moreover, all the gun instructors I spoke with recommended other forms of self-defense for certain types of threat as part of an overall self-protection strategy. Lentz's claim is ill-founded; instructors do not recommend firearms for self-protection out of a belief that women are simply biologically wired for passivity or ineptitude.

Linked to the assumption that guns are not transformative is the worry that women will think that all they need is a gun, and thus will never develop a feminist consciousness. For example, Ann Jones (1994, 44) cautions, "Please don't mistake your hardware for power." Lentz (1993, 395) argues that women's gun culture avoids social critique because she supposes that armed women assume that having a gun means they do not need a cultural critique. This ignores that women use firearms in the context of the possibility of their own victimization, and of their status as taboo for women. Things we do because of our oppression can result in a feeling of empowerment. Power is complex. Certainly guns do not provide female equality or power; but this is no reason to avoid them. Moreover, if a change of body really is a change of mind, as I have argued, then to a great extent having a gun is having a critique. Feminist skepticism of women's bodily activities is often rooted in the notion that power operates through the body. We have neglected, however, the way power is also contested through the body. As such, it follows that the body can and perhaps should be disciplined. The idea that bodily engagement somehow stands in the way of critical, mental engagement is part of a much broader assumption of a mind-body dualism in Western philosophy and culture.

Mind-Body Dualism

Feminists' skepticism about women's physical aggression may have to do with the age-old association of women with the body (immanence) and men with the mind (transcendence). Simone de Beauvoir (1952) suggested that women will not be free until they are no longer closely bound to their bodies. In contrast, Paxton Quigley likened women's gun training to women's entrance into primarily male occupations. She asked me, "Why shouldn't a woman know how to use a handgun, just because in the past it's been basically a male thing? Women strive to be doctors, lawyers, etc. and those have basically been male-oriented, so why not strive to learn how to shoot a handgun?" It may be that some feminists hesitate to associate women's emancipation with corporeal acts. Yet this hesitation itself relies on a dualism of mind and body that we might profitably reject.

John Locke and John Stuart Mill have bequeathed to us an understanding of agency that excludes the body. The body in liberal individualist discourse recedes into a passive object over which the agent ideally has sovereignty (Cohen 1991, 77-78; Diprose 1994, 3). This explains why feminists have run extensive campaigns involving the control of women's bodies. Feminists have insisted that people (and often men specifically) must look at and act upon the female body differently. Consistent with the liberal paradigm of self-propri-etorship, feminists struggle over the body's inhabitant or owner and its exploiter or appropriator. This perpetuates a mind-body dualism (Grosz 1994, 9). Simi-larly, in our debates about whether gender patterns are rooted in "nature" or "nurture," body or mind, we reproduce a dualism that, even if we side with culture over nature as the determining force, winds up dehistoricizing the body.

The body and culture are not in opposition. Rather, the body is yet another compelling and important expression of cultural norms and ideologies. Yet some feminists have tried to get away from the view of gender as deep inside one's body, a natural or inborn essence, through a de-emphasis of the body altogether. But the body is significant, although not in the patriarchal sense; it is a site of cultural significations, a place where patriarchy is embodied, in the flesh, and contested, in the flesh.

This is not to say that the notions of agency or consciousness are bad or use-less. They must, however, acknowledge the primacy of corporeality. A central implication for feminist theory is that consciousness—a category of interior-ity—is useful only if figured in a way that includes the primacy of corporeality. Rather than seeing the body as something that is irrelevant to political trans-formation, or relevant as an object only, feminists might see the body as some-thing that is politically relevant and needs to be changed along with attitudes, beliefs, and values.

All ideologies of identity are ritually enacted. It is true that we live in a world in which public texts such as films, advertisements, and fairy tales mediate dis-courses of gender. But these textually mediated ideologies must still be ritual-ized so that the meanings they have for us actually become part of us and feel real. Ideologies of masculinity and femininity may circulate through visual and other images/icons, but they are felt real through their ritualized enactment. As I have shown, self-defense training—specifically the disciplined reorganization of one's bodily comportment—amounts to a ritual undoing of femininity.

Feminists have focused less on how the body might be a source of new con-sciousness—in short, on the body as something other than a passive house of the soul. The body is not just something that gets acted on, taken over, occu-pied, constrained, or defended. Feminists might conceive the body as an agent, not just the thing that (psychical) agents struggle over (Grosz 1994, 9). Diprose (1994, 104) offers this understanding: "It is not so much that the individual stands above his or her body in appreciation of its social significance and in control of its capacities but that the capacities of the body, its habits, gestures and style, make up what the self is in relation to the social and material world."

Self-defense can encourage feminists to rethink the mind-body dualism so as to incorporate the body not as the basis of gender or social norms and not as what society is reducible to, but as part and parcel of subjectivity. If feminists are to recognize the person as a corporeal being, and yet avoid the reductionism of traditional understandings (understandings that rationalized removing a woman's uterus after labeling her hysterical), then we must refigure the relationship between consciousness and the body.

But some feminists do reject the mind-body dualism, and reject women's self-defense on the grounds that it perpetuates that very dualism. After her experience in a Model Mugging course, Shannon Jackson (1993, 116) argued that, in teaching women boundary-setting skills, self-defense instructors "leave unquestioned a liberal ideology of Western individualism, an ideology that works very hard to assure its practitioners of the possibility and the desirability of [a conception of self as a container]." Based on an argument that individualism promotes an atomistic self-containment and, ultimately, the withdrawal from others or the manipulative control of them, Jackson (ibid.) insists that such self-defense courses "teach a woman to enforce her own policy of containment" as "an unquestioned right of the individual." Of course, we are not really self-contained and the principle of bodily self-determination is founded on the transhistorical "fact" of our biological status as discrete individuals (Woodhull 1988, 174). The body is a politically regulated boundary, not a "being" (Butler 1990, 139).

While I agree with the analysis that individualism has actually benefited white men at the expense of other groups, my study of women's self-defense points to ways in which Jackson's conclusions are shortsighted. Liberal individualism claims to represent the rights of individuals but actually excludes women (Woodhull 1988, 172). The very conception of the body as a bounded entity is the precondition for our notions of political rights and ideal citizenship: Wholeness, integrity, moral soundness, and honor are all connected (Gatens 1996, 41). In popular and classical logic, women's bodies are unfit for citizenship, because they are not bounded entities the way men's are. The female body in our culture has been understood and often lived as an envelope, vessel, or receptacle (ibid.). Of course men's bodies are not any more naturally enclosed than women's; nor are women's any more naturally penetrable than men's. Conceptions of male and female embodiment may be lived and understood in this way, but only due to their fit in a social and political context. Civil society does not reflect natural differences, it creates them (ibid., 79, 83).

Women lack the privilege of the individual because they are not seen as full citizens (which are conceived as males). Liberalism's ideal of self-determination has been used by feminists to claim a right to bodily control and self-determination for women. If women are learning to enact and enforce a possessive individualism, it is because they, unlike privileged men, never were allowed to have it. Women have been seen as property rather than as proprietors. As MacKinnon (1989, 172-73) notes, "women's sexuality is, socially, a thing to be stolen, sold, bought, bartered, or exchanged by others. But women never own or possess it, and men never treat it, in law or in life, with the solicitude with which they treat property. To be property would be an improvement."

And, besides, women are processed in court not as bourgeois individuals but as possibly vindictive and masochistic feminine subjects (Innes 1976, 25). We should be striving for the eradication of the conflict women now feel between femininity and bourgeois equal citizenship. Women, being construed as objects, not agents, in a (male) search for morality, truth, ideas, and meaning (whether that is transcendental or animalistic), are not even seen as moral agents that could be violated. Women are not supposed to want or need self-determination. (Or, if they are, it is supposed to be the desire for all the things men have wanted for women—evidenced by former U.S. Vice President Dan Quayle's statement, "[My wife] has a very major cause and a very major interest that is a very complex and consuming issue with her. And that's me" [quoted in Starr 1991, 176].) Thus to insist on one's moral integrity and boundedness is to claim a status equal to men—the way they have construed what it means to be an individual with rights.

For men's sexual violence is one of the consequences of civil society's granting only men the status of individuals with inviolable boundaries. After all, if the male body has historically been understood and lived as bounded and impenetrable but the female body has been seen as an incomplete receptacle, then women's bodies can be seen, and treated, as full of holes that require filling—which, sadly, rationalizes men's attempts to "complete" the female body and renders nonsensical women's desires for bodily self-determination (Gatens 1996, 42). From this perspective, dismissing self-defense has at least as many of the problems of possessive individualism that embracing it has.

Women change the meaning of possessive individualism by forcefully inhabiting that subject position. When women demand the rights trumpeted by a social and legal system grounded in possessive individualism, demanding control over their body-selves, they demand that men stop treating them as men's property. Thus demanding women's rights to protect their bodily boundaries *does* conceptualize the body as the property of an individual self. In this sense,

defending self-defense does not entirely transform the terms of liberal possessive individualism, but it does challenge its masculine slant. Self-defensers do
not reinscribe liberal individualism but, ultimately, undermine it from the
inside. Patriarchal expectations and circumstances do not allow women to be
bounded, self-contained individuals; during self-defense training, many women
find that they have learned (or had) to be too cooperative and too worried
about alienating others.

Thus to worry about women's spreading individualism and its presumed
dangers of unbridled competition and atomistic self-containment because they
practice self-defense seems backward. The meaning of liberal individualism
cannot stay the same when women demand its privileges. That some self-
defensers feel their ability and willingness to fight make them better citizens
indicates that possessive individualism and community need not be understood
as mutually exclusive. Self-defensers fight for their entitlement to freedom from
coercive constraint—hardly a leap into manipulative, controlling, or alienating
antisocial practices. Women's self-defense is entirely compatible with social
well-being and cooperative interdependence.

Although self-defense may appear to be the enforcement of one's bodily
boundaries and the reification of the self as a container, such a practice extends
women's sphere of effective liberty. Indeed, I found that self-defensers are not
becoming increasingly "contained." The fear of rape results in containment,
while women's self-defense training results in an expansion. Women begin to
use their bodies differently, go more places, and have less fear of private spaces,
public spaces, and men. Such female entitlement, a convergence of self, body,
and world, is not containment but self-extensiveness (Brown 1991, 196). Self-
defense affords women increased mobility and an expanded sense of self.

Women's aggressive protection of their bodies, then, is less a naive retreat
into possessive individualism than an entitlement to greater agency, social space,
and mobility. It is an insistence on women's status as equal citizens, as body-
selves rather than as body-things ownable by others. Women who learn self-
defense do not and cannot pretend to learn it as gender-free subjects. In this
way, they do not embrace the illusory gender-free subject of individualist discourse, one that privileged men without admitting it. Moreover, women's self-
defense addresses a collective, not individual, problem, one that the state,
despite its claims to represent individuals regardless of sex (Woodhull 1988,
175), has not solved.

Despite her problems with the discourse of self-defense, Jackson (1993) does
not offer a new way to construe the harm of rape and the power of self-defense,
or any new metaphors for understanding the body, the self, and the individual

who claims the right to defend herself from attack. I want to offer a politically and philosophically informed way to experience and understand self-defense, however troubling some of the assumptions of any individual self-defenser or self-defense course may be at present.

As I have already noted, Lentz (1993) suggests that self-defense places a new, uncritical emphasis on the harm of rape, by making it seem as though what sexuality means to us is apparent, that sexual acts are naturally important, and that women have sacred inner violable spaces. This suggests that self-defense is the chagrined acceptance of a primal predator-prey relationship, women swallowing whole their status as victims and men's status as naturally powerful. At the same time, others may fear that self-defense will have the effect of *minimizing* the political or psychological impact of rape, rendering it akin to getting punched in the stomach. Though rape is not the only form of gender-motivated violence self-defensers prepare to resist, these worries should prompt feminists to make explicit the political reasons why rape is wrong, locating our disagreement with it not in ideas of the purity of the female body or the sanctity of (consensual) sexuality, but in the politics of social sexing.

The Harm of Rape

With the phrase "the personal is political" the women's movement of the early 1970s effectively politicized apparently nonpolitical experience. "The key instance of this, which generated campaigns, actions, and then debates and theories, like the spokes leading out from the central point in a wheel, was the woman's body" (Mulvey 1989, xii). In this light, it should hardly be surprising that for North American feminism, rape became symbolic of the injury of patriarchy. Rape has been crucial to the development of feminist practice, feminist theory, and feminist jurisprudence. Rosalind Innes (1976, 23) captures the feminist representation of rape:

> Rape is the ultimate act of sexism. Rape is the supreme assertion of masculinity. Rape is a mechanism for the social control of women. Rape is normal heterosexual intercourse stripped of its ideological veneers of "love" and "equality." Rape is a young girl's entrance into femininity. Rape is the weapon used to maintain that femininity. The Rape of One woman is the Rape of All women.

Rape, in being positioned and used as the ultimate act and symbol of male domination, has inadvertently been construed as almost ahistorical, monolithic, and, as such, seemingly unstoppable (ibid.). Of course such views were important for countering the "rape myths" that women would really relax and enjoy men's forced sex, and that various women—depending on their current social context, marital status, prior relation to the rapist, pattern of drug use, occupation, and dress style—really deserved to be forced into sex, or that the force should not actually be considered as such. But even the feminist view has its problems in that it gives "a simple vision of the oppression of women as one ultimately determined by biological differences" (ibid., 24). Such a view also slips into a simplistic, conspiratorial notion of rape. How do we construe the harm of rape in a way that avoids essentializing narratives and a mind/body dualism?

Women want to avoid rape because they think rape is wrong: It's immoral, unethical, sinful, painful, mean, ugly, humiliating, traumatizing, and just plain bad. Women may use many different constructions of womanhood, sexuality, and crime to explain why it hurts and angers them. For instance, a woman might perceive the harm of rape according to traditional, outdated laws that construe her as the precious—and after a rape, soiled—property of her husband or father. Traditionally, rape was seen as harmful because one man stole another man's property, or because innocent virtue was defiled. In contrast, Dworkin (1987) argues that the harm of rape lies in its defeat of a woman's struggle for meaning and integrity. When a woman for whom sex is "part of a human quest for human solace, human kindness" gets raped, her body is taken over, her integrity is challenged, her privacy is compromised, and her selfhood is changed (ibid., 45, 122-23).

Feminist antiviolence campaigns have often conveyed the harm of rape in dualistic terms, as though the mind-agent lost control of her body-property. Certainly self-defensers, and the anti–sexual assault movement more broadly, must claim the self-possession that has been denied women. Self-possession, however, can be a way of relating to one's personhood as a self with a body-appendage, not as an integrated body-self. The reality of violence against women forces women to enact this mode of being-in-the-world. In an ideal world, of course, women would not need to think of their bodies as things they must protect, whose boundaries must be under their constant surveillance.

This is precisely why rape is harmful and worth fighting against: It reduces a woman's mode of being-in-the-world from an absorbed lived body to a broken body with a self somewhere else or a self reduced to a body-thing. Women are regarded by men who rape (and, regrettably, by many others) as things, void of a moral will or a body-self distinct from the rapist's, or they are reduced to his (mis)interpretation: "She really wants it." Rape is harmful because it imposes an "ownable" status, effectively construing woman as passive and as property. Rape imposes a sex-class status. As such sexual violence is politically important to fight against. Foisting upon women a sex-class status may also help explain other gender-motivated attacks, such as lesbian-bashing and wife-beating.

Our bodies are the very fabric of our selves; our social identities stem from our corporeal histories; and "having" (sovereignty over) a body, rather than "being" a body, is alienating (Merleau-Ponty 1962; Diprose 1994, 108). Selfhood is changed when one's body is forcibly beaten or raped. The outward projection of self-identity with the body becomes constrained. When one is sick, the unified lived body becomes an object for reflection (Merleau-Ponty 1962, 136). When one is beaten or raped, the absorbed projection of one's embodied self becomes particularly difficult, much like when one is ill.

The women's movement has long been invested in possessive individualism. The woman for whom feminists struggle is an individual who is capable of being, and deserves not to be, violated. Though rape occurs in societies that are not capitalist, its specific meaning for North American women—as a political weapon against women's equality—takes place in a capitalist context in which the individual is an ideological construct (Innes 1976). But the possessive individualism self-defensers claim might force feminism to be a bit more corporeal.

Sexuality and its "possession" are constructs of male domination. No woman, feminist or self-defenser, wants to find the meaning of life in sexuality. Men's interest in it and entitlement to access to it are part of the oppressive social sexing that women fight. Feminist antirape work is not what turns sexuality into something prominent; rape is. Feminists cannot afford to give up the primacy of sexual violence before men do. As Plaza (1981, 32) states, "What men—situated in a patriarchal power relationship—persist in creating and perpetuating (the oppression of women, the 'difference between the sexes,' the primacy of sex) they impute to us as wanting to create and perpetuate."

Though traditionally seen as a property of individuals, sexuality is not some natural essence that is automatically important, or automatically divided as male and female. Sexuality is a regime of power that divides people and provides identities that produce power relations. At the same time, punishing rape as if it were the same as being punched in the face will have to wait until that is all it means to men (ibid.). Self-defense from a feminist perspective does not diminish the political meaning of rape; it highlights it. At the same time, self-defense from a feminist perspective does not solidify or falsely naturalize rape or sexuality.

As MacKinnon (1989, 174) points out, most attempts to explain what is wrong about rape start with what is right about sex: "Perhaps the wrong of rape has proved so difficult to define because the unquestionable starting point has been that rape is defined as distinct from intercourse, while for women it is difficult to distinguish the two under conditions of male dominance." If most rapes are not seen as violative of women, it is because sex and violence are seen as mutually exclusive rather than mutually definitive (ibid.). We must politicize sex as well as rape. Sexuality, not just rape, proceeds within a context of power relations.

Acknowledging bodies in feminist theories and politics also means acknowledging sex categories as constructed politically, rationalized in nature, and solidified in practice. Self-defense, as part of an anti–sexual assault movement, politicizes rape as well as sexuality more broadly. There are reasons for arguing against rape, for being feminists, and for taking self-defense to prevent its occurrence. These reasons are no less compelling for being historical and cultural.

Rape is harmful not only because a man claims sovereignty over that which belongs to a sovereign woman—the female body or female sexuality. The body in feminist theory cannot stand simply as an appendage that women ideally own. Rape is a violation not simply because a woman lost sovereignty over this thing, but because the body is a form of social expression and rape makes the woman's body into an object or possession of the rapist rather than a lived body. Social identity is the body-self. A broken body is the collapse of one's social expressiveness (Schneck 1986, 51). Rape turns an "open embodied engagement" into an embodiment as sexual object for men's use (Diprose 1994, 113).

Thus, a woman doing what she can to stop a sexual assault might not necessarily solidify her identity as a bourgeois liberal individual who possesses a body-thing but rather as an expanding body-self who is willing to fight in order not to be so sexed, in order not to be made female made flesh. In this sense, self-defense is as much a war of social realities as a war protecting bodily boundaries. In actively employing her body to resist being made into an object for another's abuse, the self-defenser undermines, rather than solidifies, the mind-body dualism.

Women's bodies have been construed as vessels for babies and penises. In contrast, men's bodies have been understood to have a wholeness and integrity, which makes it easier to see male citizens as whole beings who possess moral soundness and integrity (Gatens 1996, 41). This differential conception of male and female bodies contributes to the greater degree of outrage that the rape of a man generates. When self-defensers fight against rape, they are fighting for a status usually accorded only to men. Self-defense is a fight for integrity and wholeness, and rejects the status of the female body as a vessel or receptacle that is incomplete without a man or a baby. That self-defense must perpetuate some of the very same notions of the possessed individual that men's violence against women does is no reason to reject it. A theory of the harm of rape can help self-defense dismantle the possessive individualism that has guarded male privilege.

Self-defense is an attempt to refuse the imposition of the possessed status of womanhood, to fight for a different vision of self, of sexuality, of relationship, of the body. Thus self-defensers are fighting rape not only to obtain the freedom of liberal individualism—a freedom from interference from others and a rightful ownership of their bodies—but to fight for the freedom to structure the world as an absorbed lived body. This is a freedom not so much for an increased number of choices but for an enhanced way of being a person in the world.

We live in a time in which a portion of the body discourse involves a rhetoric of self-determination and choice. Could this rhetoric of the "democratic body" (Cole 1994, 16-17), combined with the increasing popularity of body projects in contemporary Western society, work in the service of women's emancipation? Rape and battery are body projects not of democracy or democratic bodies but of male dictatorship. Women need body projects that discipline their bodies in self-consciously transgressive ways. Self-defense is a disciplined body project that refines and enhances women's claims on human rights conceived within the framework of possessive individualism.

Conclusion

A series of interrelated assumptions has kept feminists from embracing self-defense as an important strategy for challenging male domination: the legacy of cultural feminism, its related debates over power and sexuality, which spill over into controversies about what kind of womanhood is resistant, what kind of resistance is feminist, how to resist co-optation, how to avoid increasing violence, and the conceptual distinction between mind and body in which women's physical activities are suspected of not transforming their minds or political attitudes.

Self-defense is not only a body-conditioning regimen, but is simultaneously a social activity, materially and symbolically linked to others, all of which challenge rape culture. Of course, women's self-defense has made some impact, but it has yet to infiltrate social institutions at large. It is not taught widely to girls, say, in public schools or Sunday schools. Nor has it attracted much attention from major feminist writers or groups such as the National Organization for Women. Until it does, it will not necessarily have the chance to spread, generate external funding, and influence related policies.

A chasm between academic feminist and self-defense cultures could keep self-defense from necessary political self-reflection. Without a feminist understanding of sexual violence, the self-defense movement is likely to perpetuate a host of rape myths that feminists have worked hard to bring to light, including myths that men usually rape strangers, that white women are the primary victims of rape, and that black men are the primary perpetrators of rape. For example, to explain why women should be armed, *Women and Guns* magazine employs a right-wing political discourse about the welfare state, the lazy, the poor, and the criminals—a rhetoric that easily feeds racist assumptions about who criminals are. Former editor Sonny Jones (1990, 6) states, "While the anti-gun, pro-crime liberals study human nature and the political machine sucks up our hard-earned money like a vacuum cleaner possessed, only to disgorge it directly into the hands of poor unfortunates who quickly convert it to drugs and alcohol, we the people are supposed to be good workers during the day and willing victims at night."

The NRA is supported by many who certainly are not feminist. They may support women's self-defense precisely because they believe the rape myths that women are incapable of self-defense without weapons. Or, they may support women's self-defense without questioning the racist (and false) assumption that the primary problem of rape culture involves black male intruders who rape white women. Firearms for self-defense may make sense to some of those people precisely because they do not consider whom women would have to shoot. (The professional women who teach women how to shoot, however, believe that a woman should have the right to self-defense regardless of her relationship with the perpetrator.)

Since guns for self-defense are usually intended for use in cases of stranger assault (where, unlike on a date, the self-defenser has a chance to get her gun), the only way that the armed self-defense movement will avoid feeding racist and sexist stereotypes would be to work closely with other self-defense subcultures, like martial arts or padded attacker courses. Gun instructors Quigley and Bates do recommend padded attacker courses, noting that unarmed techniques are appropriate forms of self-defense for many attack situations. This is an important reason for the self-defense community to have a sense of themselves as a community, rather than as groups competing with one another or arguing with one another over whose self-defense course offers the best kind of protection.

Moreover, *Women and Guns*, just like the *American Rifleman*, glamorizes success stories, ignoring the very painful emotions and financial drain of a legal trial, both of which often result from killing in self-defense. Glamorized success stories might have a different effect on women than men, however, because of women's socialized tendency to worry too much about inflicting pain on others. Nevertheless, we cannot ignore the fact that North America's paramilitary culture gives us much to worry about.[6] This worry may contribute to feminist skepticism over films like *Aliens*, in which well-armed women blast aliens to bits. Although Sigourney Weaver's character does not have military status, she wears fatigues and is on board with military members. The military imagery equates women's empowerment with nationalism and militarism and thus disturbs feminists who might otherwise enjoy the spectacle. But perhaps we should remember that right-wing antifeminist women are also against celebrations of women in the military. In any case, women's armed self-defense culture might best avoid essentializing, racist, nationalist troubles if it gets contextualized within the feminist anti–sexual assault movement and merges with other forms of self-defense, providing every self-defenser with a range of options.

If self-defense instruction incorporates a variety of training regimens and a feminist understanding of sexuality and inequality, it has a good chance of becoming a new, explicit part of the feminist movement. Paradoxically, the more feminists distance themselves from self-defense culture, the more likely self-defense is to be depoliticized and co-opted. But closing the rift between feminism and women's combative bodily practices will not be an easy task. For, as I have shown, feminists will have to rethink their own philosophical and political presumptions. In the next chapter, I discuss some specific ways a physical feminism might impact rape culture, feminist rape prevention and education efforts, and feminist reformations of self-defense law.

5

Physical Feminism
Implications for Feminist Activism

Chapter 3 showed how the combative bodily practices of self-defense disrupt the embodied ethos of rape culture. Chapter 4 suggested that self-defense prompts feminists to reconceptualize women's violent resistance to rape and battery, and the place of the body in feminist theory. This chapter considers in turn how women's self-defense impacts rape culture, rape education and prevention, self-defense law, and feminist politics and theory more generally.

Because the accomplishment and normalization of rape depend on a fantasy of both male invulnerability and female helplessness, embracing women's capacity for violent resistance might have a deterrent effect on male violence. Because rape prevention efforts have tended to position women's violence as impossible, distasteful, or insignificant, embracing women's capacity for violence opens up a new set of possibilities for rape education and feminist political symbols.

Moreover, women's self-defense and its transformation of gender ideology might clash with other efforts to reform self-defense law, bringing to a head a central tension in feminism between "difference" and "equality." Finally, because self-defense has such radical potential for disrupting rape culture and feminist activism, it exposes the need for a marriage of theory and practice, of consciousness and corporeality.

Consequences for Rape Culture

The politics of male domination are embodied; male domination is a social construction inscribed in the bodies of women and men, thus imposing itself as self-evident and natural. But this is not as bleak as it may sound, for self-defense as physical feminism disrupts the embodied ethos of rape culture. When self-defensers rehearse and enact new bodily dispositions, they challenge rape culture at its somatized core. As women embrace their power to thwart assaults and interrupt a script of feminine vulnerability and availability, they challenge the invulnerability and entitlement of men and, by extension, the inevitability of men's violence and women's victimization.

In embracing the pleasures of combat, women undermine the exclusive association between masculinity and physical aggression. Women who fight, box, and shoot enact a central performance of manhood. By infiltrating an arena that has enabled men to solidify a naturalized sense of raw and physical masculine prowess, women cease to be merely fought-over objects, pretty property, or the ones behind the scenes nursing the male warriors. Notions of manliness depend on contrasting notions of womanliness. Hence, changes in what counts as a woman will greatly impact what counts as a man.

Men can so easily believe in their superior physical strength—a strength so much more powerful and extreme than women's—because aggression is male turf. Cornering the aggression market offers a sense of natural superiority, even in the face of feminist gains women make, for instance, in the workplace. This quote from a thirty-two-year-old professional man is revealing: "A woman can do the same job I can do—maybe even be my boss. But I'll be damned if she can go out on the field and take a hit from [football star] Ronnie Lott" (Messner 1994, 70-71). A sense of physical superiority over women, in a number of ways but notably here in the way of strength, informs many men's interactions with women. Of course, the man who said this probably can't take a hit from Ronnie Lott either, but the male-only nature of football allows men, even the scrawny, older, and nonathletic ones, to identify with the men on the football field. This belief in a superior biology (even the notion of superior strength is, conveniently, based on male-centered criteria) rationalizes gender inequality, in fact it rationalizes the division of the sexes itself.

Given the way violence against women reinforces gender norms, it is no wonder that self-defensers are often seen as a direct threat or challenge to the gendered social order. Whether or not they know it or intend to, in challenging men's physical superiority over women, they are challenging gender. The social, moral, and psychological boundaries gender norms maintain are directly threatened by the self-defense movement. A sense of physical superiority over women informs many men's moment to moment interactions with women. This is why many men feel uncomfortable around strong women; they experience anxiety when gender arrangements, and gender difference itself, are called into question, particularly when the aspect of gender under threat is the one that *feels* most real. The aggressive woman can be experienced as an affront to a fleshy sensibility.

Clearly, that sensated "knowledge" of sex differences, particularly sex differences in aggression, results from social conventions concerning violence. As Jeffner Allen (1986, 38) has argued, "The heterosexual virtue that dictates what is a woman also prescribes what is violence. Violence is defended as the right to limit life and take life that is exercised by men, for men and against women. A woman, by definition, is not violent, and if violent, a female is not a woman." Too often, we think only men are entitled to have the right and responsibility of giving and taking life. Some feminists think this is why many men are uncomfortable with a woman's right to abortion. In any case, this helps explain why so many men express discomfort over the possibility of women's violence.

In addition, men know that women have reason to be furious, so allowing women's aggression as a society brings with it the scary possibility that women will seek revenge. Furthermore, men might fear an inability to distinguish what is and is not offensive to women, thus fearing women's aggression, at least until they become comfortable with their respect for women. The suppression of women's aggression is also connected with a whole host of ideologies many people might not want to challenge: heterosexuality, capitalism, nationalism, and militarism. Perhaps anxieties stem from a sense that women's self-defense is not recoverable through these ideologies.

Self-defense, then, has a number of components that can tear down rape culture. The first potential impact on rape culture is that men may actually become too afraid to pounce. Marcus (1992, 396–97) suggests that "directed physical action is as significant a criterion of humanity in our culture as words are." Thus, any move toward constructing women as agents of such action ought to have an appreciable impact on the respect with which men approach women. Second, men will not see violence (or active sexuality) as male turf, and so the gender identity available to them through violence might wither away, making violence less appealing. Third, since women are supposed to be the ones to keep the peace, and many fear that women's failure to hold out against violence will doom society, decoupling gender and violence might make men more responsible for peace and social harmony. Men might become more responsible for their communities once women are taken out of their position as moral guards of the social order. Women's aggression deconstructs the sex binarism that revolves around aggression, debunking yet another rape myth.

While some feminists, Naomi Wolf (1993, 156), for instance, are offended by other feminists' declaration that all men are emotionally capable, or politically capable, of rape,[1] most tend to believe all men are physically capable of rape (an idea that even Wolf feels comfortable with). But feminist self-defense challenges the notion that all men are *physically* capable of rape. Finally, men might not see penetrability and vulnerability as suitable only for females and "fags," thus opening up possibilities for respecting women's boundaries and, because self-defense could make men see their own bodies differently, tolerating variance in male sexuality. When sex is denaturalized, manhood ceases to be a fiction that men must live out as "real"; it ceases to be the myth that they must make true.

Old and New Symbols for Feminist Sexual Assault Awareness and Prevention Efforts

Feminists have rightly pointed out the many ways in which women are victimized. This has been an effort to counter prevailing assumptions that women actually enjoy victimization or denial of the problem altogether. However, as Wolf (ibid., 36-37) has pointed out, feminism's negative, even gruesome imagery, is becoming counterproductive. Instead of urging women to vote with ads depicting women without mouths (as Lifetime TV did), instead of distributing hangers for women to carry at pro-choice rallies (as NOW did), and instead of encouraging financial contributions by rewarding donors with bracelets engraved with the name of Becky Bell, a teenager who died from a botched abortion (as the Fund for the Feminist Majority did), the women's movement might move women by appeals to women's strength, resourcefulness, and sense of responsibility.

A ritual conducted on International Women's Day in 1978 and at some Take Back the Night marches attempted to celebrate women who have fought back (Kaye/Kantrowitz 1992, 59-60). Eight women donning white masks each took on the voice of a woman who had killed an abusive man: "My name is. . . . My husband beat me for years. . . . I shot him." The group would then chant, "I am a woman. I fought back." Many feminist activists charged the group with "glorifying violence" (ibid.). Why? The assumptions of cultural feminism have grounded women's resistance in women's difference from men. Unfortunately, however, women's victim status is a significant way women are different from men and as such has become an identity for feminist activists. The idea that any kind of violence is bad also turns the celebration of even specifically self-defensive violence into feminist taboo. Hence, it seemed to make more sense to feminist activists on college campuses in the 1980s to paint the statement "A Woman Was Raped Here" all over sidewalks and streets. Increasing public awareness, rallies, candlelight vigils, phone calls, lobbying for stiffer sentencing, and creating safe houses are all feminist moves—and well they should be. But can't we do more?

Rape education and prevention programs have maintained some of the same assumptions about women's nonviolence that ultimately wind up solidifying men's aggression and excluding women from the possibility of aggressive self-defense. A flyer on avoiding rape issued for women by a college rape prevention education program (RPEP) suggests to women who are "not getting through" ("Not Getting Through?" is the bold-face title line of the flyer) to "say no loudly and clearly." The most extreme suggestion is, "Yell." The flyer does not instruct women to twist the attacker's testicles, kick his kneecaps, or gouge out his eyes. The Rape Treatment Center of Santa Monica Hospital Medical Center distributes a handout for use on college campuses called "Prevention Information" with much the same advice. To their credit, they first list seven things men can do to stop acquaintance rape. But their list of strategies for women includes no self-defensive action. The most extreme self-protective measures they suggest to women are, "State your feelings and get out of the situation," "If you say 'No,' say it like you mean it," and "Use campus escort services."

Other attempts to keep women from being victimized involve controlling or restricting women's behavior, as if there were no other option. For instance, some college campuses still maintain curfews for women, which demand that they return to their dorms earlier than the men. RPEPs on college campuses intentionally try to increase women's sense of victimization; they have even been evaluated by researchers in terms of how successfully they instill feelings of vulnerability in women (see, e.g., Gray et al. 1990; Hanson and Gidycz 1993). The reasoning behind this is based on other studies that have shown that the greater one's perceptions of vulnerability to danger, the more one will restrict one's own "risk-taking" behaviors.

This perspective sees women's basic freedoms, which men exercise without even thinking of them as privileges (partying with buddies, hanging out at night, staying late at the library and walking home afterward, playfully kissing someone without knowing if he wants to "go farther"), as "risk-taking" behaviors that women should avoid. What kind of freedom is this? Those researchers do not consider avoiding self-defense courses as a "risk-taking behavior"; for they do not entertain the possibility of responding to a sense of vulnerability with physical training. Self-defense is not considered a behavior that might decrease one's likelihood of being victimized.

Even though the passage of the Violence Against Women Act (VAWA) has channeled government funds toward the prevention of violence, this rarely includes training women for combat with potential attackers—one of the few prevention measures that does not restrict women's behavior.[2] The VAWA, part of President Clinton's 1994 crime bill, combines tough federal penalties with financial resources channeled to prosecuting offenders and helping abused women. By October 1996, the VAWA had provided more than $130 million in federal money for states to train police and prosecutors and to assist victims of domestic violence and rape (Campbell 1996). Related to this legislation is the creation of the National Domestic Violence Hotline and the Violence Against Women Office (which coordinates the federal government's efforts to implement the VAWA) in the U.S. Department of Justice; the funding of shelters and crisis centers; the funding of efforts specifically aimed at protecting older women from domestic violence; and the enhancement of public lighting systems. The VAWA directs its resources to educating police officers, prosecutors, and health and social service providers; providing more shelters and counseling services for victims of domestic violence and rape; prosecuting offenders; and researching the causes of violence against women and educating the public about it.

The Office of Justice Program's Violence Against Women Grants Office launched a grants program called S•T•O•P, which stands for Services, Training, Officers, and Prosecutors. The S•T•O•P program obviously gets its name from the desire to stop violence against women, but the training to which it refers is that of police and prosecutors, not of women for self-defense. In fact, as specified in the program's report for applicants, each state receiving a S•T•O•P grant must allocate 25 percent of its funds to law enforcement, 25 percent to prosecution, and 25 percent to nonprofit, nongovernmental victim services. Only the remaining 25 percent can be spent the way the state chooses, within the parameters specified by the VAWA under its list of purposes. A representative of the Grants Office told me that it does not disallow a state's spending some of its discretionary grant money on self-defense training. Such training, however, is not even listed as one of the purposes of the program. The initiatives connected with the VAWA are important and necessary; but again what surfaces is the assumption that women's self-defense training is impossible or irrelevant to prevention efforts.

Rape education programs less explicitly confirm women's helplessness by focusing almost exclusively on men's privileged imperceptiveness and sexual entitlement to women. For instance, Sut Jhally's (1990) widely used rape education video, *Dreamworlds*, shows how women are depicted in an MTV male "dreamworld" where women are constantly sexually available and interested in men, a fantasy that Jhally suggests perpetuates rape culture. The video intercuts scenes of MTV rock videos with scenes of the gang rape of a woman in the movie *The Accused*. The goal of such videos is to convince viewers both that women are horribly abused and that popular images legitimize such abuse by representing as sexy the violence that many men, but few women, seek in their sex lives. But these videos perpetuate a perception of men as dangerous and women as victims with much to fear.

This approach terrorizes women and increases their sense of helplessness and responsibility for men's violence against them. Jhally (1994) notes that his video scares women. He even quotes a female student, who said that she went home and threw out all her cosmetics after seeing *Dreamworlds*, to indicate the "success" of his educational video (ibid., 160). Once again the assumption surfaces that women are responsible for keeping men from being interested in raping them. Rape education videos that feature "dangerous men" do little to unsettle the popular fantasy of superior strength that men bring to their interactions with women. Even if this "dangerous men" approach does reach men, it mobilizes them around guilt or empathy for "the weaker sex," not around the kind of respect with which men keep from attacking other men. Men that rape and beat women do it in part because they think they'll get away with it. If research has shown that an increased sense of vulnerability to danger leads to self-imposed behavioral restrictions, then why aren't we increasing men's perceptions of vulnerability to danger so that they'll restrict their abusive behavior?

Moreover, why not subvert the culturally dominant fantasy of male invulnerability and female passive sexual availability and celebrate alternative representations of womanhood? Such a celebration might expand men and women's awareness that the body is an imagined political construction, and encourage men to imagine that attempting violent assault could bring violent consequences. Wanting women to be able to celebrate images of their own heroism, and sometimes a fantasy of the respect and even terror that such heroism might inspire in others (particularly powerful men), my colleague Neal King and I developed a set of video clips consisting of images of women's verbal and physical aggression against men.[3] Some of the rape prevention educators with whom we shared this video astonished us with their hesitancy to use these images of women cursing, clobbering, and shooting men.

It seemed as though the images of men's violence against women had become so routine that educators reacted with horror only to the images of women's violence against men. But of course the images of men's violence are horrifying; this is why rape educators use them for rape education, hoping people will become more critical of the images. Yet so entrenched are images of men's violence against women as a feminist symbol that images of women's violence can seem too jarring. Feminists are so ambivalent about women's aggression (or aggression in general) that even images that spark a rage fantasy appear to be dangerous, or at least politically incorrect. It has become difficult to acknowledge women's aggression even at the level of fantasy.

Feminists and nonfeminists alike have expressed skepticism about images of violent women finding their way onto the big screen. What I find exciting about "mean women" in films is that they allow us to see that women are not as violent as men *only because women have not been entitled to violence, politically.* Women's passivity is a matter of politics, not natural inabilities or dispositions. Furthermore, the films force us to think about the relationship between fantasy and reality in new ways (Halberstam 1993, 198). Yet, as the protest of Tribe 8 at the 1994 Michigan Womyn's Music Festival illustrates, many feminists are appalled by representations or fantasized enactments of women's violence.

As mentioned earlier, in performing their song "Frat Pig," lead singer Lynn Breedlove simulated cutting off a penis (Hummel and Mantilla 1994). Punk music arose as a response to a violent society, so it can be expected that a punk band like Tribe 8 will deal with anger. Breedlove feels that this particular ritual "makes us feel better. . . . It's an effigy" (quoted in ibid., 16). Although the band did not wish to push their ritual on potentially offended festival goers and made several announcements warning audience members about their show's content, a group of women protested their show before and during the performance. During a workshop after the show that Tribe 8 hosted, many women were concerned about "whether or not anger was good and whether or not violence was good" (Breedlove, in ibid.). Violence has come to be what's wrong with patriarchy; hence violence itself, even if a fantasized enactment for a protest, is suspect. The performance may even seem like a naive "reverse sexism" that will never help us reach a social climate of peace and equality.

But such representations do not amount simply to reverse sexism. The images of violence by socially subordinated groups are not prescriptive, a simple matter of escalation, or a reversal of roles. Watching a fantasy of violence by women on stage or in film allows a disruption of the much more common fantasy/reality that I discussed in chapter 1. That more common fantasy is not easily distinguishable from reality, given men's social power to merge the two successfully through actual acts of violence and to enforce their belief that such violence is normal, natural, erotic, deserved, and desired by women.

Images of women's violence take place in a social context that presupposes its impossibility. Far from solidifying the expectations and physical dispositions of a rape culture (as images of men's violence and women's sexual availability and physical vulnerability do), such images call into question the naturalized status of gendered physical dispositions. They're not prescriptive; the films do not work at that level. They provide a fantasy of resistance that affects action not in the form of imitation or copying, but in the form of increased entitlement in everyday situations, increased skepticism about the myth of male invulnerability, increased entitlement to respect, and increased confidence with which to enforce that respect. The alternative films offer fantasies that disrupt the association of women with passivity. These images, then, are not inconsequential because they are fantasies.

Not only might more images of women's violence help real women think that violence is not simply a physical impossibility, but such images might reverse the fantasized connection between violence and sexuality that more traditional images instill in men's imaginations. That is, men might stop thinking that violence against women is sexy and heroic, as traditional fantasies suggest, and instead start appreciating a woman's self-defensive violence (as in *Aces: Iron Eagle III*), or even retaliatory violence (as in *Thelma and Louise*). The fantasy of women's brutality is not the only "unrealistic" one.

After all, the idea that women will actually start writhing and moaning with pleasure, or fall slavishly in love, after being held captive (as in *Tie Me Up, Tie Me Down; Overboard; Beauty and the Beast;* and any number of heterosexual pornographic films) is an equally unrealistic fantasy. This fantasy, however, is one that men have had the privilege of entertaining as real. Just as common fantasies that eroticize men's violence against women might have the consequence of making men (however erroneously) think "women really want it," or that the result of coercion will be a woman's enjoyment, fantasies of women's self-defensive or retaliatory violence against men might have the consequence of making men realize that "perhaps she doesn't want it" or think (however erroneously) that the result of coercion will be their violent punishment.[4]

Women's violence against men is a textual strategy that might effect a new set of social consequences—not because women will imitate those films, but because those films might instill a new unrealistic fantasy in men that will affect their behavior around women, countering or disrupting the imperceptiveness that the more common arrogant masculinist fantasies produce. The fantasies are not equivalent, or simply "reverse sexism," precisely because their institutional contexts and consequences are not the same.

In chapter 3, I suggested that popular images of women influence, and become part of, self-defense culture. Self-defensers I spoke with explained their relationships to those images in a number of ways. One instructor lamented the fact that *Thelma and Louise* depicted a woman's shooting that was not legally in self-defense. A firearms student told me that for her *Thelma and Louise* was just a "fun adventure." But I found no evidence that the women I spoke with took prescriptions from these movies or acted in ways that skeptics fear. Instead I found a critical engagement with discourses of femininity and masculinity. I saw a deep investment in popular representations of women, including a desire for better ones.

Still, though, some rape prevention educators say that they don't like the way that images of aggressive women are eroticized in popular films. In their view, this blunts the radical potential of the images. Showing images of eroticized women is routine for rape educators; *Dreamworlds* is full of them. But rape educators are hoping to increase students' distaste for those eroticized images of women's sexual availability by showing the images in the context of a serious discussion of sexual violence, whereas students are encouraged to celebrate images of tough women, however sexy students might find them.

The skepticism surrounding the eroticization of images of tough women, however, collapses the issue of the eroticization of women's helplessness into a problem of the eroticization of women, period. Feminists have become so strongly critical of the sexiness of violence against women that they are now hesitant about any images of sexiness—like the muscle-bound Cory Everson who shows off her mags in a backless catsuit and fights with Jean Claude Van Damme (who shows off his mags in a tiny tank top) in *Double Impact*. After all, being sexy isn't the problem; the problem is what has constituted sexiness. But in the same way feminists often categorically reject violence, they have come to reject eroticization or sexiness categorically. When the self-defensers say that self-defense is "sexy," perhaps they are suggesting that grace and beauty cannot coexist with the traditional feminine helplessness of days past.

Just as social movements at present are more diffuse than in the past, they are also more dependent on images, symbols, and fantasies. A social movement must capture our imaginations and our feelings. To the extent that the self-defense movement employs and contests the images of our popular culture, it might be more successful in disrupting fantasies of women's helplessness and men's invincibility. Not only might more women take up self-defense, they might also see it as a feminist project. In other words, it might replace the violence of fantasized male power and women's enjoyment of sexual subjugation with the power of fantasized female power. This is the importance of self-defense instructors' suggestion that women "rewrite" a scene from a movie in which a woman does not fight back successfully.

In much the same way, the popular psychology book *Female Rage* encourages women to rethink the Medusa story, emphasizing that Medusa was a beautiful woman who was angered when a man tried to look her over at her bath (Valentis and Devane 1994). Jane Caputi (1993) suggests women recuperate the age-old myths of horrific female monsters so as to refigure our own body-selves. She relates one woman's self-defense story carried through as the Gorgon. The woman enacted a demeanor so threatening that the assailant fled; afterwards, she realized that she'd become the Gorgon in order to scare the man away.

If I am correct about the radical impact of images of tough women, and the extent to which men's violence and women's self-defense against it depend upon fantasies of our bodies, then these new images help constitute the self-defense movement. In this light, riot grrrl bands, "bitchy" rap music, mean women movies, and Diane DiMassa's comic book series (published by Stacy Sheehan), *Hothead Paisan: Homicidal Lesbian Terrorist*, are all a part of the self-defense movement. A 1995 "Free to Fight" girl-rock concert tour and album explicitly merges the sentiments and sensibilities of riot grrrl music with self-defense. Their tour included self-defense demonstrations among songs, skits, and spoken-word performances. They put together a compilation album from the tour and a booklet emphasizing self-awareness and self-defense. Fanzines encouraging empowerment were also part of the scene at the shows (Ali 1995, F1).

Feminists' skepticism about aggression, eroticization, and women's pleasure, especially in the context of fighting sexual violence, has blunted our capacity to embrace women's popular pleasures in the gyms, the dojos, and even in the movie theaters as part of a strong antirape movement. We have assumed that our rape education videos should be horribly depressing, and our tactics for stopping rape debilitatingly angry, pure, and virtuous. But as Wolf (1993, 156-57) remarked, in the context of her experience working in a rape crisis center, "Rape, of course, must never be thought of as fun. But should it be heresy to suggest that changing attitudes about rape should sometimes be fun? . . . Rape *is* hell, *is* trauma, *is* pain; *and*, the power we have to change the world is a source of joy."

A feminist tendency to position women as victims, while strategically useful in certain instances, has blinded many to the potential of women's resistance. Feminist correctives to self-defense law have often positioned women in self-defense cases as incompetent victims. This has been shifting recently; the increasing numbers of women trained and prepared to defend themselves from violent attacks provides even more reason for reforms of self-defense law to move away from those earlier reform efforts and instead incorporate a physical feminist vision.

Implications for Feminist Reformation of Self-Defense Law

An important feminist force influencing self-defense law is the battered women's movement. Battered women have begun to claim self-defense in court regularly when they, fearful for their lives, kill or maim. Although such women usually have not had formal training in self-defense, their prior and current treatment in the legal system reflects ideologies about women and aggression. Arguments in their defense, as well as the legal reforms coming out of the battered-women's movement, negotiate self-defense law and its underlying assumptions about women and aggression in ways that are sometimes at odds with the counterdiscourse of women's self-defense.

My central concern is that feminist legal reformers in the battered-women's movement have suggested that self-defense law accommodate women's weakness, niceness, and helplessness, while the self-defense movement creates a large number of women who are strong, assertive, and far from helpless. I have argued that women's self-defense training metamorphoses the female body and hence constitutes a serious challenge to popular gender ideology, specifically that which differentiates men and women along the lines of aggression. But women who kill their batterers and claim self-defense are often defended on femininity grounds. The original frame of women's aggression as intolerable is challenged only slightly, and is sometimes preserved, in this discourse.

Women's self-defense cases are important sites in which discourses compete and provide an opportunity to understand how women have tried to make the dominant discursive system work for them. The reforms to self-defense law urged by the battered-women's movement must be evaluated not only in terms of their success defending battered women who kill in self-defense, but also in light of women who are trained in self-defense. Some reforms may wind up punishing trained women who defend themselves in an entitled way.

Feminists began to reshape self-defense law, with battered women who kill in mind, by incorporating a particular set of defense issues, namely that women's perceptions of danger are different from men's, that women are physically smaller and weaker, that women lack self-defense skills, that women cannot handle situations that may require them to be aggressive, and that women are more afraid of physical pain than men (Schneider and Jordan 1981, 22). Such reforms, however, reward womanly behaviors, prevent women from occupying a juridical status as culpable subjects with agency, and ignore the politics of legal judgments. Those changes in self-defense law have meant that a woman can best legally defend herself if she can show that she is helpless, weak, scared, and defenseless. This is in direct conflict with what the self-defense movement is doing—that is, teaching women to get mean, be angry, feel justified in fighting back, and know how to fight and use weapons.

In their self-defense manual for women, Conroy and Ritvo (1982, 7) explain that it is lawful for a person who is being assaulted to defend himself or herself from attack if, as a reasonable person, he or she has grounds for believing and does believe that bodily injury is about to be inflicted upon him or her. In doing so, he or she may use all force and means that he or she believes to be reasonably necessary and that would appear to a reasonable person, in the same or similar circumstances, to be necessary to prevent the injury that appears to be imminent.

> Since many women are concerned about being sued by their assailants after incapacitating them, we asked Chief Rappaport if this was a possibility. When he stopped laughing he replied, "Can you imagine a 210-pound burly rapist suing a 105-pound frail female for defending herself while being assaulted?" He continued, saying that when you know you are in danger, fight! If you delay because you're worried about what might happen in court, it may be too late." (Ibid.)

That the average man is nowhere near 210 pounds and the average woman far exceeds a petite 105 pounds seems to escape the chief and the authors. Women have lost self-defense cases precisely because they weighed over 105 pounds and in fact weighed more than their assailant. Women's self-defensive violence is much better tolerated when their weakness and vulnerability are highlighted. But the self-defense case of, for instance, a woman who shot her husband when he turned to hurl a pot of boiling water at her (Gillespie 1989) shows that much of men's violence, such as throwing boiling water, whether or not it occurs in a battering relationship, could be done to anyone of any size by anyone of any size. The man's size is irrelevant in some circumstances.

As long as the law accepts women's self-defensive violence as legitimate only with the idea that women really are vulnerable to physically superior men, women will not be seen as both powerful and simultaneously justified in defending themselves from attack. What justifies women's self-defense is the very same ideology of natural differences in size, strength, and aggression that perpetuates men's assaults in the first place. Thus women's self-defensive violence is most often excused, paradoxically, when it does not constitute a serious threat to the systematic violence women face in this society.

This precludes women from developing the skills to fight and ignores the many instances in which the woman defending herself does not fit the stereotype. That white women more easily fit the stereotype of feminine helplessness in the popular imagination is significant. The positioning of women as compliant and innocent, even for the purpose of claiming justifiable self-defense in court, excludes black women, who are stereotyped as less docile and compliant. Hence, black women lose under this framework.

When feminists talk about women's aggression—say, in cases of self-defense against a spouse's assault—their rhetoric sometimes takes the aggressive agency away from the woman (see, e.g., ibid.; Walker 1989). Such rhetoric on the part of legal and psychiatric professionals positions women as "harmless" (Allen 1987). If a female offender can be positioned as harmless then she has a better chance of claiming that her self-defense was justified. As Allen (ibid., 82) notes, "Against the bald facts of the criminal allegation or conviction, these reports counterpoise a subtler and more compromising version of the case, which systematically neutralises the assertion of the woman's guilt, responsibility and dangerousness, and thus undercuts any demand for punitive or custodial sanctions."

In contrast, men do not have to be construed as harmless in order to be seen as legitimately violent. We presume that men have the capacity for violence; the legal question is simply whether or not they exercised this capacity justifiably. The presumption that men but not women can act violently on their own behalf is closely associated with the assumption that men but not women can actively choose whether or not to engage in sexual relationships. As long as women are going to be thought of as wanting and liking the sex, forced or not, that men want to have with them, as long as men do not see women epistemically on their own terms, and as long as men's arrogant refusal to allow women to make their own choices has ideological support, women's self-defense will be hard to justify.

Women are currently in a no-win situation: If a woman seems too competent, she is also too assertive and unfair; if she seems too helpless, then she is incompetent or did not show enough resistance to assault. When a woman's self-defense is rendered legitimate, it is often because she can be shown to be irrational or unreasonable (though not culpably so). Instead of characterizing women's violent action in their own defense in terms of the absence of reason and will, demolished through Battered Women's Syndrome, self-defense could be understood to include the presence of reason and will. How can we see a woman's self-defensive violence as a willful and reasonable act?

In chapter 1 I noted that "passion" and "pathology" have been central concepts by which women's aggression is explained and contained. Because jurors might not find justifiable the violence of battered women who have fought back, the concept of Battered Women's Syndrome (BWS) was developed to help explain why and how a battered woman becomes trapped in an abusive relationship and does not leave. BWS implies that battered women, as a result of ongoing abuse, suffer from "learned helplessness" and therefore do not attempt to leave their batterers (Walker 1979). Although the admission of expert testimony on BWS yielded some important legal victories, BWS pathologizes the same kind of self-defensive violence for which men need no such excuse.

Feminists have suggested that the Impaired Mental State defense for women charged with homicide is troubling because women who defend themselves should not be seen as insane (Schneider and Jordan 1981). Incorporating BWS as a primary defense issue, however, still relies on a claim that the woman was driven crazy or incapacitated from years of abuse. Such a defense determines the action to be legitimate not because of the circumstances but because of the defendant's state of mind. This positions the violent action as wrong and the woman as deeply troubled psychologically. Such a legal defense strategy, though it may work to excuse battered women's self-defensive violence, removes the possibility of a woman's legal self-defensive violence when she is being threatened the first time. BWS requires women to take several years of abuse before their helplessness is learned and their violence seems legitimate. Even if incorporating expert testimony on BWS can help exonerate the woman who kills her batterer, it still reinforces the notion that women's violence is reasonable only from a place of extreme victimization, rather than as an entitled refusal of victimization.

Although originally intended to address the jury's misconceptions about battered women (which often either accept the abuse as normal, blame the woman for being abused, or blame the woman for not ending the relationship) and to expand the legal options available in defending women against charges of homicide or assault beyond the traditional insanity and incapacity pleas, the BWS defense actually replicates the old stereotypes of feminine passivity and incapacity. Indeed, the overall impact of the BWS stereotype might limit, not expand, the legal options of women who cannot conform to the stereotype (Schneider 1992a, 216-18).

Radford (1994, 195) notes that "virtuous" women, the ones who do not fight back, count as "true" victims of domestic violence. The BWS defense is in danger of perpetuating this separation of "true victims" from "viragos," victims who are undeserving of sympathy. Women should not have to hold on to nonviolence until their self-control and sanity finally give way. They should have just as much right as men to assess a situation reasonably, and use violence when reasonable for defending themselves. Although BWS might justify some women's self-defensive violence, it fails in the long run to allow women the same entitlements men have to defend themselves.

Furthermore, as both Radford (ibid., 189) and Schneider (1992a) suggest, BWS winds up making women's self-defensive action seem incomprehensible.

For if the woman has been beaten into submission, fear, dependence, and passivity, it is that much harder to imagine her taking a radical action such as killing the abuser. At the same time that the feminist battered-women's movement has tried to dispel the myth that battered women are a separate species of weak, unintelligent, or damaged women, BWS in some ways suggests exactly that, but blames it on the cycle of battering. Hart (1994, 151) points out that defending women on the grounds that they were deeply disturbed victims of sexual abuse troublingly rests on the very pathology that reproduces the social conditions in which women kill in self-defense.[5]

Charles Patrick Ewing argues for justifying battered women's killing of partners not by expanding what counts as "imminent danger" and redefining the "reasonable person" who fears imminent death (a strategy I discussed in chapter 1), but rather by saying that lethal force should be allowed to prevent *psychological* self-annihilation. Because batterers reduce their victims "to a psychological state in which their continued physical existence will have little if any meaning or value" (Ewing 1990, 587), "psychological self-defense" justifies killing that prevents such an existence.

Psychological self-defense is interesting in that it challenges the law's privileging of the corporeal aspects of human existence (physical life and bodily integrity), and favors an existential view of self. Feminists have knowingly stressed the physical aspects of woman abuse—even though it also involves extreme harassment, threats, and obsessive forms of control—precisely because they know society is more willing to redress physical harm than psychological harm (Schneider 1992b, 535–39). Still, the notion of psychological self-defense has many potential problems. For instance, it solidifies women's position as helpless victims, highlighting the contradiction in one's utter helplessness and simultaneous act of (psychological) self-defensive violence. Moreover, it leaves unanswered the question of who will get to say what counts as psychologically damaging behavior. Ewing (1990, 587) has these same problems with what he calls "battered woman defense." Lethal force can rarely be used justifiably to prevent the infliction of "extremely serious psychological injury." But if we imagine a man being held hostage by people who have not started to kill him yet, his use of lethal force might be seen as justifiable not because of his psychological terror but because he has reason to believe that anyone holding him hostage will also kill him.

Then again, as Ewing points out, in the castle and true man doctrines, the law already privileges psychological issues over physical life for specific circumstances. The law that permits the use of deadly force to protect one's home privileges things other than life (Ewing 1990, 589). Of course, the castle doctrine may not be a psychological issue as much as it is a last retreat for the threatened person. Still, women have found it relatively difficult to justify legally self-defensive violence on the grounds that being in their homes was a last retreat justifying life-preserving actions. Nor have they been able to justify legally self-defensive violence on the grounds that a man's threatening behavior produces a reasonable fear that he could kill them at any moment, the way a hostage would feel with a terrorist.

The citizen's right to use deadly force to resist being ousted from her or his own home rarely works in women's self-defense cases. Battered women who defend themselves from their abusers are almost always in their homes at the time. But the notion that "a man's home is his castle" does not seem to apply to women; battered women who defend themselves are inevitably asked why they didn't leave. For instance, an Idaho chief of police who had investigated the case of Thelma Griffiths, convicted of involuntary manslaughter for shooting her husband after he shoved her violently and lunged at her with the same expression on his face that he had had when he attempted to strangle her (Gillespie 1989, 17-18), wrote this to the judge: "We could find no reason for anyone to shoot him. . . . Why didn't she leave the house, she had plenty of opportunity to do so . . . [she] followed him [into the bedroom]. She claimed that he had been hitting her. Was she asking for more?" (quoted in ibid., 18). Often women are expected to retreat even when in their own homes, while the castle doctrine has allowed men an exemption from self-defense law's requirement to retreat before using violence (ibid., 82).

Battered women should not have to "just leave." The dearth of shelters, financial resources, child care, housing, and employment opportunities prevent many battered women from doing so. Many stress the need for more institutional resources to which women could turn so that they are not forced to stay with violent partners. Many women no doubt want to leave abusive relationships and need such resources to accomplish this safely and successfully. Recent data suggest that learned helplessness does not characterize most battered women because they make a number of attempts to escape the violent relationship, seek help, and reform their partners. This is a view of "Battered Women As Survivors" (Callahan 1994).

Because many people (relatives, clergy, teachers, counselors, employers, doctors) and social services offer little help for many battered women who seek it, and because the risks of job loss, homelessness, and/or "separation attack" are so great, the relationship and the abuse continue (Mahoney 1991, 65-66). This understanding of the battered woman's behavior is more likely to render a woman's lethal self-defensive measures reasonable. The revised view of battered women as survivors, however, still leaves out women's self-defensive violence against men who have not been battering them for a long period of time.

Positioning women as victims (of either learned helplessness or a lack of social services) and then defending their self-defensive violence on those grounds, can leave unexplained and unjustified cases where women take self-defensive violent action against men who assault them the first time. In this light, other courtroom strategies become important, such as a jury instruction regarding the right to bear arms. If cultural stereotypes lead juries to mistrust a woman who has knowledge of self-defense tactics and readiness to use them if threatened—for instance in the 1959 case of Mary Ellen Nelson, who was convicted of voluntary manslaughter for fatally shooting her battering husband (who had already beat her, blinded her in one eye, slashed her arm with a knife, and came toward her with the fireplace poker with which he had blinded her) with a gun from the dresser drawer which she knew to be loaded and knew how to use—then juries should be reminded that women, like men, have a right to bear arms (Blodgett-Ford 1993, 552-53).

If a woman does not act stereotypically, juries may very well have a difficult time understanding her behavior as reasonable. A group of psychologists found that, in experiments involving stranger and date rape, women who resisted their assailants both verbally and physically were perceived as having been more guilty of precipitating the attack (Branscombe and Weir 1992). Also, research subjects placed more blame on women who competently shot a burglar than on women who handled the gun incompetently and made a lucky hit (Branscombe, Crosby, and Weir 1993). A woman's knowledge of shooting and fighting can already make her look like an aggressor.

African American women often do not fit the stereotype of the "good victim" because they are stereotyped as either very strong or inherently bad (Ammons 1995, 1007). The dominant gender ideal is the yardstick against which all women's actions are measured, and so such racist stereotyping makes black women even less likely than white women to be rendered harmless in courtroom trials. For instance, at the 1994 trial of Pamela Hill, an African American woman sentenced to five to twenty-five years for killing her battering boyfriend with whom she lived (she pleaded self-defense), the prosecutor contrasted Hill to a "good victim" when he told the jury: "[A] lot of people would have you believe Pamela Hill is carrying the banner of Nicole Simpson" (quoted in ibid., 1006). Hill is black, poor, an unwed mother, and already considered aggressive simply because she does not fit the stereotype of femininity.

Despite the facts that race does not predict one's likelihood of suffering violence by intimates (U.S. Department of Justice 1995, 4) and that studies of social services' responses to African American women reveal preferential treatment to white women who seek help, many find it difficult to imagine that an African American woman could be trapped in an abusive relationship, and are more likely to dismiss her as a combative person, as if her race predisposed her to engage in and enjoy violence (Ammons 1995).

This explains why one study revealed that jurors are more likely to discount the accounts of rape by black women than by white women (Lafree, Reskin, and Visher 1985, 402). If racist imaginations don't entitle the black woman to bodily boundaries, then of course they could have the related difficulty of seeing her self-defensive violence as legitimate. Hence, jurors, regardless of race and sex, must be educated first about battering relationships and then about how myths about African American women operate. Even positive perceptions of African American women, such as attributions of independence and strength of character, can work against them when used to stereotype individual black women who actually can be emotionally dependent and even "trapped" in an abusive relationship (Ammons 1995, 1078).

Unlike white women, women of color must face the double burden of sex and race oppression when confronting violence in their lives. Asian women may be reluctant to report battering because of commonly held attitudes toward family honor (Rimonte 1989). Immigrant women face extreme social isolation and fears of deportation. Black women must confront racist beliefs that black men are more aggressive than white men, and a racist social structure in which black men are already oppressed. They may even attempt to understand the battering as "displaced aggression" that results from their oppression (Coley and Beckett 1988, 483). When judges and juries don't understand these issues, these women's status as victims becomes harder to see; hence their self-defensive violence becomes difficult to see as reasonable or excusable.

Not only can positioning women as victims leave unstereotypical women indefensible in real-life courtroom situations, it can also wind up including some cases where women commit homicide that is not self-defensive. This is exemplified by some feminists' reaction to the case of Aileen Wuornos, the "lesbian serial killer" to some, but the feminist sex-worker who needed to kill in self-defense to others. Wuornos shot several men dead (on separate occasions), and, despite her claim that these killings constituted justifiable self-defense, never reported the killings to the police. That some rallied around "Lee's" cause, claiming she shot those men in self-defense and was being jailed because she was a lesbian, indicates a failure to distinguish responsible self-defense from irresponsible violence.

Heroizing or even excusing Wuornos, by positioning her as a victim of sexist laws, fails to give women responsibility for the consequences of legitimizing their aggressive self-defense. Help for Lee seems to indicate an unwillingness to see justice as a contract. Women who exercise what is currently a constitutional right to own a gun for self-defense undertake a serious social responsibility. Treating women as responsible citizens means allowing their justified self-defense *and* punishing their unjustifiable violence. This is the social contract, and women, like men, who violate it must be taken to task. Seeing women as totally acted upon prevents responsible distinctions between cases of women's violence.

Here's how feminism is now tied into a knot: Elements of feminism fight against notions of women as helpless while simultaneously sustaining and promoting the logic of denial and exculpation of women's violence (Allen 1987, 82). A woman's violence not only disturbs a prevailing understanding of women as peaceful and passive, but certain feminist ideals as well. Thus feminists and society more broadly seek to reposition the violent woman in some other less uncomfortable status (ibid., 93). Attempts to position women as victims in order to defend their violence reveals a central tension in feminism between victimization and agency: women are not seen as justified agents of violent acts, and so their victimization is invoked to construe them as nonagents.

Feminists have had good reason to emphasize the victimization, rather than the agency, of the battered woman who kills in self-defense. Highlighting a woman's agency can feed into popular dismissals of her abuse and to questions about why she did not leave the battering relationship. But as I have discussed, fixating on a woman's victimization has other problems. Requiring a battered woman to leave the relationship holds her to a higher standard of conduct than most would have for themselves or for men (Schneider 1992b). Requiring that battered women be thoroughly victimized nonagents before their self-defensive violence is understandable also holds women to a higher standard of conduct. Women's self-defensive actions must be put into the context of their victimization, but they must also be understood as actions (ibid.). Feminists might best get around the victim versus agent dichotomy by emphasizing the complexity of women's everyday lives, lives which include both victimization and active resistance to it, both desires for intimacy and compromise, and desires for respect and safety.

Allen's (1987, 93) work suggests that legal professionals consider the circumstances (psychological, economic, degree of harmfulness to society, etc.) of men and women equally, and to invoke the offender's statuses in order to enlighten, rather than to preempt, the serious examination of women's (and men's) actions and responsibilities. She states,

For what is potentially oppressive to women—criminal or otherwise—is for the frailties and disadvantages that do tend to characterize their position in society to be treated as exhaustive of their condition as social or legal subjects. There is every reason for feminist analysis to retain an awareness of those personal vulnerabilities of criminal women that are so insistently portrayed in the professional reports. The delicate task is to do so without also following these reports into suppressing the recognition that these women can also—even at the very moment of their victimization and coercion—be conscious, intentional, responsible, and potentially dangerous and culpable subjects of the law. (Ibid., 93-94)

As Kelman (1991) notes, all self-defense claims are political. He points out that many liberals support a battered woman's violence against her abuser, but not Bernard Goetz's violence against black robbers on a subway, as justifiable self-defense. This illustrates that the perception of who is the oppressed or victimized one determines whose defensive violence seems legitimate. Thus anyone who sees women and blacks as victims will not want to see them killed. For conservatives, the converse may be true: The subway killer's violence is understandable but the battered wife's is not, because they think whites and men are victims, not blacks and women in these circumstances. Liberals see blacks and women as the victims, and therefore side with them. As Kelman (ibid., 810-11) observes, liberals

are ultimately persuaded by two propositions. First, the notion that suffering is intrinsically both (morally) ennobling and (cognitively) clarifying—a notion vaguely derivative of liberation theology—seems appealing to many. Second, privileging the insights of the oppressed may seem an appealing reaction formation to what is seen as smug, elitist dismissals of their competence. Neither argument, though, is likely to speak clearly to the nonconverted. Suffering is surely as compatible with paranoia as insight, bitterness as well as compassion, self-centeredness as well as altruism.

BWS actually positions women as oppressed people who, by virtue of the conditions of their oppression, have special insight on one hand (for instance, that a battered woman really "knows" her abuser and when he will kill her), and, on the other hand, are totally victimized nonagents unable to think counterhegemonic thoughts (ibid., 811-12). In contrast,

The subway killer is seen for the purposes of legal judgment to have developed his paranoid and racist worldview on his own; we invoke the idea that only oppressors are intentioned subjects, not determined objects, suppressing the awareness that a determinist account of the subway killer is readily constructed, and that leftists frequently construct just such accounts outside the trial context in theorizing about unconscious or institutional racism. (Ibid., 812)[6]

Thus the problem is not that anyone is trying to turn a neutral self-defense law or a neutral concept of the right to self-defensive violence into a political tool for a special group. Anyone using, applying, or reshaping self-defense law is using a political concept, a political law, for political ends, with a political vision of gender relations in mind.

In this light, I suggest that physical feminism is a particular kind of vision that those struggling with self-defense law keep in sight. Self-defense law must work for women not through the inclusion of a set of properly womanly behaviors that the law can reward. It must work for women by acknowledging women as responsible, culpable agents who have the same right as men to defend themselves from violence. Self-defense law was construed with men in mind; this must be changed so that a greater number of legitimate women's self-defense cases are legally recognized as reasonable.

But justifying women's self-defensive violence on the grounds that women lack fighting skills, for whatever reason, ignores the growing number of women who have trained to defend themselves from assault. Their actions will not be seen as womanly in the eyes of the law; thus the project of changing self-defense law must go beyond accommodating women's inability to fight and women's victimization, in a way that punishes neither those women who happen to weigh a slight 105 pounds nor those who are trained to fight and do so immediately, without ever developing Battered Women's Syndrome. If self-defense law includes a separate standard for women (e.g., battered women in particular) then women who don't fit the stereotype of the good victim—such as black women and women who are trained in self-defense—are left without justification for defending themselves.

The conflict between the battered-women's self-defense cases and the self-defense movement brings to a head a central tension in feminist theory. That conflict, between equality and difference, has frequently emerged in a variety of contexts of concern to feminists. Emphasizing women's sameness with men, chalking up differences to gender socialization and trying to get women to be treated the same as men, is seen as a route to equality, but can also wind up comparing women against a subtly androcentric standard. As I showed in chapter 1, women lost ground in courts when self-defense law was applied to them the same way it was applied to men, because self-defense law is implicitly male-centered. A woman who defends herself usually does so in circumstances dif-

ferent from those in which a man usually defends himself, has a different relationship with her attacker, and is likely to be perceived differently by jurors
because she is a woman. Expert testimony on BWS emphasizes how women's
perceptions that lead to violent action in self-defense might be different from a
man's but still reasonable or at least excusable. Women's demand for equal legal
status, then, is not always as simple as being treated the same as men. The inherent sex bias of self-defense law indicates the failure of the formal equality model
to accommodate women's experiences and perspectives.

Emphasizing women's different bodies and social contexts, on the other
hand, while capable of opposing male-centered values and norms, has its own
drawbacks. Specifically, the difference approach has perpetuated the idea that
men and women are naturally different, and has often rationalized unequal legal
treatment. In the case of self-defense, the law exempts a person from criminal
responsibility for her/his behavior, as a person is assumed not to have free will
at that moment. Otherwise, people are assumed to have free will and thus must
take legal responsibility for their criminal actions. The law has allowed women
not to take responsibility for their criminal assaults more often when they can
be proven to be appropriate feminine subjects (i.e., the good victim). Self-
defense law and its application have rewarded "womanly" behaviors just as they
have rewarded "manly" behaviors. If women trained in self-defense fight back
and are charged with assault or murder, they will not benefit from the difference approach to self-defense law.

How can the tension between equality as sameness and difference, played
out in this instance between feminist reforms of self-defense law and potential
trained self-defensers who wind up in court be resolved? If women's difference
is acknowledged in a way that keeps the historical construction of the sexed
body in sight, then women's particular histories and circumstances can be discussed in court but in a way that is not essentializing, in a way that does not
generalize, say, helplessness as a condition of womanhood. Women will lose if
positioned as different from men, or the same as men, when either status is used
to preempt rather than enlighten the examination of their actions in court.

While emphasizing difference is important for overcoming male-centered
frameworks, sex difference must be understood as historically constructed and
embodied in order to avoid both the trap of essentialism and frameworks that
conceive of the body as irrelevant to gendered personalities. Emphases on difference and equality are not opposed then. The emphasis on difference "is concerned with the mechanisms by which bodies are recognized as different only
in so far as they are constructed as possessing or lacking some socially privileged
quality or qualities" (Gatens 1996, 73). Difference must eventually accommo-

date not just how women and men have been historically constituted differently, but also a wider variety of forms of embodiment among women.

The Physical *and the* Feminism *of Physical Feminism*

I have described a social movement of women who, without necessarily identifying as feminists, are challenging some of the assumptions that support rape culture. Women's self-defense is not only empowering, pleasurable, and transformative for women, or unsettling for men. Self-defense shakes some assumptions driving feminism—particularly how we have been thinking of rape, sexuality, and the body. The association of aggression and masculinity that undergirds rape culture comes a little unhinged when women get on the mats, step up to the punching bag, kick the shit out of a mock assailant, and take aim at the gun range.

Feminists all agree that systematic power relations can be changed; that's what makes feminism a theory as well as a social movement. But we have often proceeded as if men's violence against women could not be stopped. Ordinary North American women are contesting the inevitability of that violence. When women learn self-defense, and begin to take pleasure in a construction of womanhood that includes the capacity for violence, it confounds and alters the way we think about power operations. We have inadvertently reified male power. And, as we have argued that "rape is about power and not sex," we have construed consensual sex as free and good (MacKinnon 1989, 135, 173-74; Woodhull 1988, 170), and positioned womanhood as virtuous and pure.

Keeping women away from violence, or denying the aggressive potential in them, preserves the association of violence and masculinity, and upholds a false similarity within the category "women." It also maintains men in a class of "protectors" and women in a class of "the protected" (Stiehm 1982)—an ideological arrangement that justifies heterosexism and perpetuates men's violence against women. In this way, the anti–sexual assault movement and feminist theory more broadly have failed to challenge rape culture at its core. Women's self-defense culture casts the association between masculinity and violence radically into question. It challenges the rape myth that men rape because of size and strength. It contests the distinction between sexuality and politics. Finally, it encourages feminist theorists, educators, legal reformers, and activists to reconsider the importance of physicality to consciousness and, specifically, the radical impact training women in self-defense could have in women's lives and on rape culture.

Feminist antiviolence education and activism might better challenge prevailing social/power relations if we emphasized the historical production of gendered identities at the level of social interaction *and* at the level of the body. A karate student explained the significance of self-defense as it relates to the body: "Martial arts, everything that goes into being able to think of ourselves as fighters or as strong or as having a certain kind of body, a strong body, all of that has the effect of making us a counter example to what women are supposed to be" (in Turaj 1993, 59). As I discussed in chapter 1, male domination is already an embodied politics; hence feminism would do well to get physical too.

I have suggested that feminists' neglect, and sometimes outright skepticism, of self-defense actually perpetuates and solidifies some of the very assumptions of rape culture. More than this, it obscures a primary "consciousness raising" arena—one that involves not simply a discussion of one's oppression, but one that, by enlisting the body as part of one's consciousness, involves the reenactment and undoing of one's oppression. Hence a feminism that gives primacy to the (re)construction of the body is a physical feminism. If theories *are* practices, then feminism, like the patriarchy it hopes to eliminate, is physical.

Feminists have argued that women, rather than men or the state, should get to control their own bodies. But the body, not just a disembodied female subject, can be seen as an agent. Put differently, agency must include embodied subjectivity. The self-defense movement encourages us to see women as agents, and understand (practically and theoretically) our bodies as subjects instead of objects. Sexual violence is oppressive precisely because it reduces one's body to an appendage of another. Several feminist scholars have critiqued the construction of sexuality, individualism, and the mind/body dualism in much of feminist thought. Women's self-defense illustrates well these tensions within feminism. I have suggested that women's practical action in self-defense courses seeks a freedom that pushes beyond traditional notions of liberal individualism.

Although the aggressive female body is defiant of ideologically produced gender boundaries that perpetuate rape culture and male dominance, it is still an ideological production—one reflecting an ideology of female entitlement. The new bodily comportment women learn in self-defense destabilizes those processes through which the differentiating forms of difference are naturalized. The fighting habitus of the self-defenser is a new female body, and a transgressive female body. This transgressive body is much like the lesbian body, which, making the "wrong" sexual object choice, disrupts the ideology that women are "naturally" attracted to men. But of course, the self-defense movement can and should make the aggressive female body not simply transgressive, which in some ways reinforces the norm of female pacifism, but an acceptable norm of female embodiment.

I have examined the place and significance of representations of femininity and gender relations in specific cultural commodities—such as music, clothing, movies, and self-defense lessons themselves—in the lives of self-defensers and simply as the cultural backdrop of the increasing popularity of women's self-defense. Women involved with self-defense consume and make sense of these images in particular ways that relate to their involvement with self-defense training. That is to say, the realm of self-defense as a popular cultural form and the realm of representational cultural texts such as "mean women" movies are interrelated and mediate one another.

The efforts of self-defensers to make sense of these representations and commodities, as well as the efforts I have made to understand them in the context of a self-defense movement, amount to a struggle to transform the many contradictions of "being" feminine in a social milieu of often conflicting inequalities of gender, race, class, and sexual orientation (Roman, Christian-Smith, and Ellsworth 1988, 4). Insofar as images of mean women actually push the bounds of gendered bodies and celebrate a fantasy of female physical power, they allow women to tell new stories about who they are, and support an emerging pleasure in politically reflexive physicality.

Embedded in self-defense are both dominant ideologies of gender, violence, and morality, and resistance to and transformation of those ideologies. Of course the popularity of self-defense among a diverse group of women with diverse political commitments shows that as a cultural form self-defense is capable of generating many different meanings. I have offered a specific reading that might help women and feminist theorists to capitalize on the transformative aspects of self-defense. If a woman takes self-defense just to get a leg up on some primordial male aggressive advantage, and does not deconstruct her social position or see her body project in a feminist way, it may be because some of the assumptions and political dynamics of feminist organizing have distanced feminism from the body project of self-defense.

That is why this book has emphasized the connections between sexual violence, naturalized sex difference, male domination, and the cultivation of feminine bodily comportment. Although women are not necessarily shown this connection in self-defense classes, and some self-defensers might not see it, I have argued that self-defense throws into sharp relief, and simultaneously helps women unlearn, a cultivated physical comportment that makes them easy targets for men's violence. In drawing this connection, I have proposed a way of experiencing self-defense: as physical feminism. Since male domination demands specific bodily investments, its transformation will require new bodies. And it will require a critical feminist skepticism of biological theories of sex differences as well as culturalist theories of stable, unchanging dueling (yin/yang, Mars/Venus) gender psychologies. This is the importance of a self-defense movement that is both an explicit part of an anti–sexual assault movement and an explicit project for the aesthetics and politics of a new womanhood.

Freedom can be understood as "the open embodied engagement with others in the world. . . . A woman's freedom is jeopardized by the reduction of her lived body to a thing through various forms of intolerance including the appropriation of her experience by another" (Diprose 1994, 113). Of course rape culture diminishes women's freedom in this sense. When women get the fighting spirit they get the energy and resolve with which to protect themselves around violent men. The fighting spirit is simultaneously a new feeling, a new body, and a new idea. This is the political, and feminist, importance of learning self-defense, beyond its ability to enforce women's refusal of attack. By declaring the body an idea, a construction, and a materiality, the fighting spirit defies the traditional duality between body and spirit.

If a freedom comes from women's self-defense, then, it is not simply the freedom of having more choices like going out for a jog at night or standing up to a bully without fear of being pulverized. Self-defense offers a freedom to resignify one's body. This is not the same as "freedom" construed as a discovery of what womanhood "really" means; it is a freedom that lies in rebelling against the ways in which "woman" has been defined. Self-defense does not, should not, and cannot tell women who they "really are" or put them in touch with some repressed aggressive inner core. Self-defense can free us from certain ways of experiencing ourselves and the world. It can tell us who we do not have to be at the same time that it reveals how we came to think of ourselves as we did. This is Foucault's understanding of freedom (Rajchman 1985, 38, 62). It is a notion of freedom that is not voluntarist or humanist; it allows for constant attempts at self-disengagement and self-reinvention, without the idea of a will or fundamental choice as to who and what we are. It is a freeing of possibilities (ibid., 44-45).

I have not claimed to represent the will or consciousness of North American women's self-defense culture. Nor have I suggested that this group alone can be the agent of some sort of fundamental transformation of gender ideology. Instead, I have suggested that the configurations that oppose womanhood and aggression are historical and cultural, and therefore contingent rather than natural or necessarily enduring. We have the freedom to question these configurations and transform our relationships to traditional gender ideology. This freedom is what feminist politics is all about.

Of course corporeal self-fashioning, and freedom more generally, has its limits in any given cultural and historical circumstance. Chapter 1 pointed to some of the very real sanctions on women who dare to step out of, or whose life situations make it difficult to fit into, a feminine bodily schema. Women lack freedom in this sense; this is another important component of the oppression feminists have decried. My hope is that this analysis enables a way to experience and appreciate women's self-defense training with all its transformative possibilities.

As I suggested in chapter 1, the aesthetic, the moral, and the "normal" are intertwined with the political. And when we opt for a new body stylization, bodily comportment, or body project, we defy the patriarchal/feminine aesthetic. Freedom is changing our relationship to tradition, not predicting the future. Thus, if embracing women's aggression created more violence in the world and only subordinated women further, we would then have to change our relationship to the arguments advanced in this book.

Self-defensers are disembodying a social order of female subordination and embodying a feminist order of entitlement. As these become solidified as permanent dispositions, they imagine and create a new social order. Even feminists, who already have a differential political vision, find in self-defense the opportunity to develop the routines, the gestural and visceral scripts, of those political commitments. To the extent that we have some choice over what sorts of bodily habits we will don, self-defense becomes a compelling option, and a forceful route to the transformation of traditional gender ideology and the sexual violence it supports.

Often bodily habits precede consciousness. Self-defense offers a critical standpoint from which to deconstruct accepted ideas about sex differences and aggression. Self-defense enables a "de-essentialized embodiment," a central route, according to Braidotti (1994, 171), for the achievement of transformed psychic reality. As the body gets reconditioned in self-defense classes, and women inhabit their bodies in ways previously not imagined, their consciousness as to what kinds of women they are, and what it means to have a female body, is transformed. Herein lies the power and potential of a feminist self-defense movement and of a physical feminism.

Self-defense offers women a new sensibility in which to invest their energy. Any set of bodily dispositions makes the social world meaningful—that is, mean something particular—and self-defense endows the world with a meaning and value more compatible to the aims of feminism. It brings feminism into the realm of expression, into the sensual world in a new way. Feminism at its best is more than just a willful commitment to a set of values; its passions motivate and sustain feminism (ibid., 167).

Self-defensers present us with an energized, passionate set of inscribed bodily proclivities. I have suggested that this bodily resignification is an affirmative one. Ed Cohen (1991, 84) remarks that "political movements are engendered by personal and political (e)motions that impel people . . . to put their bodies on the line." In this sense, self-defense is a feminist (e)motion, which moves women to act to rescript bodily boundaries. Self-defense as physical feminism gives women the feeling and the knowledge that impels them to put their bodies to use for the preservation of an idea, a body, a spirit.

Conclusion

A commentary on women's self-defense, as one self-defenser put it, opens a Pandora's box. Though I do not hope to close that box, from which emerge a series of arguments, fears, philosophical positions, ethical dilemmas, conflicting political strategies, and practical concerns, I shall conclude by suggesting three main controversial questions that I believe this study raises.

First, it raises the question of what will happen when increasing numbers of women develop an efficacious and pleasurable relationship to aggression. Of course, as much as we might prefer that everyone embrace an ethic of caring, and as much as the ideal society we strive for is free of coercive violence, women cannot embrace a position of pacifism when that will only cause their further victimization. That said, will self-defensers use their abilities in a socially responsible manner or a socially irresponsible manner? However we answer that question, we must first acknowledge the many conflicting definitions of a socially responsible woman.

I believe that anyone who wants to use fighting techniques or weapons responsibly must not escalate conflicts in order to use those techniques or weapons. She must determine her ethical limits and thresholds for violence. She must be willing to handle and store weapons safely. And we must treat women as culpable subjects in the law, understanding both women's victimization and agency, while we scrutinize the law for the ways in which it subjugates women.

Feminism as a social movement seeks to change women's situation and has often suggested that the lives of men, children, and even the planet will be improved if feminist demands are met. We must be careful, however, not to position women as responsible for occupying a moral high ground from which they must reject all forms of power and domination. Women must be responsible enough to admit that they seek power. Moreover, the idea that women are the ones who keep men tame, who need to be peaceful in order to keep society together and to keep men from destroying everything, presumes that men cannot be counted on to act ethically and to control themselves and positions women as the moral barometers of society.

Many fear that acknowledging women's capacity for violent behavior, and embracing their right to violent self-defense, while necessary for self-protection, does not get at the root causes of violence. Of course it may not. But women are entitled to it anyway. By analogy, women did not deserve the right to vote because of the ethics they would bring to the voting booths; they deserved the right to vote because it was a right of citizenship. We must consider to what extent we will hold women responsible for changing the violence of our society. Others may fear that if women's self-defense became a bigger part of the women's movement, we would see a naive gender-peace-through-strength mentality, where both men and women would get more and more heavily armed. We might remember, though, that women are not superpowers equal to men. Hence, it is unlikely that self-defense training turns women into equal-opportunity violators by allowing equal access to the means of coercion.

It is possible that seeing women as subjects capable of violence, and violence between men and women as subject-subject violence, will make men pick fights and escalate pride conflicts with women as much as they currently do with men. It's also possible that men will shoot female strangers as often as they currently shoot male strangers. Does a component of chivalry keep men protecting women from much of the violence they dish out to one another? Even if that is the case, this protected class of citizens (women and children) are often the excuse men use to engage in that violent conflict with one another, so any challenge to the existence of such a class might remove one of men's rationales for violence. In any case, chivalry has not protected women from violence by male intimates—women's supposed protectors are still the men most dangerous to them. Further, if men attack women because they think they can and/or because they are so callously imperceptive that they misconceive or ignore women's desires altogether, then imagining that women might very well use violence to stop them could help snap those men out of that privileged imperceptiveness. Creating for women the status of citizens equal to men equally capable of and entitled to justifiable self-defense might reduce the role that women's current social standing as objects of violence plays in perpetuating rape culture.

Then again, some might insist, a women's self-defense movement may lead to greater violence. Maybe women do keep the peace. At what cost to women, however? If the only thing that keeps us from changing firearms laws, self-defense laws, rape and domestic violence laws, social programs, and so forth is women's refusal to get into the arenas deemed negatively consequential for society, then perhaps women's entrance into those arenas will force them to change.

This study raises the related question of what is the best way to resist sex inequality, and male violence specifically. Is self-defense effective or subversive? Since we lack any objective criteria for deciding what counts as subversion, we must decide what actions, goals, and policies do or will subvert existing hierarchies. There is a long-standing tension in feminism over whether emphasizing women's difference from men or sameness to men will help women the most. Some feminists have been skeptical of the kind of political efforts that seem only to include women into the mainstream/malestream. This, to them, signifies a failure to understand the more radical critique women might have on culture and society. So, is getting women the rights of men the goal? Or is this just getting women equal access to the means of violence? Is it getting in the pigsty with the pigs? In other words, is questioning the patriarchal definition of it all the goal? Or should women get into male-dominated institutions in order to critique and transform them? The difference versus equality debate looms large here.

Those in favor of the difference approach and against equality-as-sameness might protest that self-defensers are only getting sucked into an androcentric model of power. This line of argument insists that emphasizing difference forces us to change our value system. Those who herald sameness for blurring the boundaries between men and women, on the other hand, oppose emphasizing how women are different on the grounds that it makes women and men seem inherently, essentially different which only fuels rationalizations for inequality and belies the power/knowledge regime differentiating men and women as members of distinct sex categories. One way to resolve this debate is to understand that women's differences are historical, constructed, and real. Only by historicizing the body can we emphasize difference in a way that avoids the problems of essentialism. At the same time, though, we must think about how women's entrance into "male" symbolic and institutional terrain might alter, not solidify or exacerbate, power inequality.

As Grosz (1995, 49-54) points out, feminism initially attempted to secure women's access to institutions from which they were excluded—access to educational institutions and male-dominated professions, equal pay, and so on—and affirmed women's ability for equal intelligence, ability, and social value. Yet feminism has also been committed to questions of social transformation and critique—questioning taken-for-granted knowledge, social structure, and work life—stressing women's specificity as the basis of visionary social transformation. Paxton Quigley's remark that women's striving to shoot a handgun fits right in with women's striving to be doctors and lawyers might be questioned by feminists with the latter bent toward questioning male-defined values, norms, and goals. These feminists would urge women to redefine themselves and the world according to women's perspectives. Grosz points out that both the sameness and the difference orientation in feminism can be accused of selling out, but both ultimately must admit their involvement in patriarchal power relations. One crucial political question that Grosz (ibid., 57) poses is: "Which commitments, despite their patriarchal alignments, remain of use to feminists in their political struggles?"

For many, the role of consciousness is important for determining whether or not self-defense will have subversive effects. If self-defense is a pleasurable practice that's popular among women who do not always identify as feminists, is that OK? Is pleasure, particularly when "individual" rather than public and part of a collectively articulated political consciousness, automatically suspected of being complicitous with oppressive regimes? How might women's enjoyment of combative bodily practices upset a culture of normalized male violence against women? Can self-defense really offer critical consciousness? Will women be seduced by violence if it's pleasurable? Or does the attraction of women's self-defense to a broad range of women who do not identify as feminists hold the promise of making self-defense an issue and practice around which a mass-based movement coalesces? Could self-defense draw more women to the feminist movement?

The third question comes up when trying to answer the second question of how best to resist male domination: What is the relationship between individual change/empowerment and social change? Even those convinced that self-defense training transforms and empowers women might dismiss it as a mere individual solution to a social, political problem. The skepticism that individual transformation will not cause collective social transformation presumes, however, that women's self-defense is only about increased confidence or increased chances of stopping assault. I have shown that self-defense affects women's lives and perspectives in a much broader sense. That skepticism also neglects the ways in which women's self-defense involves the organizing, fundraising, and educational efforts that many other classic feminist activist ventures do.

Yet the question of where individual change fits into broader social changes has plagued feminism for a century. Susan Cayleff's (1987) study of a nineteenth-century women's health movement illustrates the tension. Women in the health- and dress-reform movements shed their corsets, raised the length of their skirts, and donned bloomers to escape from the literal and figurative confines of femininity. They saw this personal empowerment as a necessary step toward women's liberation in all social and political spheres. The suffragists, while potential allies of the era, rejected the bloomers on the grounds that such individual, personal change would have to come after the larger political gains were made. They didn't want to turn anyone off from the cause of women's rights; they fought, and won, the vote for women in their corsets and long skirts.

The same tension between personal reform and formal legislative change could emerge here. How much should women focus on changing themselves? How much of a social, political impact will such changes have? Self-defense culture clearly values personal change, and sees it as a prerequisite for social change. For instance, self-defenser Lisa Sliwa (1986, 126-27) insists that the social order can not be changed without individuals who try to change their own lives:

> Every woman has two options: constant paranoia or using the lessons of self-defense to stand tall. One person can make a difference; all revolutions start with an individual. Before the quality of life can be improved on this planet, people must make an effort to better their own lives. That begins with taking a hard look at yourself and asking, "Is my life worth fighting for?" I hope you say yes.

The idea that "the personal is political" has been interpreted in two ways worth mentioning. Some women have reduced "the personal is political" to the search for personal satisfaction, neglecting collective change for women, or assuming that their own individual advancement will simply trickle down to other women. This makes feminism into a sort of therapy movement or female culture movement, possibly with only individual empowerment effects. Others recast "the personal is political" in a prescriptive way that compels women to make sure their lives conform to abstract feminist political ideals, leading to lengthy debates over specific sexual practices and over whether or not to shave one's legs, wear makeup, own a business, or get legally married (Echols 1989, 18).

Women's self-defense could be viewed cynically as evidence of the first interpretation of "the personal is political," where women concern themselves only with their individual chances of victimization and feelings of assertiveness, and fail to make collective change. Then again, the diligence with which many feminists have tried to distinguish the practices that express or perpetuate patriarchal values leads to the kind of disabling political correctness characteristic of the second version. In that framework, orthodoxy begets orthopraxis; hence self-defense gets ignored or rejected altogether because violence is a "male" way of handling conflicts and defining power.

Some might still object, the concern over "male" ways aside, that self-defense only changes an individual's feelings of safety and consequent freedom, and does not challenge the rape culture. I have suggested that rape culture demands specific bodily investments, for instance that the female body is a violable hole. Women's self-defense targets that embodied ethos and by extension a prevailing social perception that women are second-class citizens who cannot and do not deserve to fight for bodily boundaries. Embodiment is substantial for maintaining and legitimizing the social structure of sex inequality; thus a critique and restructuring of that embodiment through self-defense does not simply address "symptoms" of sex inequality—it addresses what can be considered a "cause."

An important implication of my investigation of women's self-defense is that the individual and the social are not clear and distinct categories with easily separable social effects. The self-empowerment found in women's self-defense affects the way women understand and experience social, political, and economic issues. Of course women's readiness to fend off assailants will not necessarily stop men's violence outright. But a woman's engagement in self-defense does seem to provide access to a series of questions about equality that had not been on the table before in quite the same way. Though learning self-defense is not the same as dealing with occupational sex segregation, for example, learning self-defense did make the nurse I interviewed question the way the male doctors she worked with treated her. Self-defense can increase women's sense of entitlement to justice and drive for self-accomplishment in a variety of arenas. Furthermore, by enfeebling rape culture, self-defense helps undermine the very discourses of sexual difference that rationalize and sustain sex inequality in a variety of settings.

Of course, a change in women's consciousness about violence does not erase the many men who commit and/or condone acts along the continuum of violence against women. In the 1970s, the feminist anti–sexual assault movement fought hard to achieve the conditions to speak of previously unspeakable acts of violence against women. Sexual violence didn't, and won't, end with the raising of female consciousness, the education of the police, or even the changing of laws. But consciousness raising led to many great social changes, individual and structural. Self-defense raises consciousness in a way that includes the body as part of consciousness, and it too can lead to structural change.

The view that suspects self-defense of being too individualistic to change society positions women's self-defense as an individual, privatized solution to a social problem that really demands collective action and legislative change. Training in self-defense certainly should not be the only solution to the social problem of violence against women. But neither should legal reforms or Take Back the Night rallies. Laws should reflect and spread a devout intolerance for violence against women. Batterers and rapists should face the criminal justice system. Feminist health centers, bookstores, theater groups, newspapers, and women's studies programs should challenge sexist ideas and practices. Women's self-defense affects women in positive ways that complement these efforts, and in fact can accomplish some things that they cannot, namely the corporeal change that disrupts the embodied ethos of rape culture.

The physical feminism of women's self-defense has policy implications. It has implications for reforms of self-defense law, for the funding of social services, and rape prevention education. It has implications for women's studies scholarship and for many other feminist organizations and activist efforts. Women's self-defense can change these institutions, not only by helping women embody de-essentialized notions of womanhood but also by pushing those social institutions to question the categories with which they have been operating.

Legal precedents with regard to rape, domestic violence, and self-defense might include a physical feminist vision. Some of the money that states get from the Violence Against Women Act needs to be directed toward "preventative" measures that go beyond street lights. Gun control strategies must be evaluated for how adequately they serve the needs of those whose lives could be saved by the self-defensive use of a firearm, for instance battered women (see Blodgett-Ford 1993). Women's shelters and rape crisis centers could offer far more self-defense training and keep as a more explicit part of their missions the dismantling of rape culture's myths that insist upon men's natural physical superiority and women's natural violability. Rape prevention education programs could be evaluated for how well they keep men from assaulting women, or for how well they have increased women's freedom to move around in the world. Physical feminism is not just the practice of self-defense, then. It involves the reevaluation of policies, legislation, and other strategies for change with the counterdiscourse of self-defense in sight. Moreover, the strategies of physical feminism cannot be pursued, or seen, in isolation. A physical feminism adds the muscle the women's movement needs to bring rape culture to its knees.

Appendix: Conceiving the Kick of Self-Defense Methods of Investigation

This appendix explains the methods of investigation and political concerns that have informed my study. First I explain the logic and significance of my participant observation, interviews with self-defense instructors and students, immersion in the culture of women's self-defense, and examination of the legal treatment of women's self-defense. Then I discuss the ways in which feminist cultural analysts have studied women and popular culture, situating my analysis in terms of such approaches. Specifically, I argue that my involvement and pleasure in the culture I interpret has affected my analysis in ways that are not only important for my interpretation of self-defense culture but for feminist debates surrounding women's popular pleasures more broadly.

Participant Observation

I spent over 120 hours participating in self-defense classes, and another 15 hours observing them. Why does my participation give me the authority to interpret the phenomenon? My feminist theoretical insights put me in the unique position to go through the self-defense experience and make sense of the instruction in a way that is appropriate to answering questions about gender, aggression, and rape culture. Judith Rollins (1985) wanted to know how white women treat the women of color they hire as domestic workers, so she became a domestic worker to find out. Rollins took field notes and used her experiences as an important source of insight into the dynamics between women in such employment situations. She simultaneously used her understanding of racism, sexism, and social psychology to explain her experiences and the experiences of other domestic workers she interviewed. In much the same way, I analyze my experiences in self-defense courses, and the observations that self-defensers shared with me, through a feminist theoretical lens. During my interviews and participant observation, I paid careful attention to the different ways women spoke of their training and its influence in their lives. While no one's experiences in self-defense are the same as anyone else's, my interviews with self-defensers reveal that my experiences are in fact not so different from theirs.

Traditional ethnographic researchers maintain a "critical distance" and often a lack of identification with the group under study. In this situation, the scholar reports to an academic group with which she identifies to describe the "other" group. Not only did I want to describe self-defensers in ways that would enable them to recognize themselves and their perspectives, but I did so as someone who identifies with those experiences and perspectives.

I feel my "insider" status has facilitated, not hindered, my accountability to those women. Researchers are typically more skeptical of those with whom they do not identify, exhibiting a greater willingness to dismiss the practices under investigation as examples of "false consciousness" (Kurzman 1991). Not only was I unwilling to consider these women fools—after all, I was going through similar experiences, having similar reactions—but I became a fan of the movement and its potential. My position within the movement made me committed to enhancing it rather than dragging it down with a set of sophisticated but distanced academic criticisms. Certainly most self-defensers do not have the time or the interest that I have had to analyze women's combative bodily practices. Thus I offer a set of feminist insights for self-defense culture, in the spirit of making it more connected to a broader feminist anti–sexual assault movement. At the same time, my insider status enhances the story I can tell to interested scholars, and I tell that story in the spirit of encouraging feminism to embrace women's self-defense.

Of course, having an academic engagement with self-defense made the instruction different for me than for those women in my classes who, for instance, took up self-defense because their lives were being threatened. I do not personally know what learning self-defense would be like under those conditions. But I did share with self-defensers the transformative experience of learning to fight back. I learned that I, like so many other women, had become accustomed to holding back my voice, my anger, and my physical strength. I felt the fear of a gun and the exhilaration of shooting one. I knew the encouragement of instructors and fellow students. I spent time in the company of women who discussed the significance of self-defense training. Through this immersion, I developed an appreciation for what self-defense culture can offer to women, and why self-defense instructors devote themselves to training women to fight.

Becoming a self-defenser also proved educational in terms of how it feels to live in a predatory culture after having learned self-defense, and how men react to women who take up self-defense. Throughout my research, which has consisted of increasing degrees of familiarity with self-defense, I have been harassed and intimidated by men in many situations. I have thus kept track of how learning self-defense has changed my feelings and reactions in such situations.

I have also had the opportunity to hear men react, over and over, each time I explained what I was studying. The most common reaction involved a declaration to be careful around me ("Don't mess with her, man"; "I'll have to watch my step around you"), which could indicate either that men know that ignoring women's boundaries will usually bring no consequences or that men think women with self-defense know-how will use it inappropriately. Also, one man lectured me about how weak I was, telling me that he felt like beating me up to prove that he was (men were) stronger than me. Interestingly, this man is five feet seven inches tall and weighs 140 pounds. Another male friend unexpectedly pinned me on the ground; he bulldozed me, rather artfully and painlessly as he had some experience in the martial arts, because he wanted to see what I could do to get him off.

Self-defense instructors say this sort of thing happens to their students all the time; in fact, they make a point of recommending that women not discuss their self-defense classes with men who might give them a hard time. I heard about a woman who was jumped by her boyfriend who wanted to see if she could really fight him off. I witnessed a man's telling his girlfriend, who was about to take a padded attacker course, that she should save her money because he'd stuff a few pillows in his shirt and let her practice her moves on him. Of course she could do enough damage to hurt him and is powerful enough to warrant training with a seriously padded mock assailant, but the message seems to be, "I don't believe you can do it." The myth that men are so strong and powerful relative to women is one in which some men are deeply invested. After all, during adolescence boys sometimes remind each other that they could take a girl and rape her; some, secure in their power over the opposite sex, even tell girls that they're going to rape them; others actually do it, alone or in groups. Even the men who welcome challenges to their privileged place in the world might still be more or less naively committed to the myth of male strength and female weakness.

Then again, many men have been thrilled by my self-defense training. Some, so invested in my abilities—even excited that I could be attacked as I'd "get the chance" to beat a man—have boasted about me to other men. A few of these men offered me weapons or other personal protection items as gifts, including pepper spray, a British police whistle, a knife, and a handgun. While many women have been enthusiastic about my project, they have neither offered me weapons nor tried to pin' me on the ground.

By having casual experiences and discussions with students and instructors in the self-defense classes I took and by reading self-defense publications, I collected information informally. I collected information more systematically by conducting formal interviews with self-defensers outside of class and by taking field notes after class. This "insider" knowledge informs my analysis throughout the book, but especially in chapters 2 and 3, in which I explain what happens in self-defense classes and interpret the significance of women's self-defense, respectively, and in chapters 4 and 5, in which I discuss the significance of women's self-defense for feminism.

Interviews

I interviewed twenty-five people for this study, including students and instructors from padded attacker courses, martial arts courses, and firearms courses, by asking for volunteers during my classes and also by word of mouth. A few self-defensers were not interested in speaking to me. My sense was that those who were not interested in talking with me either simply did not like me personally, were skeptical of academic research and of being studied, or were too busy or emotionally overwhelmed to spend the energy discussing their involvement in self-defense with me. Still, many more volunteered to be interviewed than I could actually interview.

I conducted some interviews over the telephone (when the student or instructor lived far away), some in person while we were taking the class (at a break during a class, or at a restaurant after class), and some in person after the student had already taken the self-defense course one month to three years prior. Most of the instructors I interviewed were teaching me, or had taught me self-defense prior to the interview. Some, though, were instructors whose classes I observed either before or after the interview. And in two cases, I interviewed an instructor whose course I could only read about and not take or observe.

All of the in-person interviews were tape-recorded, and most of the telephone interviews were done with my computer in front of me so that I could record interviewees' responses verbatim. In one instance, though, an instructor whose course I was observing spoke with me informally, without my tape recorder, while her students were practicing exercises, and then answered more formal questions on tape after the first part of the interview was over. In another instance, my tape recorder malfunctioned during one portion of an in-person interview. In these cases, I simply tried to write down everything that the people told me during, and immediately after, the interviews. All of the student interviews, and some of the instructor interviews, were anonymous. Some instructors chose to be identified either because they were already known publicly for their opinions or because they wanted their views to be known publicly and associated with their self-defense organizations.

Interviewing students who were in the midst of or fresh out of self-defense class, as well as students who took the course two or three years prior, enabled me to talk with women who had had different amounts of time to be affected by and reflect on their involvement with self-defense. This is important because immediately following self-defense classes women often have a particularly heightened awareness about the possibility of assault, which several weeks or months abate. For the same reason, interviewing students who were not then taking self-defense possibly gave me access to the type of student who felt overwhelmed, and thus would not have granted an interview, in the midst of her self-defense class. Some of the women were students with me, and some were not. I was referred to the latter through another student or instructor. Once I attempted to interview women in the martial arts by posting a sign at a martial arts dojo asking to speak with people about their experiences learning self-defense, but I gained access to no one this way.

I tried to interview a variety of women, although in the end I took whoever volunteered. The sample is predominantly white. I do not know, however, whether or not self-defense students nationwide are mainly white. This was not a national survey of self-defense courses and students, and that data is not available. I asked interviewees for demographic information but some refused to reveal their age and race. In these cases I made note of what my inferences were. Four volunteered their sexual identities (one lesbian, one bisexual, and two heterosexual) in the course of their interviews with me, although most did not. I considered making inferences about sexual identity, for instance if a woman mentioned that she had a husband, but decided against it because even an obvious status such as married does not necessarily indicate that a woman identifies as heterosexual. Thus I was unable to make any conclusions about differential effects of self-defense lessons based on women's sexual or racial identities.

I interviewed students to understand how they experienced their self-defense classes, how they framed what they were learning, and how they talked about its effects in their lives. My interview data helps establish a theoretically informed picture of the relationship of self-defense to gender ideology. During the course of my research, I discovered Gaddis's (1990) doctoral dissertation for which he interviewed students of Model Mugging and was given a copy of Turaj's (1993) master's thesis for which she interviewed students of karate. While the foci of their studies are different from the focus of mine, I occasionally quote their interviewees.

Some of the students I interviewed did not just tell me their personal feelings about their involvement with self-defense but rather shared their critical analyses of their self-defense instruction, or of feminism and the antirape movement. For instance, one interviewee said that she felt she could not be a full-fledged feminist without knowing how to keep men from bullying her. She said self-defense is feminism applied or "feminism on the physical level." This same interviewee wanted to make clear that women are not automatically passive, vulnerable, or afraid to fight. When she told me about her ex-lover who battered her, she said, "I always fought back. I just kept losing the fights. I needed training."

In a similar spirit of intellectual and political engagement with women's self-defense, some of the instructors I interviewed offered criticisms of rape culture, self-defense instruction, and even my project. For instance, as I conducted interviews for what was at that time a doctoral dissertation, a few questioned my original title, "Getting Mean," explaining that they did not want people to think women were "mean" when they defended themselves. Instructors spend so much of their time working to counter the popular stereotype that women's assertiveness is mean that they preferred I use the word *assertive* instead of *mean* and *aggressive*. Of course, I wanted my title to call attention to that issue and embrace the very behaviors thought unbecoming for a lady. Nevertheless, I felt it was necessary to respond to instructors' concerns by changing the dissertation title. I called it "Physical Feminism," based on the aforementioned interview with a self-defense student. This conveys the importance of the body in self-defense and its relationship to feminism. But I changed the title yet again when I turned the dissertation into a book since the word *feminism* alienates as many women as the word *mean*. To many women, *feminism* has come to stand for disempowered victims complaining about their powerlessness—not what this book is about. I was determined to retain "physical feminism" somewhere in the title after reading Elizabeth Grosz (1994) on "corporeal feminism."

The aim of my study is to explore gendered notions of aggression and women's aggressive refusal of men's aggression. I wanted to investigate what makes possible women's freedom to defend themselves from sexual assault legitimately. My interview questions thus involved the following topics: How have women changed? How do people react to the women's transformations? Against whom do women see themselves using self-defense? And how, if at all, have women's understandings of themselves and their relationships with popular culture (including imagistic discourses of femininity) changed?

One purpose of the interviews with instructors was to understand how they see what they are doing. I wanted to know the philosophies behind their courses. My feminist aims made me question self-defense instructors in specific ways. For instance, I "tested" their knowledge of sexual violence, and feminist critiques of gender, with specific questions such as, "Who are the assailants you are training your students to defend themselves from?" and "How do you incorporate self-defense law into your class?" Since the instructors had much more experience watching women get tough than I did, the other purpose of interviews with instructors was informational. Many of my questions allowed instructors to tell me their impressions of students' transformations. For instance, I asked, "In your experience teaching, what is the most challenging thing for women to learn?" I also asked, "What do you say or do to help students meet that challenge?"

The participant observation research, which I present in chapter 2, enabled me to interpret the interview data rather than simply use the interviews in the service of description. In chapter 3, I tell the story of self-defense *analytically*. In other words, I use my participant observation to tell the story of self-defense and then use interview data, combined with participant observation data, to develop a theoretically informed interpretation of it.

Published Materials

I read the manuals published for women on self-defense because doing so familiarized me with the kind of advice that is available to women who do not necessarily take self-defense courses. Documents such as Corporal William J. Underwood's *Self-Defense for Women: Combato* (1944), the California State Police's *Safety Tips for Women* (1976), and Lisa Sliwa's *Attitude: Commonsense Defense for Women* (1986) reveal various assumptions about gender and violence as they suggest the means by which women might achieve safety and freedom. Self-defense books, manuals, and pamphlets—like the examples I used from popular culture, rape law, and self-defense law—provide a sense of the traditional understandings about women and aggression, which in turn enables an understanding of the ways in which hands-on self-defense instruction challenges those understandings. By examining how those assumptions are contested and not contested, I gained insight into common understandings of women and aggression, including how women's relationship to aggression is seen in the first place and how it is reorganized. In this way, self-defense manuals are a source of information about both traditional and developing assumptions.

In addition to reading self-defense manuals, I collected the current newsletters and magazines for self-defensers throughout my research. I read the current self-defense-oriented publications for women because this helped me become familiar with the culture of self-defensers. I read them as both a researcher and a blooming self-defenser. Reading these publications as I went through the self-defense courses enabled me not only to get my study off the ground but also to understand better the subtle differences in perspective of various self-defense disciplines. Organizational newsletters make up part of the discourse of self-defense instruction. I include items from them in my book because such items are artifacts that reflect the agendas and activities of their corresponding organizations (Jenness and Broad 1994, 407). I examined the following publications: in the martial arts, the newsletter of the National Women's Martial Arts Federation, *Shuri-Spiral News*, and *Fighting Woman News*; in firearms, *American Rifleman* (specifically the sections on women) and *Women and Guns*; and in padded attacker programs, *emPOWERment News* and *Self-Defense and Empowerment News* (formerly *Model Mugging News*).

One interesting development in women's self-defense culture did not exist when I began this research but deserves noting here. Since the fall of 1994, the Assault Prevention Information Network (APIN) has provided a fascinating dialog about women's self-defense on the internet (http://galaxy.tradewave. com/editors/weiss/APINintro.html). I was still completing this book at the time that I discovered the APIN World Wide Web site, with over one hundred screens of information about self-defense, workplace violence, conflict resolution, and related topics. For instance, net-surfing self-defensers will find stories of "real-life self-defense" (including armed self-defense), lists of domestic and international self-defense organizations, a discussion of legal issues, guidelines for choosing a self-defense course, a list of self-defense books and videos, and articles about the importance of self-defense training. Judith Weiss is the originator, researcher, and maintainer of the APIN web site, which began as a school project but has continued as a labor of love. Its only institutional connection is the Galaxy Web Directory, which provides it as a public service through their Guest Editor program. Since the discussions on the web were not a means by which I became familiar with the world of self-defense, nor a means by which I arrived at my theoretical argument, I do not include them here.

Throughout the reading and fieldwork I asked specific questions to learn about the ways in which gender is implicitly or explicitly challenged in self-defense culture. I coded data from fieldwork, interviews, and nontechnical literature that pertain to the specific phenomenon of women's learning self-defense. Other coding categories pertained to conditions and contexts related to, and actions that manage, that phenomenon. I use this data, then, to enhance my interviews and field observations. My claims involve a set of knowledges produced in particular settings and in particular materials, as they are experienced by a group of women (a group that does not necessarily represent women as a whole). I suggest a way of reading and experiencing self-defense from the theoretical vantage point of gender (including the sexed body) as a social construction, because I think it would have the consequence of challenging the gender ideology that undergirds rape culture.

Self-Defense Law

In chapter 1, I discuss the historical rejection of women's aggression in the legal system, because I suspected that the discourses around gender, aggression, and sexual assault that distinguish women who use aggressive force legitimately from those who do not, are similar in the legal system, in crime prevention advice, and folk wisdom. Many women are punished legally for defending themselves. This may explain why other women do not defend themselves—not because they know certain statistics or the law but because they inhabit the same set of discourses that distinguish (in)appropriate uses of violence. To the extent that self-defense instruction challenges the commonly accepted assumptions about women and violence, I consider how these opposing discourses might meet one another when, say, a Model Mugging graduate or a former student of Paxton Quigley is on trial for assault and battery. Thus, in chapter 5, I examine the possibly clashing consequences of women's self-defense training and struggles over the legal treatment of women who fight back. Here, I also examine feminist efforts to reform self-defense law.

My participant observation, interviewing, reading of published materials, and analysis of self-defense law familiarized me with self-defense culture and enabled me to have the kinds of discussions I wanted to have with the people I interviewed. While some of the women I interviewed were not in my self-defense class, they all knew that I had taken self-defense and that I could relate to what they were talking to me about. The methods I employed have helped me answer my original questions about how self-defense culture challenges traditional notions of the gendered body. They have also raised some new questions about the relationship of feminism to women's popular pleasures and resistance to rape. Hence I want to situate this research in a larger terrain of feminist examinations of women's engagement with popular culture. I suggest that my participant observation gives me a sense of the pleasure of self-defense training, and my identification with self-defensers allows me to avoid the distanced skepticism typical of many feminist studies of popular culture. To make this argument, it will be important to review the ways in which feminists have theorized the relationship between women and popular culture.

Feminism, Women, and Pleasure

Feminists have increasingly become interested in women's engagement with popular cultural activities. Since a key concern of mine, and theme in self-defense, is women's growing appreciation for and pleasure in their own aggression, I have paid particular attention to the ways in which feminist cultural analysts have understood women's relationship to popular culture and popular pleasures. Feminist studies of women and popular culture have focused on the following: the romance novel (Radway 1991); soap operas (Modleski 1982); television shows (Flitterman-Lewis 1987); popular scientific knowledge about women's bodies (Martin 1992); women's literary advice seeking (Simonds 1992); and specific subcultures of women engaged with cultural objects in some unique and interesting way, such as the production of "slash zines" in which *Star Trek* stories feature Kirk and Spock as lovers (Penley 1992). With the exception of Penley (ibid.), studies of women's popular pleasures often seek to answer the question, Why do women take pleasure in this cultural practice, and how does this pleasure serve patriarchal and capitalist interests?

This is probably why feminist books, consciousness-raising groups, and music festivals have not been considered popular cultural objects worthy of investigation. While Simonds (1992) and no doubt other feminists have had their worldviews shaped by these books and activities, they conduct academic studies of *other* women, seeking to understand the tastes of nonfeminist, nonacademic women. Indeed, it is hard to imagine an article explaining "how and why women read feminist books" or "how and why women attend women's music festivals," as such pleasures are already seen as political and appropriate. Ang (1988, 180) remarks that studies such as Radway's *Reading the Romance* (1991) reflect feminist attempts to "cope" with those female pleasures deemed problematic. As Simonds (1992, 215) puts it, "Writing about culture is done in the hope of understanding it better; but it is also done to make more culture and to articulate alternatives." Feminists' cultural critiques have both shared and challenged various theoretical and epistemological legacies of cultural criticism, such as Marxism.

For Marxists, the culture industry disseminates capitalist ideology. The Marxist critique suggests that capitalism creates false needs that people see as real. People seek the satisfaction of these created needs at the expense of seeing themselves as members of a class with a collective interest that is in conflict with capitalist interests. This is how social control operates (Marcuse 1964). Put bluntly, people are manipulated cultural dopes, trapped into supporting their own domination by naively following the interests of the economic machine (Horkheimer 1974). "The deceived masses are today captivated by the myth of success even more than the successful are" (Adorno and Horkheimer 1972, 359). Researchers make such imputations of false consciousness most often when they are interpreting a group with whom they do not identify (see Kurzman 1991). Herein lies an implicit assumption that the academic knows the liberating truth about popular culture and is capable of representing the interests of the oppressed class.

Traditional Marxist theorists have clung to an epistemology that assumed a privileged standpoint on the part of the oppressed. Claiming that all knowledge is political and socially constructed would, they feared, wind up maintaining the status quo. Thus, studies of popular culture were approached in a way that deconstructed popular culture to reveal its bourgeois interests or "distortions of reality." This, of course, presumes that there could be a pure resistance independent of distortions, interests, and ideology. Further, this perspective assumes that intellectuals, while not necessarily being in the position of the oppressed, can represent the interests of the oppressed and can therefore achieve an undistorted, or less distorted perspective. Marxists have presumed that an intellectual's revealing perspective was necessary because people are so swallowed up in an ideology promoted through popular culture that they will not develop a critical consciousness, which is needed for transformative social action. The notion that social change must be preceded by a critical consciousness or intent of some sort is an assumption that my study challenges.

Many early feminist views of popular culture took a leftist approach. Indeed, the feminist contempt for beauty pageants and images of femininity in film, television, pornography, and advertising assumed an adversarial relationship to the cultural powers that be (Denning 1991). For instance, Douglas (in Radway 1994, 3) argued that romance novels were part of a backlash against feminism: "Popular culture is out to get the so-called liberated woman." But a Marxist perspective provides too limited an understanding of women's relationship to popular culture. I wanted to analyze self-defense culture without the failings of Marxist theories. Therefore I did not interview self-defensers to "prove" that self-defense created in women a critical consciousness or a "false" consciousness. My argument that self-defense can potentially challenge rape culture does not imply that rape culture changes once women gain a critical consciousness of it. I offer an interpretation of self-defense culture that is not necessarily shared by those in it. Nor do I consider it my task to decide whether self-defensers are exercising free will or socially determined choices; whether they are displaying resistance or "playing into the patriarchy"; or whether they are successfully enacting resistance or getting recuperated by capitalism.

Some contemporary feminist studies of women and popular culture maintain some Marxist assumptions while rejecting others. These studies reflect the idea that women are so immersed in the patriarchal ideologies flowing through romance novels and self-help books that they need the help of the feminist intellectual to develop the ideological maturity necessary to "rechannel" their values. This maintains some of the arrogance of the intellectual/researcher but not quite as much as in traditional Marxist research. This is because some feminist studies have focused not on women who have bought false needs as real ones, but whose real needs are treated as false.

For instance, Simonds (1992) argues that advice to heterosexual women about how to get along with men sexually involves invalidating what many women want sexually and encouraging them to get a sexuality more in line with the sexuality men want women to have. Simonds' goal is to validate women's desires. In the case of romance novels, Radway (1991) argues that women do not get their needs for commitment, affection, and passion met from the men in their lives and that the novels enable women to feel that this need is valid. (She also hints that women should rechannel their needs and not use romance novels to meet them.) A strict Marxist might argue that women's desires for faithful, loving male companionship are imposed needs that only keep them cooperating with their own oppression. For Radway, however, this would miss the feminist point. Rather than claiming that women are wrongly taught to need romance novels or the values of heterosexual commitment and passion expressed within these novels, and that women's liberation depends on renouncing those needs, Radway validates these needs and argues that women's use of these cultural objects expresses needs that do not get met because of patriarchy. Thus women are not necessarily participating in their own domination by choosing to spend their time reading romance novels. Women can be seen as resisting patriarchy by reading such novels.

While I was doing my fieldwork, I began an intensive strength-training and cardio-endurance program. I had been an athlete in high school and self-defense reminded me how much I enjoyed physical challenges. In addition, taking so many self-defense courses made me want to improve my performance and reduce my chances of injury. A colleague approached me to inquire about the "self-loathing" I must have to do weightlifting and aerobics. This question assumes that women must account for the very same activities for which men do not have to account, that women engaged in exercise forms must be doing it to please men, and, further, that women would not look as pleasing to men if they did not go through such effort. It also keeps the things my colleague does with his body—computing, cycling, and so on—closed for critical consideration. I can think of no woman (or man) who is not implicated in capitalist, technological relations; an iron-pumping aerobicizer is not necessarily more implicated than a popcorn-eating moviegoer or coffee-drinking café dweller.

There is no way to escape capitalism, and sometimes cultural studies scholars will invoke capitalist relations to reject a practice they do not like, while ignoring the inevitable capitalist relations of the practices that they do not find problematic. "Capitalist relations" thus becomes a new God-trick: something to invoke when one wants to hold someone accountable. Accusing a woman of buying into "patriarchal relations" works much the same way. Furthermore, the charge that subjects are naively contradicting themselves becomes an easy way to dismiss one's research subjects. Another way to "prove" one's subjects wrong is to call them essentialists. The trouble is, the decision that one's subjects are naive or wrong about something usually *precedes* the charge of self-contradiction or essentialism (Smith 1993).

In sum, although Marxism provides a valuable perspective about economic relations that cannot be ignored, many left-wing cultural critics maintain a distrust of ordinary people, reproduce the elitism inherent in the assumption that the intellectual knows best, and preserve the epistemological assumptions that falsely disconnect truth/resistance from politics/ideology. The Marxist notion that the intellectual can determine which needs are true and which are false upholds an idea that authority on these political matters should be left to the intellectual rather than to lay people. The Frankfurt school's assumption that culture produces certain kinds of consciousness and that such a consciousness is the prerequisite for political action and social change is one that feminist psychoanalytic and New Left–Birmingham school studies of popular culture seem to avoid.

The Birmingham school in England uses Gramsci's (1971) ideas about hegemony but rejects the elitism of the Frankfurt School, which imputed false consciousness and cultural dopeness whenever hegemony was discussed. This is perhaps because the connection between individuals' intentions or consciousnesses and the larger social order is less strict for the Birmingham school than for the Frankfurt school. But the New Left approach is not pluralist. For

Gramsci, hegemony works through the naturalization of the ruling class's right to rule. The ruled consent to the arrangement because they see it as natural and sensible. The Birmingham School's approach to popular culture has involved studies of particular subcultures of resistance, such as punks, gangs, or rock music listeners, and has examined the containment and resistance that are both part of popular cultural forms. Until recently, most of the subcultures under study have been male, and the theorists tended to extol their revolutionary virtues while ignoring the sexism of the subcultures. Much feminist work on women's popular pleasures relies on a Gramscian notion of ideological hegemony, in which women's practices with which they do not agree or identify are rejected on the grounds that the women in question are silenced or otherwise unable to do what is truly in their interests as women.

One of Stuart Hall's meanings of *popular* comes from viewing cultural forms in a particular period as in tension with the dominant culture. The focus, then, is "the relation between culture and questions of hegemony" (Hall 1981, 235). *Popular* may mean the culture of the excluded or oppressed. But then this ignores people whose status simultaneously puts them in the position of oppressed and oppressor, such as married women (whose gender subordination and heterosexual privilege operate together). Further, in order to fight against pornography, women have employed the association between popular culture and the filthy, low culture "other" of high culture. Since pornography is produced and consumed primarily by the dominant group, men, popular culture cannot simply be defined as that which is consumed by the oppressed. Ultimately, Hall concludes that there is never total freedom from hegemony nor total encapsulation.

Hall contends that the popular is the culture of the people, versus the "power-bloc" which is "the side with the cultural power to decide what belongs and what does not" (Hall 1981, 23). Cultural forms are never whole and coherent; everyone has an ongoing dialectical and contradictory engagement with popular culture. Simonds (1992) echoes this notion in the introduction to her book on women and self-help literature. She argues that the connection between personal perception and cultural ideology is not clear and simple, that even cultural objects that seem easy to read and similar are strikingly variable when you note women's varied responses to such cultural objects.

Applying Lacanian theory to a societal level, Althusser argues that our subjectivities develop through the mirror of ideology, or by reflecting the value of others. Culture then becomes a place of political struggle because it is not simply determined by capitalist relations but is complexly involved with identities, ideologies, and discourses, themselves all intertwined. This is different from the traditional Marxist notion of false consciousness because, for Althusser, the self is constructed and contradictory. Thus, popular culture is seen as neither prohibiting political action nor necessitating it. Ideology can be used by the masses in popular culture to their benefit. This, however, still leaves the researcher with the authority to decide when something is to the masses' benefit. Much feminist concern over women's use of firearms simply assumes that what women see to be in their benefit is actually not (e.g., Jones 1994).

Given that everything is commodified in consumer capitalist society, Jameson (1979) and Hall (1981) see popular culture as a site of political contest, wherein both hegemony and resistance occur simultaneously. Radway (1991) uses Jameson's (1979) idea that there is always implicitly a utopian element in any cultural product to argue that there is always some aspect that is critical of the social order or utopian in the romance novel: "It seems apparent, then, that an oppositional moment can be said to characterize even the production of the romantic story if that process is understood as the women themselves conceive it" (Radway 1991, 214). A popular cultural form does not contain within itself a certain meaning or value.

The researcher's own political distinctions sometimes will, however, decide what counts as ideology and what counts as utopia. For instance, does the engagement with firearms culture (guns, gun clubs, gun magazines, gun lessons, etc.) on the part of some women count as a utopian impulse or is this the ideological repression of their feminine/feminist resistance? Answering this question could depend upon whether or not women as the keepers of morality and "family values" in their properly heterosexual feminine roles is a way of resisting patriarchy (hence guns mean they're duped by patriarchy) or a way of being duped by patriarchy (ergo guns mean they're resisting patriarchy). It could also depend upon whether or not women's properly heterosexual feminine roles are solidified by their use of guns or challenged by their use of guns.

Deciding what counts as resistance and what counts as hegemony has been tricky for feminists, especially because they have criticized the arrogance with which researchers make such distinctions. However, taking one's subjects at their word, something Radway (ibid.) suggests makes her method more feminist and less authoritarian, masks a different type of arrogance. Any cultural object is interpreted by the researcher or those more directly engaged with it, the research subjects. Research subjects are similarly interpreted by the researcher. Thus, I consider my research feminist precisely because I do not pretend that my interpretations are the same as those of whom I study, nor do I mask my disagreements as therapeutic concern. Here is where my identification with self-defensers becomes important.

The pleasures of the people I studied were fully apparent to me. That I did not disagree with the general practices of those I studied makes me less likely to mask my disagreements in ways that are ultimately only superficially accountable—that is, that explain away the women's pleasures so as to claim that they "really" need something other than that with which they are engaged. This is not to say, however, that identifying with my research subjects means that I will swallow whole every pleasure, chalking everything up to resistance. I do not see self-defense as an arena of women's free expression in an otherwise male dominant world. I see self-defense as an arena that brings to light the ideologies that perpetuate rape culture as much as it is an arena in which women might resist rape culture.

Taking multiple oppressions and contradictory identities (such as white woman) seriously, which feminists have encouraged, complicates cultural interpretation and renders impossible any simplistic claims that something is resisting. For example, while pop star Madonna can be seen as challenging images of femininity (oppressed woman's resistance), this is accomplished through the reliance on a contrast between pure white feminine innocence and a "nasty blackness" (hooks 1992, 157) (white oppressor's hegemony). Therefore, embracing aggression may counter particularly white standards of femininity, while it may be in black women's interests finally to get to be seen as traditionally feminine and therefore respectable. In my analysis I have tried to pay attention to the multiple locations in the power structure that any self-defenser might have, considering the differential social causes and consequences of many women's, and feminism's, uneasiness with combative bodily practices.

Another approach to women's popular pleasures, psychoanalysis, addresses some of my concerns. Psychoanalysis does not problematize pleasure the way that Marxist approaches have, but rather argues that resistance can occur with fantasy, play, and pleasure. Psychoanalysis postulates resistance on the grounds that the effects of culture are never fully determined or predictable. Further, psychoanalysis offers an account of what appeared to Marxists to be simple consent to oppression. In psychoanalysis, subjectivity is a process, not a thing from which a process stems.

Post-Lacanian psychoanalysis and feminist theory disrupt cultural studies by reposing questions about sexuality, subjectivity, the unconscious, representation, and language. Psychoanalysis argues that women do not naturally or easily, but painfully and imperfectly, fit into roles. Thus, psychoanalysis rejects simplistic views of identity and of the relationship between the social and identity. Psychoanalytic approaches are taken not to show how oppression is internalized, but to show how oppression is resisted. As Rose (1986) remarks, psychoanalysis provides a basis for discussing the incoherence and contradictory character of identities and thus the impossibility of total indoctrination.

Many popular culture scholars coming from a psychoanalytic perspective have spent time debunking the leftist myth that psychoanalysis is inherently conservative because it individualizes collective problems. De Certeau (1984) argues that psychoanalysis helps to undermine the authority of the researcher. Thus, the researcher listens to the research subjects, rather than imposing her interpretive framework onto her subjects. Like a psychoanalyst, the scholar researching a group consuming some popular cultural object must beware of the influence of her own fantasies and omissions. Also, the researcher must be able to study popular culture in a way that will enable her to learn more about her own political commitments and identifications. For instance, feminist researchers of popular culture have noted that they have had to take women's tastes and activities seriously, reexamine their own assumptions about such activities, and possibly rechannel their feminism. Further, because popular culture operates at a subconscious level in addition to a conscious level, psychoanalysis is particularly important for popular culture studies.

Penley (1989, 178) suggests that feminism's reliance on the reified category "woman" is perhaps the greatest obstacle to the acceptance of psychoanalysis. By arguing that there is no universal feminine essence, psychoanalysis may threaten traditional feminists. However, some feminist skepticism of psychoanalysis may be based less on a push toward essentialism and more on an uneasiness with what they perceive to be psychoanalytic theory's own essentialism. Flitterman-Lewis (1987, 173) says that psychoanalysis "seeks to analyze the fundamental structures of desire that underlie all human activity." To some feminists, this statement may reflect an unnecessary essentialism and absolutism.

I want to analyze femininity, particularly in the women's self-defense movement, as an ideological category without making the totalizing claim that women (or men, for that matter) are by nature aggressive. Put differently, it is possible to analyze the political stakes of seeing women as aggressive or not without claiming that they *are* inherently anything. This might be the more complex view of subjectivity, which is still compatible with feminist politics.

Psychoanalytic approaches to popular culture have historically been less squeamish about pleasure, fantasy, and play than other approaches. Feminist cultural criticism has contributed to women's feelings of guilt about "politically incorrect" fantasies or desires. Politically incorrect desires are those that feminists have assumed should be painful. Feminists have said that domination is bad because it is painful, thereby framing pleasure as the ultimate good. In so doing, feminists then trouble themselves with women's pleasure in the "wrong" things. While traditional feminist critiques inadvertently police women's pleasures, steering them in the "right" direction, psychoanalysis urges feminism to change in response to women's pleasures, not the other way around.

Feminists have also assumed that political endeavors are public, and not particularly pleasurable or playful (hence Radway's misgivings about the private pleasures of romance novels). This is especially true for political resistance to horrendous, violent, and deadly serious matters such as sexual violence. That the pleasures of the women I studied take place in the context of violence against women—a subject that is supposed to be serious and concerned with the harms and injuries to women—might exacerbate the concern surrounding women's popular pleasures and resistance to domination. Feminist psychoanalysis rejects the assumption that "real" social change is separate from fantasy or from pleasure. Penley's (1992) study of women *Star Trek* fanzine writers asks what feminism can learn from the pleasures women experience consuming and producing erotic stories of two male media characters. Thus psychoanalysis can make room for stories about resistance, and we can imagine that self-defensers' activities are no less politically significant for being personal and pleasurable.

A final authority issue to consider is the researcher's relationship with producers and consumers of popular culture. Researchers may participate in shaping the agendas of the groups they study. This is because, as Simonds (1992) notes, popular culture studies themselves become part of popular culture. Thus an ongoing reflexivity may develop whereby those engaged with particular popular cultural objects see themselves accountable to their respective ethnographers. Radway (1994, 14) discusses the recent changes in the romance novel genre: "I see great ambivalence at the heart of recent romances as the genre's writers attempt to think through the apparent contradiction between a more active and autonomous feminine identity and traditional assumptions that relationality and connectedness are not only woman's work but woman's desire as well." Similarly, romance writers who once claimed they were writing harmless escape stories now fancy themselves as active participants in social change through the narration of pleasurable fantasies about newly imagined individuals and relationships (ibid., 7). Even if Radway is now arguing that romance novels can teach feminism that emotional connectedness and assertiveness can go together in women's lives, feminism has obviously taught romance writers new possibilities for male and female characters. (The latter, not the former, was Radway's original focus.)

While critical ethnographers and popular culture scholars have been explicit about their goals of shaping the direction of various movements and subcultures, they seem less willing to take responsibility for their influence once they see it happening. After all, is it not possible that Radway's work provided a new narrative for romance writers? This is not necessarily a bad thing, as long as researchers acknowledge having such effects on the cultural forms about which they write. Thus, acknowledging that the researcher might become a new source for the meaning of cultural objects to their consumers is important.

Donna Haraway (1991, 309) has remarked that research is like "a modernist work of art," in which we interpret events and shape a culture in a way we find pleasing. As critical ethnography, my project is not simply a representation of the movement I set out to study but an active intervention in and shaping of it. As a researcher, I created a story that could influence the direction the activities I studied take. The larger political context that makes some consequences of self-defense (like serving a jail sentence) more likely than others will help determine the outcome of the self-defense community, but so also will my intervention in the community. Therefore, questions about how the researcher influences the direction of the group she studies and how she can do this more consciously and explicitly are crucial.

My insider status has enabled me to make explicit my desire to shape the self-defense movement in particular ways. Many of the self-defense instructors I met read *Her Wits about Her* (Caignon and Groves 1987) and *Stopping Rape* (Bart and O'Brien 1985), and expressed great interest in reading my work when it was complete. Though I initially feared that instructors would be skeptical when I told them I would be writing a book on women's self-defense, it became clear that they were glad that someone was finally writing about, theorizing, and sharing with others the important work they were doing. Because self-defensers are an eager audience for my work, I realize that I am in a position to influence the direction of the self-defense movement.

Not only could the final product of my research help shape the self-defense movement, but the research process itself was an intervention in self-defense culture. For instance, in order to see a particular self-defense videotape, I had to request that my neighborhood video store stock the video. My enthusiastic discussions of my research prompted several friends, students, and colleagues to seek instruction in some form of self-defense. I became an advocate for self-defense. I was one of a few students to demonstrate self-defense techniques for a local television news spot. The organization then used a videotape of this broadcast as a promotional device in Europe. My investigation not only involved my own transformation—namely, using guns that I'd always refused to, strength training at a gym, learning some forms of martial arts, and learning to deliver knockout blows—but also involved my monetary support of a number of organizations to which I wouldn't normally belong. During the course of the study, I belonged to the National Women's Martial Arts Federation, the National Rifle Association, and the Pacific Association for Women in the Martial Arts, and I subscribed to *American Rifleman*, *Fighting Woman News*, the National Women's Martial Arts Federation newletter, *Self-Defense and Empowerment News*, and *Women and Guns*. However, my study was not financially supported or endorsed by any of these groups.

Conclusion

Social scientific knowledge is an instrument of political power (Brown 1987). I have tried to proceed with this kind of methodological conscience. I want this work, as feminist research, to be clear about my values and desires (to the extent I can even know them [see Gordon 1990]). I have created a story about self-defense that I want people to consider. I have woven the experiences and events of *Real Knockouts* into a story that could have been woven together differently, along different dimensions reflecting different political commitments.

I investigated self-defense not because involved with it are a group of women who are smarter or freer or more feminist than others, but because it is an exciting place where traditional discourse is exposed and reworked. There is no form of popular recreation that is authentic or pure or free from power relations. While some may have expected that this study of women's engagement with self-defense, particularly their engagement with firearms, would involve the problematization of their pleasure and an accompanying explanation of what went wrong to make them enjoy what they are doing, I sought to appreciate women's enjoyment of all forms of self-defense training critically.

I have examined a group with whom I identify. My reluctance to see the members of the self-defense community as completely socially determined fits Kurzman's (1991) observations that field workers tend to impute free will to those groups with whom they identify while assuming those with whom they do not identify are victims of social forces beyond their control. Feminist cultural studies have often investigated the "false beliefs" of ideological enemies. Academic interpretations of women handgun advocates, for instance, have been conducted by those who do not identify (see, e.g., Jones 1994). Predictably, such women are construed as naive dupes under the control of patriarchal organizations.

Elshtain (1981, 312) laments the arrogant attitude with which feminists have approached their female adversaries in the Right-to-Life movement. What she suggests is relevant for any feminist attempt to understand women who do not identify as feminist or women with whom feminists do not always agree:

Without allowing Right-to-Life women to speak the truth as they understand it; without engaging them from a stance that respects their human possibility for the creation of meaning through uncoerced dialogue, which requires of the investigator a stance of empathy, openness, and a willingness to entertain and explore alternatives she may not share, [feminists] will continue to treat them in distorted, presumptuous, and prejudicial ways.

My exploration of women's self-defense culture is useful precisely because I identify with the carnal pleasures of learning to resist sexual violence. That identification has prompted the particular analysis I offer; it puts me in the position to understand, and pass on, the "kick" of self-defense.

Notes

NOTES TO THE PREFACE

1. Lists, updated periodically, of self-defense programs and other resources for women are available over the telephone at 1-800-345-KICK; in *Women and Guns* magazine each month; and over the internet at http://galaxy.tradewave.com/editors/weiss/SDtheory.html.

2. The National Coalition against Sexual Assault also offers guidelines for choosing a self-defense program over the internet at http://galaxy.tradewave.com/editors/weiss/NCASAGuidelines.html.

3. See Dworkin (1974, 174-93; 1979, 14-15) and MacKinnon (1987, 117-19; 1989, 90-93, 112-14) for their explicit statements about the political construction of sex categories in a system of compulsory heterosexuality. Early radical feminism did contain more essentialist elements, however. For example, Susan Brownmiller (1975, 4) suggested that rape is connected with "man's structural capacity to rape and woman's corresponding structural vulnerability," an idea that, although not intended to suggest that rape is natural or inevitable, was, as Echols (1989) notes, later criticized by other radical feminists for its failure to recognize rape culture's influence on how we conceptualize sexed bodies.

4. The appendix provides a detailed account of the methods of investigation and political concerns informing the study.

NOTES TO THE INTRODUCTION

1. The publicity surrounding this attack had much to do with the facts that the victim was white and middle-class and that the perpetrators were black and Latino. Evidence for this position is that twenty-eight other first-degree rapes or attempted rapes took place in New York City that same week about which we didn't hear much, if anything (Terry 1989, 25). Two weeks after the Central Park attack, a black woman was beaten and raped at knife point by two men. That such cases do not receive national attention indicates the racist biases informing assumptions of who can be victimized and who can be aggressors.

2. I regard research that strips data on violent acts of their context and uses them to claim that women and men are equally violent (e.g., Strauss and Gelles 1990) as

less credible than other research that indicates that men victimize women far more than vice versa (see Dobash et al. 1992).

3. That masculinity and violence are far from incongruous does not mean that all men are seen as the same kind of potentially violent agent. Black men are more likely to be seen as potential agents of illegitimate violence against whites and of legitimate violence against black women, while white men's violence stands a better chance of being perceived as legitimate, period (Marcus 1992, 392). Black men have been demonized as inappropriately aggressive, even when their social position kept them from being particularly dangerous or threatening. Further, they have been aggressively punished for the same aggression (even if they were innocent) that white men have practiced with impunity. The idea during Reconstruction that white women were in danger of rape from black men served to justify white men's control of black men. White men inflicted violence—often sexual violence in the form of castration—against black men for supposedly attacking white women. This was routinely the justification for lynching, a form of racist social control (Davis 1983, 172-201). This victimization of black men, rationalized by racist ideologies and institutions, has led some to suggest that racism "emasculates" the black man— precisely because of the link between masculinity and violent agency, on one hand, and femininity and being violated on the other.

4. This definition of rape culture, adapted from Buchwald, Fletcher, and Roth (1993), is meant to avoid a narrow definition which might exclude forms of male violence that women commonly experience and fear, and that are as bound up with normative gender expectations as rape is. Hence "rape culture" denotes a culture that not only supports and excuses rape but also woman beating, incest, and other forms of sexual assault. Such crimes have been deemed "gender-motivated assaults" by the Judiciary Committee on the Violence Against Women Act of 1990 because they are not simply individual or personal injuries but rather gender-motivated forms of discrimination (Biden 1990, 40-41).

5. An important exception must be noted here. Most rapes are intraracial (as are most violent crimes more generally) and committed against someone the assailant knows (United States Department of Justice 1993, 30-31). But under statistically less probable circumstances, such as when a man sexually assaults a stranger or when a male ethnic minority assaults a white woman, the act of rape is more likely to be seen as aggressive and inappropriate and a woman's self-defense, if it occurs, is regarded with less skepticism. It should also be noted that FBI data are somewhat misleading because so many date and acquaintance rapes are not even reported to the police.

6. Unfortunately, statistical data that lead to any definitive answers to questions about how often and how effectively women use weapons in self-defense have not been collected. For instance, the 1993 National Crime Victimization Survey (NCVS) provides some information on defensive responses to sexual assailants, which suggests that self-protective measures help the situation in most cases, but we

can only assume that those are responses by women (see, e.g., United States Department of Justice 1993, 73, 77). Crime victims were surveyed about the effectiveness of the resistance strategies they used against their attackers, but such responses are not coded by sex of resister (ibid., 76-77). Based on NCVS data for recent years, Roth (1994, 4-5) found that 30 percent of all surviving assault victims were injured, 27 percent of assault victims who did not resist attackers in any way were injured, and 12 percent of assault victims who used a firearm to resist attackers were injured. Of course, because responses are not coded by sex of resister, we cannot conclude anything about the use of firearms for self-defense among women specifically. That this data is not often divided by sex indicates that the idea that women will be endangered if they use a firearm in self-defense is merely hearsay.

7. Although I argue that the self-defense movement can impact North American culture as a whole, I do not attempt to argue that women outside of the self-defense movement are affected in the same ways as women who have taken up self-defense.

NOTES TO CHAPTER I

1. The sexual organs and brains of men were thought to be competing in the same way. Men, however, were directed to use the energy of their brains (Ehrenreich and English 1978, 126).

2. Thomas assumed that the premarital sex was consensual, ignoring the reality of rape and reinforcing the punishment of women for rape.

3. Of course, sexology and psychoanalysis are discourses that also made possible the deconstruction of the very categories they established, as they gave "deviants" something with which to identify, mobilize around politically, and eventually critique. For instance, the professional discourse of psychoanalysis might now be invoked to justify as normal a woman's aggression, sexual interest in other women, or desire for "favorable notice, distinction, and freedom."

4. See Haraway 1989; Longino 1991; and Martin 1992 for feminist critiques of specific scientific accounts of sex difference.

5. Perhaps because she so accurately captures how men experience, and rationalize, their own superiority, Dworkin is often seen as believing it herself, and is therefore accused of espousing the very biologism that she is trying to expose as patriarchal myth. I have cited Dworkin and MacKinnon extensively here along with Marcus precisely because I see their work as compatible. MacKinnon (1987, 49) argues that sexuality (its predominant structure is heterosexuality) is a social process that creates desire and, while it is taken for a natural essence, creates men and women. MacKinnon historicizes the patriarchal construction of the female body as a violable, occupiable space. She also comments that women's self-defense, far from being futile—which she would have to believe if she really did propose "essentialized conceptions of female and male sexualities" (Gatens 1996, 78)—can

change the way women understand their bodies and selves. No doubt MacKinnon's years practicing karate ground her claims as much as her radical constructionism does (see MacKinnon 1987, 117-24).

6. This male fantasy is depicted in the extreme in mainstream heterosexual pornography, if only because it is more explicit. In such films, commonly a man enters a room in which women to whom he has no emotional connection and who are usually far more attractive than he devour him sexually and enjoy the very things which make him sexually aroused. Or, the plot may involve the kidnaping, entrapment, or "innocent" discovery of already enslaved women whom the male protagonists then devour sexually to the women's great delight. That the women are trapped, tied up, bound, or gagged is simply exciting for the women in the story. This is how mainstream pornography perpetuates as erotic fantasy what men in real life force upon women.

7. African American men were often represented in films and early television shows as asexual, nonthreatening clowns (i.e., the "happy darky"), and sometimes as sexual threats to white women (who, before being raped, would either commit suicide or be saved by a white hero). However, as more black men have represented themselves, such representations often compete with those of white men for their sexual and aggressive heroism.

8. The murder counts in the Uniform Crime Reports exclude those murders by law enforcement officers and private citizens that are legally deemed justifiable homicide. Ex-spouses are included in the category "spouses," hence these figures include those murdered by ex-husbands and ex-wives. These UCR data for 1994 vary little from data for 1995, which are still tentative, and for 1993. It is worth noting that statistics comparing the *percentages* of female and male murder victims killed by intimates (instead of comparing raw numbers of intimate murders, as I have done) are misleading because far more men are murdered than women each year. Comparing percentages tells us that 28 percent of female murder victims and 3 percent of male murder victims are killed by romantic partners, married or not (Uniform Crime Reports for the United States 1994). Even if such figures don't really tell us how violent husbands and boyfriends are relative to wives and girlfriends, they do point to women's relatively greater likelihood to be victimized by an intimate. In 1995, U.S. women were six times more likely than men to be the victim of violence committed by an intimate, and moreover, women were more often injured when victimized by an intimate's violence than when victimized by a stranger's violence (U.S. Department of Justice 1995, 3).

9. The Olympic Games tested female athletes for sex by physical inspection from 1936 through the 1960s, and through the present by employing buccal smears and chromatin screening to determine the chromosomal karyotype of female competitors (Cole 1994, 20).

10. Garcia's conviction of second-degree murder was overturned on appeal because the judge had made an error in the jury's instructions regarding reasonable

doubt. At the new trial, Garcia's lawyer argued that she acted in self-defense, trying to prevent the "something worse" which may have meant murder (Gillespie 1989, 75).

11. Gardner (1990), however, ignores the set of rape prevention advice that is implicitly or explicitly connected with a feminist understanding of sexual violence and gender, which I discuss here last. Thus, the self-protection advice she covers, and with which women are familiar, is similar to the police pamphlets and the self-defense instruction books like them that I discuss here first.

12. I have not provided the page numbers of this booklet from which I have taken quotations because the booklet is not numbered.

NOTE TO CHAPTER 3

1. This handout is taken from *The New Assertive Woman* (Bloom, Coburn, and Pearlman 1975, 23).

NOTES TO CHAPTER 4

1. The raw number of fatal firearms accidents increased 8 percent from 1992 to 1993, mostly due to a 15 percent increase among persons between the ages of fifteen and twenty-four (National Center for Health Statistics 1996). The fatal firearms accident rate was lower than the rate of other fatal accidents for all persons including poisonings (3.3), fires (1.5), drownings (1.5), and chokings on an ingested object (1.2) (ibid.). It should also be noted that the Children's Defense Fund claimed that 5,751 children died firearm-related deaths in 1993 because they included nineteen-year-olds and under as "children." The actual number was 5,715, and 4,758 of those deaths were in the fifteen- to nineteen-year-old category, which includes 3,082 homicides, 1,273 suicides, 321 accidents, and 82 unexplained.

2. This figure includes deaths from commonly recognized poisons, drugs, medicines, mushrooms, and shellfish, but excludes deaths from spoiled foods, salmonella, etc., which are classified as deaths from diseases.

3. Some (e.g., Hekman 1995, 195) equate radical feminism with cultural feminism, citing, for instance, Mary Daly's (1978) condemnation of male womb envy and celebration of female difference as a political principle—which Daly calls radical feminism. As Echols (1989) has noted, many contemporary cultural feminists of the 1970s defined themselves as radical feminists, the group from which they emerged and departed. And of course forms of feminism overlap. This makes distinguishing feminist camps difficult. In the framework I use here, Daly is clearly a cultural feminist because of her insistence on feminism as a spiritual movement that creates a revolutionary female "counterworld" in opposition to masculinist culture.

4. Bowker studies women who have been abused over several months or years. If the women who immediately left or stopped battering relationships were

included in this study, her statistical data on the ineffectiveness of counterviolence might be different. Moreover, Bowker's study did not control for the severity of the threats or fighting on the part of the battered women. Thus we do not know exactly which kinds of counterviolence are most likely to be effective.

5. In her study of violence among the Australian Aboriginal people of Mangrove (a fictitious name for the Arnhem Land community), Burbank (1994) finds that aggression can be a dramatic bodily means for speaking about relationships, and as such even enjoyed. In the small community of Mangrove, where the people live in the public gaze, aggression has specified limits. Further, relationships are understood as organic processes "that can overcome many perturbations" (ibid., 96), rather than (as in the Western framework) things that can be broken easily by aggression.

6. See Gibson (1994) on paramilitary culture and its relationship to mass murderers, combat pistol shooting, and arguments over gun control.

NOTES TO CHAPTER 5

1. Self-defense does not suggest that men are emotionally incapable of rape; its first priority is not the exculpation of men from their position in a system of sex inequality.

2. Summaries of what each state is doing with funds provided by the Violence Against Women Act is available on the internet through the Violence Against Women Grants Office at http://www.ojp.usdoj.gov/VAWGO/

3. See McCaughey and King (1995) for the proposal that rape prevention educators employ the unconventional approach of screening women's violent action instead of eroticized victimization.

4. Helen Zahavi hopes that her book *Dirty Weekend* (1991) will have this same effect. The female revenge novel's main character, Bella, breaks into the home of the man who'd been harassing her by telephone and beats him to death with a hammer. The book's plot involves Bella's moving on to more violence against more sexist men. The author wants men to approach women differently, and thinks that they would if they feared the consequences that the men in her book face at the hands of Bella. In response to some who are horrified by the book's fantasy of violent retaliation, Zahavi declares, "It's not a liberal book, it's not saying, 'understand these men,' it's saying, 'eliminate them' and that's a very frightening idea for many people, very foreign. I believe that if the state doesn't protect the weakest members of society, they have a complete right to protect themselves. . . . Feminine behaviour is rooted in the fear of offending the male, bruising his ego and arousing him to violence. I wanted to reverse that situation" (quoted in Grant 1994, 4). Zahavi's book is not evidence that "relations between men and women seem to have turned murderous," as Grant (1994, 3) suggests. One significant difference between Zahavi's book and Bret Easton Ellis's book *American Psycho* (1991) is that men's fantasies of violence against women are politically, legally, economically, and socially

legitimated through networks of power, whereas women's fantasies of violence against men are not (Gatens 1996, 147).

5. Hart discusses this issue in the context of a discussion of Aileen Wuornos, who was found guilty and sentenced to death for the murder of seven men. Regardless of the innocence or guilt of Wuornos, Hart's point about Wuornos's defense surely is valid for less controversial cases of women's self-defensive violence.

6. It is true, as Kelman (1991, 815) notes, that the average subway self-defenser may kill many innocents by mistakenly judging them, perhaps solely on the basis of their race, as lethal criminals, while the average battered wife self-defenser who makes the same judgmental error and kills a man who was not about to kill her is still killing an established assaulter. For my purposes, Kelman's point that women are not construed as having agency is the most relevant one.

References

Adorno, Theodor, and Max Horkheimer. 1972. *Dialectics of Enlightenment*. New York: Seabury Press.

Ali, Lorraine. 1995. "Free to Fight." *Los Angeles Times*, June 25, F-1.

Allen, Hilary. 1987. "Rendering Them Harmless: The Professional Portrayal of Women Charged with Serious Violent Crimes." In *Gender, Crime and Justice*, ed. Pat Carlen and Anne Worrall, 81-94. Philadelphia: Open University Press.

Allen, Jeffner. 1986. *Lesbian Philosophy: Explorations*. Palo Alto, Calif.: Institute of Lesbian Studies.

Alpert, Jane. 1973. "Mother Right: A New Feminist Theory." *Ms.*, August, 52-55, 88-94.

Althusser, Louis. 1971. "Ideology and Ideological State Apparatuses." In *Lenin and Philosophy and Other Essays*. Trans. Ben Brewster. New York: Monthly Review Press.

Ammons, Linda L. 1995. "Mules, Madonnas, Babies, Bathwater, Racial Imagery and Stereotypes: The African American Woman and the Battered Woman Syndrome." *Wisconsin Law Review* 5:1003-80.

Ang, Ien. 1988. "Feminist Desire and Female Pleasure: On Janice Radway's *Reading the Romance: Women, Patriarchy, and Popular Literature*." *Camera Obscura* 16:179-90.

Bandura, Albert. 1977. "Self-Efficacy: Toward a Unifying Theory of Behavior Change." *Psychological Review* 84:191-215.

Barringer, David. 1993. "Under the Gun." *Details*, September, 112, 117.

Bart, Pauline B., and Patricia H. O'Brien. 1985. *Stopping Rape: Successful Survival Strategies*. New York: Pergamon Press.

Bateman, Py. 1978. *Fear into Anger: A Manual of Self-Defense for Women*. Chicago: Nelson-Hall.

Bem, Sandra L. 1993. *The Lenses of Gender*. New Haven: Yale University Press.

Benavídez, Patricia. 1979. "Chicana Women." In *In Defense of Ourselves*, by Linda Tschirhart Sanford and Ann Fetter, 161-63. Garden City, N.Y.: Doubleday.

Beneke, Timothy. 1982. *Men on Rape*. New York: St. Martin's Press.

Biden, Joseph R., Jr. 1990. "The Violence Against Women Act 1990." October 19 (legislative day, October 2). Calendar No. 1007. Report 101-545. Washington, D.C.: U.S. Congress, Congressional Budget Office.

Blacksmith, E. A., ed. 1992. *Women in the Military*. New York: H. W. Wilson.

Blodgett-Ford, Sayoko. 1993. "Do Battered Women Have a Right to Bear Arms?" *Yale Law and Policy Review* 11:509-60.

Bloom, Lynn Z., Karen Coburn, and Joan Pearlman. 1975. *The New Assertive Woman*. New York: Delacorte Press.

Bochnak, Elizabeth, ed. 1981a. *Women's Self-Defense Cases: Theory and Practice*. Charlottesville, Va.: Michie.

Bochnak, Elizabeth. 1981b. With the assistance of Elissa Krauss, Susie Macpherson, Susan Sternberg, and Diane Wiley. "Case Preparation and Development." In *Women's Self-Defense Cases: Theory and Practice*, ed. Elizabeth Bochnak, 41-85. Charlottesville, Va.: Michie.

Bourdieu, Pierre. 1990. *The Logic of Practice*. Trans. Richard Nice. Stanford: Stanford University Press.

Boutilier, M. A., and L. C. SanGiovanni. 1983. *The Sporting Woman*. Champaign, Ill.: Human Kinetics.

Bowker, Lee H. 1986. *Ending the Violence: A Guidebook Based on the Experience of 1,000 Battered Wives*. Holmes Beach, Fla.: Learning Publications.

Braidotti, Rosi. 1994. *Nomadic Subjects: Embodiment and Sexual Difference in Contemporary Feminist Theory*. New York: Columbia University Press.

Branscombe, Nyla R., Paul Crosby, and Julie A. Weir. 1993. "Social Inferences Concerning Male and Female Homeowners Who Use a Gun to Shoot an Intruder." *Aggressive Behavior* 19 (2): 113-24.

Branscombe, Nyla R., and Julie A. Weir. 1992. "Resistance as Stereotype-Inconsistency: Consequences for Judgments of Rape Victims." *Journal of Social and Clinical Psychology* 11:80-102.

Bromley, Marion. 1982. "Feminism and Nonviolent Revolution." In *Reweaving the Web of Life*, ed. Pam McAllister, 143-55. Philadelphia: New Society Publishers.

Brown, Gillian. 1991. "Anorexia, Humanism, and Feminism." *Yale Journal of Criticism* 5 (1): 189-215.

Brown, Richard Harvey. 1987. *Society As Text: Essays on Rhetoric, Reason, and Reality*. Chicago: University of Chicago Press.

Brownmiller, Susan. 1984. *Femininity*. New York: Linden Press.

———. 1975. *Against Our Will: Men, Women, and Rape*. New York: Bantam Books.

Buchwald, Claire. 1993. "Training for Safehouse." In *Transforming a Rape Culture*, ed. Emile Buchwald, Pamela R. Fletcher, and Martha Roth, 247-54. Minneapolis: Milkweed.

Buchwald, Emilie. 1993. "Raising Girls for the Twenty-First Century." In *Transforming a Rape Culture*, ed. by Emile Buchwald, Pamela R. Fletcher, and Martha Roth, 179-200. Minneapolis: Milkweed.

Buchwald, Emilie, Pamela R. Fletcher, and Martha Roth, eds. 1993. *Transforming a Rape Culture*. Minneapolis: Milkweed.

Burack, Cynthia. 1994. *The Problem of the Passions: Feminism, Psychoanalysis, and Social Theory*. New York: New York University Press.

Burbank, Victoria Katherine. 1994. *Fighting Women: Anger and Aggression in Aboriginal Australia*. Berkeley and Los Angeles: University of California Press.

Burg, Kathleen Keefe. 1979. *The Womanly Art of Self-Defense*. New York: A and W.

Butler, Judith. 1993. *Bodies That Matter: On the Discursive Limits of "Sex."* New York: Routledge.

———. 1990. *Gender Trouble: Feminism and the Subversion of Identity*. New York: Routledge.

Cabreros-Sud, Veena. 1995. "Kicking Ass." In *To Be Real: Telling the Truth and Changing the Face of Feminism*, ed. Rebecca Walker, 41-47. New York: Anchor Books.

Caignon, Denise, and Gail Groves. 1987. *Her Wits about Her: Self-Defense Success Stories*. New York: Perennial Library.

California State Police. 1976. *Safety Tips for Women*. Sacramento: California State Police Division Department of General Services.

Callahan, A. Renée. 1994. "Will the Real Battered Women Please Stand Up? In Search of a Realistic Legal Definition of Battered Woman Syndrome." *The American Journal of Gender and the Law* 3 (Fall): 117-52.

Campbell, Anne. 1993. *Men, Women, and Aggression*. New York: Basic Books.

Campbell, Bonnie J. 1996. "Implementing the Violence Against Women Act." *Womansword* 1 (10): 2-5.

Canning, Kathleen. 1994. "Feminist History after the Linguistic Turn: Historicizing Discourse and Experience." *Signs* 19 (2): 368-404.

Caputi, Jane. 1993. *Gossips, Gorgons, and Crones: The Fates of the Earth*. Santa Fe, N.M.: Bear and Company Publishers.

Cayleff, Susan E. 1987. *Wash and Be Healed: The Water-Cure Movement and Women's Health*. Philadelphia: Temple University Press.

Chauncey, George, Jr. 1982-83. "From Sexual Inversion to Homosexuality: Medicine and the Changing Conception of Female Deviance." *Salmagundi* 58-59 (Fall and Winter): 114-46.

Clarke, A., and J. Clarke. 1982. "'Highlights and Action Replays'—Ideology, Sport, and the Media." In *Sport, Culture, and Ideology*, ed. Jennifer Hargreaves, 62-87. London: Routledge and Kegan Paul.

Clarke, D. A. 1993. "A Woman with a Sword: Some Thoughts on Women, Feminism, and Violence." In *Transforming a Rape Culture*, ed. Emilie Buchwald, Pamela R. Fletcher, and Martha Roth, 393-404. Minneapolis: Milkweed.

Cline, Sally, and Dale Spender. 1987. *Reflecting Men at Twice Their Natural Size*. London: Deutsch.

Cock, Jacklyn. 1994. "Women and the Military: Implications for Demilitarization in the 1990s in South Africa." *Gender and Society* 8 (2): 152-69.

Cohen, Ed. 1991. "Who Are 'We'? Gay 'Identity' as Political (E)motion (A Theoretical Rumination)." In *Inside/Out: Lesbian Theories, Gay Theories*, ed. Diana Fuss, 71-92. New York: Routledge.

Cole, Cheryl L. 1994. "Resisting the Canon: Feminist Cultural Studies, Sport, and Technologies of the Body." In *Women, Sport, and Culture*, ed. Susan Birrell and Cheryl L. Cole, 5-29. Champaign, Ill.: Human Kinetics.

Coley, Soraya M., and Joyce O. Beckett. 1988. "Black Battered Women: Practice Issues, Social Casework." *Journal of Contemporary Social Work* 69 (8): 483-90.

Conroy, Mary. 1972. *The Rational Woman's Guide to Self-Defense*. New York: Grosset and Dunlap.

Conroy, Mary, and Edward Ritvo. 1982. *Every Woman Can: The Conroy Method to Safety, Security, and Self-Defense*. New York: Grosset and Dunlap.

Coward, Rosalind. 1992. *Our Treacherous Hearts: Why Women Let Men Get Their Way*. London: Faber and Faber.

Daly, Mary. 1978. *Gyn/Ecology: The Metaethics of Radical Feminism*. Boston: Beacon Press.

Davis, Angela. 1983. *Women, Race, and Class*. New York: Vintage Books.

de Beauvoir, Simone. 1952. *The Second Sex*. Trans. H. M. Parshley. New York: Vintage Books.

de Certeau, Michel. 1984. *The Practices of Everyday Life*. Berkeley: University of California Press.

de Lauretis, Teresa. 1990. "Eccentric Subjects: Feminist Theory and Historical Consciousness." *Feminist Studies* 16 (1): 115-50.

DeMasco, Steve. 1992. *Steve DeMasco's Aerobic Self-Defense Workout*. Global Action Video. Newark: PPI Entertainment Group.

Denning, Michael. 1991. "The End of Mass Culture." In *Modernity and Mass Culture*, ed. James Naremore and Patrick Brantlinger, 253-68. Bloomington and Indianapolis: Indiana University Press.

Diamond, Irene, and Lee Quinby. 1988. "American Feminism and the Language of Control." In *Feminism and Foucault: Reflections on Resistance*, ed. Irene Diamond and Lee Quinby, 193-206. Boston: Northeastern University Press.

Diprose, Rosalyn. 1994. *The Bodies of Women: Ethics, Embodiment, and Sexual Difference*. New York: Routledge.

Dobash, Russell P., R. Emerson Dobash, Margo Wilson, and Martin Daly. 1992. "The Myth of Sexual Symmetry in Marital Violence." *Social Problems* 39:71-91.

Donovan, Josephine. 1992. *Feminist Theory: The Intellectual Traditions of American Feminism*. New York: Continuum.

Draper, Robert. 1993. "Why 15 Million Women Own Guns." *Glamour*, May, 260-61, 302-4.

Dumaresq, Delia. 1981. "Rape—Sexuality in the Law." *m/f* 5-6:41-59.

DuShane, Carol. 1979. "Native American Women." In *In Defense of Ourselves*, by Linda Tschirhart Sanford and Ann Fetter, 164-65. Garden City, N.Y.: Doubleday.

Dworkin, Andrea. 1987. *Intercourse.* New York: Free Press.

———. 1979. *Pornography: Men Possessing Women.* New York: Perigree.

———. 1974. *Woman Hating.* New York: Dutton.

Echols, Alice. 1989. *Daring to Be Bad: Radical Feminism in America 1967-1975.* Minneapolis: University of Minnesota Press.

Ehrenreich, Barbara, and Deirdre English. 1978. *For Her Own Good: 150 Years of the Experts' Advice to Women.* New York: Anchor.

Eisler, Riane. 1987. *The Chalice and the Blade: Our History, Our Future.* San Francisco: Harper and Row.

Ellis, Bret Easton. 1991. *American Psycho.* New York: Vintage.

Elshtain, Jean Bethke. 1981. *Public Man, Private Woman: Women in Social and Political Thought.* Princeton: Princeton University Press.

Estrich, Susan. 1987. *Real Rape.* Cambridge: Harvard University Press.

Ewing, Charles Patrick. 1990. "Psychological Self-Defense: A Proposed Justification for Battered Women Who Kill." *Law and Human Behavior* 14 (6): 579-94.

Fairbairn, William. 1942. *Hands Off! Self-Defense for Women.* New York: D. Appleton-Century.

Faludi, Susan. 1991. *Backlash: The Undeclared War against American Women.* New York: Crown.

Fein, Judith. 1981. *Are You a Target? A Guide to Self-Protection, Personal Safety, and Rape Prevention.* Belmont, Calif.: Wadsworth.

Felson, Richard B. 1996. "Big People Hit Little People: Sex Differences in Physical Power and Interpersonal Violence." *Criminology* 34 (3): 433-52.

Flax, Jane. 1990. *Thinking Fragments: Psychoanalysis, Feminism, and Postmodernism in the Contemporary West.* Berkeley and Los Angeles: University of California Press.

Fletcher, Pamela R. 1993. "Whose Body Is It, Anyway? Transforming Ourselves to Change a Rape Culture." In *Transforming a Rape Culture,* ed. Emilie Buchwald, Pamela R. Fletcher, and Martha Roth, 427-41. Minneapolis: Milkweed.

Flitterman-Lewis, Sandy. 1987. "Psychoanalysis, Film, and Television." In *Channels of Discourse: Television and Contemporary Criticism,* ed. Robert C. Allen, 172-210. Chapel Hill: University of North Carolina Press.

Foucault, Michel. 1980. *History of Sexuality.* Vol. 1, *An Introduction.* New York: Vintage.

———. 1970. *The Order of Things: An Archaeology of the Human Sciences.* New York: Vintage.

Franks, David. 1985. "Role-Taking, Social Power, and Imperceptiveness: The Analysis of Rape." *Studies in Symbolic Interaction* 6:229-59.

Fraser, Nancy. 1989. *Unruly Practices: Power, Discourse, and Gender in Contemporary Social Theory.* Minneapolis: University of Minnesota Press.

Gaddis, John. 1990. "Women's Empowerment through Model Mugging: Breaking the Cycle of Social Violence," doctoral dissertation, University of California, Santa Barbara.

Gardner, Carol Brooks. 1990. "Safe Conduct: Women, Crime, and Self in Public Places." *Social Problems* 37 (3): 311-28.

Gatens, Moira. 1996. *Imaginary Bodies: Ethics, Power, and Corporeality.* New York: Routledge.

Gay, Peter. 1993. *The Cultivation of Hatred: The Bourgeois Experience, Victoria to Freud.* New York: W. W. Norton.

Gibson, James William. 1994. *Warrior Dreams: Paramilitary Culture in Post-Vietnam America.* New York: Hill and Wang.

Giddens, Anthony. 1991. *Modernity and Self-Identity: Self and Society in the Late Modern Age.* Stanford: Stanford University Press.

Gidycz, Christine A., Christie N. Coble, Lance Latham, and Melissa J. Layman. 1993. "Sexual Assault Experience in Adulthood and Prior Victimization Experiences: A Prospective Analysis." *Psychology of Women Quarterly* 17 (2): 151-68.

Gillespie, Cynthia K. 1989. *Justifiable Homicide: Battered Women, Self-Defense, and the Law.* Columbus: Ohio State University Press.

Gilmore, David D. 1987. *Aggression and Community: Paradoxes of Andalusian Culture.* New Haven: Yale University Press.

Gordon, Avery. 1990. "Feminism, Writing, and Ghosts." *Social Problems* 37 (4): 485-500.

Gordon, Margaret T., and Stephanie Riger. 1989. *The Female Fear.* New York: Free Press.

Graham, Dee L. R., with Edna I. Rawlings and Roberta K. Rigsby. 1994. *Loving to Survive: Sexual Terror, Men's Violence, and Women's Lives.* New York: New York University Press.

Gramsci, Antonio. 1971. *Selections from the Prison Notebooks.* London: Lawrence and Wishart.

Grant, Karla. 1989. *Transforming the Victim Role: Psychological Aspects of Self-Defense for Women.* Sacramento: Shinko Video.

Grant, Linda. 1994. *Sexing the Millennium: Women and the Sexual Revolution.* New York: Grove Press.

Gray, Michael D., Diane Lesser, Edna Quinn, and Chris Bounds. 1990. "The Effectiveness of Personalizing Acquaintance Rape Prevention: Programs on Perception of Vulnerability and on Reducing Risk-Taking Behavior." *Journal of College Student Development* 31:217-20.

Grieco, Helen. 1997. *Demystifying Violence: What Women and Girls Need to Know to Be Safe.* Berkeley: Celestial Arts.

Grindstaff, Laura, and Martha McCaughey. 1996. "Re-membering John Bobbit: Castration Anxiety, Male Hysteria, and the Phallus." In *No Angels: Women Who Commit Violence*, ed. Alice Myers and Sarah Wight, 142-60. London: Pandora.

Grosz, Elizabeth. 1995. *Space, Time, and Perversion: Essays on the Politics of Bodies.* New York: Routledge.

————. 1994. *Volatile Bodies: Toward a Corporeal Feminism.* Bloomington: Indiana University Press.

Gustuson, Donald, and Linda Masaki. 1970. *Self-Defense for Women.* Boston: Allyn and Bacon.

Halberstam, Judith. 1993. "Imagined Violence/Queer Violence: Representation, Rage, and Resistance." *Social Text* 11 (4): 187-201.

Hall, Stuart. 1981. "Notes on Deconstructing 'The Popular.'" In *People's History and Socialist Theory,* ed. Raphael Samuel, 227-240. London: Routledge and Kegan Paul.

Hanson, Kimberly A., and Christine A. Gidycz. 1993. "Evaluation of a Sexual Assault Prevention Program." *Journal of Consulting and Clinical Psychology* 61 (6): 1046-52.

Haraway, Donna. 1991. *Simians, Cyborgs, and Women: The Reinvention of Nature.* New York: Routledge.

————. 1989. *Primate Visions: Gender, Race, and Nature in the World of Modern Science.* New York: Routledge.

Hart, Lynda. 1994. *Fatal Women: Lesbian Sexuality and the Mark of Aggression.* Princeton: Princeton University Press.

Hekman, Susan. 1995. "Subjects and Agents: The Question for Feminism." In *Provoking Agents: Gender and Agency in Theory and Practice,* ed. Judith Kegan Gardiner, 194-207. Urbana: University of Illinois Press.

Henley, Nancy M. 1977. *Body Politics: Power, Sex, and Nonverbal Communication.* Englewood Cliffs, N.J.: Prentice-Hall.

Herman, Judith Lewis. 1992. *Trauma and Recovery.* New York: Basic Books.

Heyden, Margaret, and Allan V. Tarpenning. 1970. *Personal Defense for Women.* Belmont, Calif.: Wadsworth.

Highwater, Jamake. 1990. *Myth and Sexuality.* New York: American Library.

Hoagland, Sarah. 1988. *Lesbian Ethics: Toward New Value.* Palo Alto, Calif.: Institute of Lesbian Studies.

Hochschild, Arlie Russell. 1983. *The Managed Heart: Commercialization of Human Feeling.* Berkeley and Los Angeles: University of California Press.

Hodges, Michael. 1993. "Up in Arms." *Detroit News,* December 6, 1C, 6C.

hooks, bell. 1994. "Giving the Party: Aunt Jemima, Mammy, and the Goddess Within." *Ms.,* May-June, 22-25.

————. 1992. *Black Looks: Race and Representation.* Boston: South End Press.

————. 1981. *Ain't I a Woman: Black Women and Feminism.* Boston: South End Press.

Horkheimer, Max. 1974. *Critical Theory: Selected Essays.* Trans. Matthew J. O'Connel. New York: Seabury Press.

Hummel, Amy, and Karla Mantilla. 1994. "Punk Band Sparks Michigan Controversy." *Off Our Backs* 24 (9): 16-17.

Innes, Rosalind. 1976. "'What She Needs Is a Good Fuck': Rape and Femininity." *Hecate* 2 (2): 23-30.

Jackson, Shannon. 1993. "Representing Rape: Model Mugging's Discursive and Embodied Performances." *Drama Review* 37 (3): 110-41.

Jameson, Fredric. 1979. "Reification and Utopia in Mass Culture." *Social Text* 1:130-48.

Jeffreys, Sheila. 1990. *Anticlimax: A Feminist Perspective on the Sexual Revolution*. New York: New York University Press.

Jenness, Valerie, and Kendal Broad. 1994. "Antiviolence Activism and the (In)visibility of Gender in the Gay/Lesbian and Women's Movements." *Gender and Society* 8 (3): 402-23.

Jhally, Sut. 1994. "Intersections of Discourse: MTV, Sexual Politics, and *Dreamworlds*." In *Viewing, Reading, Listening: Audiences and Cultural Reception*, ed. Jon Cruz and Justin Lewis, 151-68. San Francisco: Westview Press.

———. 1990. *Dreamworlds: Desire/Sex/Power in Rock Video*. Amherst, Mass.: Foundation for Media Education.

Jones, Ann. 1994. "Is This Power Feminism?" *Ms*, May-June, 38-44.

———. 1980. *Women Who Kill*. New York: Fawcett Crest.

Jones, Sonny. 1990. "From the Editor." *Women and Guns*, February, 6.

Kandel, Minouche. 1993. "Women Who Kill Their Batterers Are Getting Battered in Court." *Ms.*, July-August, 88-89.

Kates, Don B., Jr. 1989. "Firearms and Violence: Old Premises and Current Evidence." In *Violence in America*. Vol. 1, *The History of Crime*, ed. Ted Robert Gurr, 197-215. Thousand Oaks, Calif.: Sage.

Katz, Jack. 1988. *Seductions of Crime: Moral and Sensual Attractions in Doing Evil*. New York: Basic Books.

Kaufman, Doris, Robert Rudeen, and Carol Morgan. 1980. *Safe within Yourself: A Woman's Guide to Rape Prevention and Self-Defense*. Alexandria, Va.: Visage Press.

Kaye/Kantrowitz, Melanie. 1992. *The Issue Is Power: Essays on Women, Jews, Violence and Resistance*. San Francisco: Aunt Lute Books.

Kellerman, Arthur L., and Donald T. Reay. 1986. "Protection or Peril? An Analysis of Firearm-Related Deaths in the Home." *New England Journal of Medicine* 314 (24): 1557-60.

Kelman, Mark. 1991. "Reasonable Evidence of Reasonableness." *Critical Inquiry* 17 (4): 798-817.

Kessler, Suzanne J. 1990. "The Medical Construction of Gender: Case Management of Intersexed Infants." *Signs* 16 (1): 3-26.

Kleck, Gary. 1991. *Point Blank: Guns and Violence in America*. New York: Aldine de Gruyter.

Koss, Mary P., and Mary R. Harvey. 1991. *The Rape Victim: Clinical and Community Approaches to Treatment*. 2d ed. Newbury Park, Calif.: Sage.

Kurzman, Charles. 1991. "Convincing Sociologists: Values and Interests in the Sociology of Knowledge." In *Ethnography Unbound: Power and Resistance in the Modern Metropolis*, ed. M. Burowoy, A. Burton, A. Ferguson, H. Fox, J. Gamson, N. Gartrell, L. Hurst, C. Kurzman, L. Salzinger, J. Schiffman, and S. Ui. Berkeley and Los Angeles: University of California Press.

Lafree, Gary D., Barbara F. Reskin, and Christy A. Visher. 1985. "Jurors' Responses to Victims' Behavior and Legal Issues in Sexual Assault Trials." *Social Problems* 32 (4): 389-407.

Lakeland, Mary Jo, and Susan Ellis Wolf. 1980. "Questions Féministes: Variations on Some Common Themes." *Feminist Issues* 1 (1): 3-21.

Lehrman, Karen. 1992. "Boy Toys." *New Republic*, March 30, 45.

Lentz, Kirsten Marthe. 1993. "The Popular Pleasures of Female Revenge (Or Rage Bursting in a Blaze of Gunfire)." *Cultural Studies* 7 (3): 374-405.

Lerner, Harriet Goldhor. 1988. *Women in Therapy*. Northvale, N.J.: Jason Aronson.

Leung, Debbie. 1991. *Self-Defense: The Womanly Art of Self-Care, Intuition and Choice*. Tacoma, Wash.: R and M Press.

Levin, Milt. 1990. Letter to the *Times*. *Los Angeles Times*, January 20, B11.

Liddle, A. Mark. 1989. "Feminist Contributions to an Understanding of Violence against Women—Three Steps Forward, Two Steps Back." *Canadian Review of Sociology and Anthropology* 26 (5): 759-75.

Lombroso, Cesare. 1911. *Crime: Its Causes and Remedies*. New York: Little, Brown.

Lombroso, Cesare, and William Ferrero. 1895. *The Female Offender*. New York: D. Appleton.

Longino, Helen E. 1991. *Science As Social Knowledge: Values and Objectivity in Scientific Inquiry*. Princeton: Princeton University Press.

Lorber, Judith. 1993. "Believing Is Seeing: Biology As Ideology." *Gender and Society* 7 (4): 568-81.

Lorde, Audre. 1984. *Sister Outsider: Essays and Speeches by Audre Lorde*. Freedom, Calif.: Crossing Press.

Luchsinger, Judith A. H. 1977. *Practical Self-Defense for Women: A Manual of Prevention and Escape Techniques*. Minneapolis: Dillon Press.

MacKinnon, Catharine A. 1989. *Toward a Feminist Theory of the State*. Cambridge: Harvard University Press.

———. 1987. *Feminism Unmodified: Discourses on Life and Law*. Cambridge: Harvard University Press.

Mahoney, Martha R. 1991. "Legal Images of Battered Women: Redefining the Issue of Separation." *Michigan Law Review* 90 (1): 1-94.

Maines, John. 1992. "Can Females Be Friends with Firearms?" *American Demographics*, June, 22-24.

Mangan, J. A., and Roberta J. Park. 1987. *From Fair Sex to Feminism: Sport and the Socialization of Women in the Industrial and Post-Industrial Eras*. London: Frank Cass.

Marcus, Sharon. 1992. "Fighting Bodies, Fighting Words: A Theory and Politics of Rape Prevention." In *Feminists Theorize the Political*, ed. Judith Butler and Joan W. Scott, 385-403. New York: Routledge.

Marcuse, Herbert. 1964. *One-Dimensional Man: Studies in the Ideology of Advanced Industrial Society.* Boston: Beacon Press.

Martin, Emily. 1992. "Body Narratives, Body Boundaries." In *Cultural Studies,* ed. Lawrence Grossberg, Cary Nelson, and Paula Treichler, 409-23. New York: Routledge.

————. 1991. "The Egg and the Sperm: How Science Has Constructed a Romance Based on Stereotypical Female Roles." *Signs* 16 (3): 485-501.

Mashberg, Tom. 1994. "Armed Camp." *Chicago Tribune,* December 30, Sec. 5, pp. 1, 3.

Matthews, Nancy A. 1994. *Confronting Rape: The Feminist Anti-Rape Movement and the State.* New York: Routledge.

McCaughey, Martha, and Neal King. 1995. "Rape Education Videos: Presenting Mean Women Instead of Dangerous Men." *Teaching Sociology* 23 (4): 374-88.

McGurn, Thomas P., and Christine N. Kelly. 1984. *The Woman's Bible for Survival in a Violent Society.* New York: Stein and Day.

Merleau-Ponty, Maurice. 1962. *Phenomenology of Perception.* Trans. Colin Smith. London: Routledge and Kegan Paul.

Messner, Michael A. 1994. "Sports and Male Domination: The Female Athlete As Contested Ideological Terrain." In *Women, Sport, and Culture,* ed. Susan Birrell and Cheryl L. Cole, 65-80. Champaign, Ill.: Human Kinetics.

————. 1990. "Masculinities and Athletic Careers: Bonding and Status Differences." In *Sport, Men, and the Gender Order,* ed. Michael A. Messner and D. F. Sabo, 97-108. Champaign, Ill.: Human Kinetics.

Meyer, Alice. 1993. "Meditation on Women, Firearms, and Survival." *Village Voice,* January 19, 132.

Miedzian, Myriam. 1993. "How Rape Is Encouraged in American Boys and What We Can Do to Stop It." In *Transforming a Rape Culture,* ed. Emile Buchwald, Pamela R. Fletcher, and Martha Roth, 153-63. Minneapolis: Milkweed.

Modleski, Tania. 1982. *Loving with a Vengeance: Mass-Produced Fantasies for Women.* New York: Methuen.

Monkerud, Donald, and Mary Heiny. 1980. *Self-Defense for Women.* Dubuque, Iowa: Wm. C. Brown.

Morgan, Robin. 1989. *The Demon Lover: On the Sexuality of Terrorism.* New York: W. W. Norton.

Mulvey, Laura. 1989. *Visual and Other Pleasures.* Hound Mills, Eng.: Macmillan.

Mynatt, Clifford R., and Elizabeth Rice Allgeier. 1990. "Risk Factors, Self-Attributions, and Adjustment Problems among Victims of Sexual Coercion." *Journal of Applied Sociology* 20 (2): 130-53.

National Center for Health Statistics. 1996. *Deaths from 282 Selected Causes, By Five-Year Age Groups, Race, and Sex.* Washington, D.C.: National Center for Health Statistics, a division of the U.S. Department of Health and Human Services.

National Safety Council. 1995. *Accident Facts, 1995 Edition*. Itasca, Ill.: National Safety Council's Research and Statistical Services Group.

Ozer, Elizabeth, and Albert Bandura. 1990. "Mechanisms Governing Empowerment Effects: A Self-Efficacy Analysis." *Journal of Personality and Social Psychology* 58 (3): 472-86.

Paglia, Camille. 1992. *Sex, Art, and American Culture*. New York: Vintage.

Penley, Constance. 1992. "Feminism, Psychoanalysis, and the Study of Popular Culture." In *Cultural Studies,* ed. Lawrence Grossberg, Cary Nelson, Paula A. Treichler, 479-94. New York: Routledge.

————. 1989. *The Future of an Illusion: Film, Feminism, and Psychoanalysis*. Minneapolis: University of Minnesota Press.

Peri, Camille. 1990. "Below the Belt." *Mother Jones*, September-October, 44-67.

Peterson, Susan Goldner. 1979. *Self-Defense for Women: The West Point Way*. New York: Simon and Schuster.

Phillips, Julie. 1995. "Equality? Why Is Brown University Fighting Its Women Athletes and Why Don't Brown's Feminists Care?" *Village Voice*, February 28, 31-34, 116, 118.

Plaza, Monique. 1981. "Our Damages and Their Compensation; Rape: The Will Not to Know of Michel Foucault." *Feminist Issues* 1 (3): 25-36.

Plummer, Ken. 1984. "The Social Uses of Sexuality: Symbolic Interaction, Power, and Rape." In *Perspectives on Rape,* ed. June Hopkins, 37-53. New York: Harper and Row.

Quigley, Paxton. 1989. *Armed and Female*. New York: St. Martin's Press.

Rabinow, Paul, ed. 1984. *The Foucault Reader*. New York: Pantheon.

Radford, Lorraine. 1994. "Pleading for Time: Justice for Battered Women Who Kill." In *Moving Targets: Women, Murder, and Representation,* ed. Helen Birch, 172-97. Berkeley and Los Angeles: University of California Press.

Radway, Janice A. 1994. "Romance and the Work of Fantasy: Struggles over Feminine Sexuality and Subjectivity at Century's End." In *Viewing, Reading, Listening: Audiences and Cultural Reception,* ed. Jon Cruz and Justin Lewis, 213-32. San Fransisco: Westview Press.

————. 1991. *Reading the Romance: Women, Patriarchy, and Popular Literature*. Chapel Hill: University of North Carolina Press.

Rajchman, John. 1985. *Michel Foucault: The Freedom of Philosophy*. New York: Columbia University Press.

Rand, Michael R. 1994. "Guns and Crime." United States Department of Justice. April, NCJ-147003. Washington, D.C.: Office of Justice Programs, Bureau of Justice Statistics.

Reinelt, Claire. 1995. "Moving onto the Terrain of the State: The Battered Women's Movement and the Politics of Engagement." In *Feminist Organizations: Harvest of the New Women's Movement,* ed. Myra Marx Ferree and Patricia Yancey Martin, 84-104. Philadelphia: Temple University Press.

Reskin, Barbara, and Irene Padavic. 1994. *Women and Men at Work*. Thousand Oaks, Calif.: Pine Forge Press.

Rich, Adrienne. 1980. "Compulsory Heterosexuality and Lesbian Existence." *Signs* 5 (4): 631-60.

Rimonte, Nilda. 1989. "Domestic Violence against Pacific-Asians." In *Making Waves: An Anthology of Writings by and about Asian American Women*, ed. Asian Women United of California, 327-37. Boston: Beacon Press.

Roiphe, Katie. 1993. *The Morning After: Sex, Fear, and Feminism on Campus*. Boston: Little, Brown.

Rollins, Judith. 1985. *Between Women: Domestics and Their Employers*. Philadelphia: Temple University Press.

Roman, Leslie G., Linda K. Christian-Smith, and Elizabeth Ellsworth, eds. 1988. "Introduction." In *Becoming Feminine: The Politics of Popular Culture*, 1-34. Philadelphia: Falmer Press.

Rooney, Ellen. 1983. "Criticism and the Subject of Sexual Violence." *Modern Language Notes* 98 (5): 1269-78.

Rose, Jaqueline. 1986. *Sexuality in the Field of Vision*. London: Verso.

Rosen, Ruth. 1993. "Domestic Disarmament: A Women's Issue?" *Dissent* (Fall): 463-66.

Roth, Jeffrey A. 1994. "Firearms and Violence." United States Department of Justice. February, NCJ-145533. Washington, D.C.: Office of Justice Programs, National Institute of Justice, Research in Brief.

Sanford, Linda Tschirhart, and Ann Fetter. 1979. *In Defense of Ourselves: A Rape Prevention Handbook for Women*. Garden City, N.Y.: Doubleday.

Sawicki, Jana. 1991. *Disciplining Foucault: Feminism, Power, and the Body*. New York: Routledge.

Scheppele, Kim Lane, and Pauline B. Bart. 1983. "Through Women's Eyes: Defining Danger in the Wake of Sexual Assault." *Journal of Social Issues* 39 (2): 63-81.

Schickel, Richard. 1991. "Gender Bender." *Time*, June 24, 52-56.

Schneck, David. 1986. "The Texture of Embodiment: Foundation for Medical Ethics." *Human Studies* 9 (1): 43-54.

Schneider, Elizabeth M. 1995. "Epilogue: Making Reconceptualization of Violence against Women Real." *Alabama Law Review* 58:1245-52.

———. 1992a. "Describing and Changing: Women's Self-Defense Work and the Problem of Expert Testimony on Battering." *Women's Rights Law Reporter* 14 (2-3): 213-41.

———. 1992b. "Particularity and Generality: Challenges of Feminist Legal Theory and Practice in Work on Woman-Abuse." *New York University Law Review* 67 (3): 520-68.

Schneider, Elizabeth, and Susan B. Jordan, with Cristina C. Arguedas. 1981. "Representation of Women Who Defend Themselves in Response to Physical or

Sexual Assault." In *Women's Self-Defense Cases: Theory and Practice,* ed. Elizabeth Bochnak, 1-39. Charlottesville, Va.: Mitchie.

————. 1978. "Representation of Women Who Defend Themselves in Response to Physical or Sexual Assault." *Women's Rights Law Reporter* 4 (3): 149-63.

Scott, Joan Wallach. 1988. *Gender and the Politics of History.* New York: Columbia University Press.

Scraton, Sheila. 1987. "Boys Muscle in Where Angels Fear to Tread: Girls' Subcultures and Physical Activity." In *Sport, Leisure, and Social Relations,* ed. John Horne, David Jary, and Alan Tomlinson, 160-86. New York: Routledge.

Scribner, Marilyn. 1988. *Free to Fight Back: A Self-Defense Handbook for Women.* Wheaton, Ill.: Harold Shaw.

Scully, Diana. 1990. *Understanding Sexual Violence: A Study of Convicted Rapists.* Boston: Unwin Hyman.

Searles, Patricia, and Ronald J. Berger. 1987. "The Feminist Self-Defense Movement: A Case Study." *Gender and Society* 1 (1): 61-84.

Searles, Patricia, and Patti Follansbee. 1984. "Self-Defense for Women: Translating Theory into Practice." *Frontiers* 8 (1): 65-70.

Shilling, Chris. 1993. *The Body and Social Theory.* Newbury Park, Calif.: Sage.

Simonds, Wendy. 1992. *Women and Self-Help Culture: Reading between the Lines.* New Brunswick, N.J.: Rutgers University Press.

Sliwa, Lisa. 1985. *Lisa Sliwa's Common Sense Defense.* Vestron Video.

Sliwa, Lisa, with Keith Elliot Greenberg. 1986. *Attitude: Commonsense Defense for Women.* New York: Crown.

Smith, Barbara, ed. 1983. "Introduction." In *Home Girls: A Black Feminist Anthology,* xix-lvi. New York: Kitchen Table: Women of Color Press.

Smith, Barbara Herrnstein. 1993. "Unloading the Self-Refutation Charge." *Common Knowledges* 2 (2): 81-95.

Smith, Dorothy E. 1988. "Femininity As Discourse." In *Becoming Feminine: The Politics of Popular Culture,* ed. Leslie G. Roman and Linda K. Christian-Smith, 37-59. Philadelphia: Falmer Press.

Smith, Susan E. 1986. *Fear or Freedom: A Woman's Options in Social Survival and Physical Defense.* Racine, Wisc.: Mother Courage Press.

Spanier, Bonnie. 1995. *Im/partial Science: Gender Ideology in Molecular Biology.* Bloomington: Indiana University Press.

Spock, Benjamin, M.D. 1945. *Baby and Child Care.* New York: Pocket Books.

Starr, Tama. 1991. *The "Natural Inferiority" of Women.* New York: Poseidon Press.

Steiner, Bradley J. 1976. *Below the Belt: Unarmed Combat for Women.* Boulder, Colo.: Paladin Press.

Stiehm, Judith Hicks. 1982. "The Protected, the Protector, the Defender." *Women's Studies International Forum* 5 (3-4): 367-76.

Stock, F. Patricia Pechanec. 1968. *Personal Safety and Defense for Women.* Minneapolis: Burgess.

Stoltenberg, John. 1993. "Making Rape an Election Issue." In *Transforming a Rape Culture*, ed. Emile Buchwald, Pamela R. Fletcher, and Martha Roth, 213-24. Minneapolis: Milkweed.

———. 1989. *Refusing to Be a Man: Essays on Sex and Justice*. Portland: Breitenbush Books.

Storaska, Frederick. 1975. *How to Say No to a Rapist and Survive*. New York: Random House.

Strachey, James, ed. 1981. "Femininity." In *Sigmund Freud: New Introductory Lectures on Psychoanalysis*, ed. James Strachey, with Angela Richards, trans. James Strachey, 145-69. New York: Penguin.

Strain, Connie Rae. 1992. "Martial Arts: Self Defense or Self Delusion?" *Women and Guns*, March, 34-36.

Strauss, Murray A., and Richard J. Gelles. 1990. *Physical Violence in American Families*. New Brunswick, N.J.: Transaction.

Swasey, Elizabeth J. 1993. "NRA Woman's Voice." *American Rifleman*, February, 18.

Székely, Éva. 1988. *Never Too Thin*. Toronto, Ont.: Women's Press.

Tegner, Bruce, and Alice McGrath. 1967. *Self-Defense for Girls: A Secondary School and College Manual*. Los Angeles: Thor.

Terdiman, Richard. 1985. *Discourse/Counter-Discourse: The Theory and Practice of Symbolic Resistance in Nineteenth-Century France*. Ithaca, N.Y.: Cornell University Press.

Terry, Don. 1989. "A Week of Rapes: The Jogger and Twenty-Eight Not in the News." *New York Times*, May 29, A-25.

Thomas, William I. 1923. *The Unadjusted Girl: With Cases and Standpoint for Behavior Analysis*. Boston: Little, Brown.

Turaj, Johanna. 1993. "Finding the Kiai: Training at a Women's Karate School and Its Relationship to Self-Esteem." Manuscript, Smith College School for Social Work.

Twin, Stephanie, ed. 1979. *Out of the Bleachers: Writings on Women and Sport*. Old Westbury, N.Y.: Feminist Press.

Ullman, Sarah E., and Raymond A. Knight. 1993. "The Efficacy of Women's Resistance Strategies in Rape Situations." *Psychology of Women Quarterly* 17:23-38.

Underwood, William J. 1944. *Self-Defense for Women: Combato*. Garden City, N.Y.: Blue Ribbon Books.

Uniform Crime Reports for the United States. 1994. *Crime in the United States, 1994*. Washington, D.C.: Federal Bureau of Investigation, U.S. Department of Justice.

United States Department of Justice. 1995. "Violence against Women: Estimates from the Redesigned Survey" (National Crime Victimization Survey), by Ronet Bachman and Linda E. Saltzman. NCJ-154348. Washington, D.C.: Office of Justice Programs, Bureau of Justice Statistics.

———. 1993. *Criminal Victimization in the United States, 1993: A National Crime Victimization Survey Report,* by Craig A. Perkins, Patsy A. Klaus, Lisa D. Bastian, and Robyn L. Cohen. May 1996, NCJ-151657. Washington, D.C.: Bureau of Justice Statistics, U.S. Department of Justice.

———. 1977. *Be on the Safe Side for Your Personal Protection.* Washington, D.C.: Law Enforcement Assistance Administration, U.S. Department of Justice.

Valentis, Mary, and Anne Devane. 1994. *Female Rage: Unlocking Its Secrets, Claiming Its Power.* New York: Carol Southern.

Vance, Carole S. 1989. "Pleasure and Danger: Toward a Politics of Sexuality." In *Pleasure and Danger: Exploring Female Sexuality,* ed. Carole S. Vance, 1-27. London: Pandora.

Walker, Lenore E. 1989. *Terrifying Love: Why Battered Women Kill and How Society Responds.* New York: Harper and Row.

———. 1979. *The Battered Woman.* New York: Harper and Row.

Weedon, Chris. 1987. *Feminist Practice and Poststructuralist Theory.* New York: Basil Blackwell.

White, Deborah. 1985. *Ar'n't I a Woman? Female Slaves in the Plantation South.* New York: W. W. Norton.

Wilson, Margo I., and Martin Daly. 1992. "Who Kills Whom in Spouse Killings? On the Exceptional Sex Ratio of Spousal Homicides in the United States." *Criminology* 30 (2): 189-215.

Wolf, Naomi. 1993. *Fire with Fire: The New Female Power and How It Will Change the Twenty-First Century.* New York: Random House.

———. 1991. *The Beauty Myth: How Images of Beauty Are Used against Women.* New York: W. Morrow.

Wong, Elaine Kanzaki. 1979. "Asian Women." In *In Defense of Ourselves,* by Linda Tschirhart Sanford and Ann Fetter, 156-60. Garden City, N.Y.: Doubleday.

Wong, William. 1993. "Feeling Vulnerable? Try Self-Defense." *Oakland Tribune,* December 17, A-15.

Woodhull, Winifred. 1988. "Sexuality, Power, and the Question of Rape." In *Feminism and Foucault: Reflections on Resistance,* ed. Irene Diamond and Lee Quinby, 167-76. Boston: Northeastern University Press.

Wyatt, Gail Elisabeth, Donald Guthrie, and Cindy M. Notgrass. 1992. "Differential Effects of Women's Child Sexual Abuse and Subsequent Sexual Revictimization." *Journal of Consulting and Clinical Psychology* 60 (2): 167-73.

Young, Iris Marion. 1990. *Throwing Like a Girl and Other Essays in Feminist Philosophy and Social Theory.* Bloomington: Indiana University Press.

Zahavi, Helen. 1991. *Dirty Weekend.* London: Harper Collins.

Index

sodomy laws, 45
Spender, Dale, 37
Spock, Benjamin, 19
sports: feminine attractiveness and, 42–43;
feminist concerns over women in, 155,
156, 158–59; and heterosexuality,
42–43; increasing participation of
women, 42; and masculinity, 43, 156;
sex tests, 236n. 9; those in which
women are encouraged to participate,
42; women and men compared, 41–43;
women's status dilemma in, 138. *See also*
boxing
spousal battering. *See* battering
spousal homicide, 152–53
Steinem, Gloria, 158
Steiner, Bradley J., 55
Stiehm, Judith Hicks, 157
Stoltenberg, John, 13
Stopping Rape: Successful Survival Strategies
(Bart and O'Brien), ix, 230
S•T•O•P program, 182
Storaska, Frederick, 54–55
strangers: guns for use against assault by,
175; as perpetrators of sexual violence,
52, 53–55, 95–96; resistance to, seen as
precipitating assault by, 194
stun guns, 76
Swasey, Elizabeth J., 91

Take Back the Night: celebrating women
who fight back, 180; in claiming
women's rights, xi, 211; as emphasizing
victimization, 1; Roiphe's criticism of,
xii
Tegner, Bruce, 53
temporary insanity plea, 47
Terminator 2 (film), 5, 98
Thelma and Louise (film), 5, 22, 99–100,
185–86
therapeutic discourse, 97
Thomas, Matt, 60
Thomas, William I., 22, 235n. 2
tiger claw, 86
Title IX of the Educational Equity Act of
1972, 42, 156
training in self-defense. *See* self-defense
training
Transforming a Rape Culture (Buchwald,
Fletcher, and Roth), 13

Trias, Robert A., 80
Tribe 8 (band), 5, 14–15, 184
true man rule, 48, 192–93
Truth, Sojourner, 146
Turaj, Johanna, 217

Underwood, William, 50–51, 218

Valentis, Mary, 186
Valley Women's Martial Arts, Inc., 80–82
VAWA (Violence Against Women Act),
181–82, 211; Web site, 238n. 2
Violence Against Women Grants Office,
182; Web site, 238n. 2
violence: as begetting violence, 152–54, 206;
as control mechanism, 10; cultural concern with, 4; fantasized connection
between sexuality and, 185; feminists
rejecting, 2, 14, 150–51, 155–57, 180; and
masculinity, 139, 234n. 3; nonbodily
oppression as violent, 155; responsibility
placed with the perpetrator, xiv; against
women compared with men, 37–38,
236n. 8; women defined as not violent,
179; women's fear of, 90, 116. *See also*
aggression; male violence; sexual violence
Violence Against Women Act (VAWA),
181–82, 211; Web site, 238n. 2
Violence Against Women Office, 182

weapons: concealed weapons, 70, 71, 143;
in defense against sexual assault, 11,
234n. 6; nonlethal weapons, 76; in
padded attacker courses, 67; and physical self-defense, 111–12; self-defense
manuals on, 52, 57; women's use of,
3–4. *See also* guns
Web sites: of Assault Prevention Information Network (APIN), 219; funds spent
by the Violence Against Women Act
(VAWA), 238n. 2; guidelines of
National Coalition Against Sexual
Assault (NCASA) for choosing a self-
defense program, 233n. 2; on self-
defense programs and other resources,
233n. 1; of the Violence Against
Women Grants Office, 238n. 2
Weiss, Judith, 219
white men: black women raped by, 24; and
violence, 234n. 3

About the Author

Martha McCaughey is Assistant Professor of Women's Studies in the Center for Interdisciplinary Studies at Virginia Tech. A third-wave feminist active in anti–sexual assault education since 1989, she developed, with colleague Neal King, an alternative method for such education using images of women verbally and physically overpowering men. McCaughey's scholarly work examines the embodied discourses of gender, sexuality, and aggression. Focusing on scientific narratives, popular culture, and feminist theory, her work has been published in *Hypatia, Science as Culture, GLQ, masculinities, Teaching Sociology*, and in *No Angels: Women Who Commit Violence*, edited by Alice Myers and Sarah Wight (Pandora 1996). She is currently coediting a book on violent women in film and teaches courses in women's studies, science and technology studies, and sociology. She received her Ph.D. in sociology from the University of California at Santa Barbara. McCaughey serves on the editorial board of *Gender & Society* and is a member of several academic associations in her areas of study. She does not represent any self-defense or self-defense-related organization.